How to Build and Furnish
A DOLLHOUSE
for $100 or Less

How to Build and Furnish
A DOLLHOUSE
for $100 or Less

by PATRICIA MAIDMENT

The Bobbs-Merrill Company, Inc.
Indianapolis/New York

Published by The Bobbs-Merrill Co., Inc.
Indianapolis/New York
Manufactured in the United States of America
First Printing
Photographs by Randall Corbin and Patricia Maidment

Library of Congress Cataloging in Publication Data

Maidment, Patricia.
   How to build and furnish a dollhouse for $100 or less.

   1. Doll-houses.   2. Doll furniture.   I. Title.
TT175.3.M34   1983   745.592'3   82-17778
ISBN 0-672-52745-6

DESIGN & PAGE MAKE UP
BARBARA BERT/NORTH 7 ATELIER LTD.

To my husband, Carl.

CONTENTS

8 THE DINING ROOM   165

9 THE LIBRARY/DEN   177

10 STORAGE ITEMS   190

11 FINISHING TOUCHES   195

ADDING IT ALL UP   206

Dear Reader:

To list crafts shops would be a book in itself and would be outdated almost before publication. Miniature shops come and go faster than one can list them, and they mostly contain the expensive objects we are avoiding in this book. Most items used for the dollhouse and furnishings can be found in hobby shops, hardware, paint, variety, drug, and department stores as well as in crafts stores.

Here are the names of two wholesalers of hard-to-find items. They can send you a list of stores in your area that carry their items.

Houseworks, Ltd.
2388 Pleasantdale Rd.
Atlanta, Georgia 30340

J. Hermes
P.O. Box 4023
El Monte, California 91734

How to Build and Furnish
A DOLLHOUSE
for $100 or Less

INTRODUCTION

This book is written for those who have always desired to own a dollhouse—and all the delightful Lilliputian furnishings that go with it—but cannot afford to bring their dreams to life.

Miniature enthusiasts have made the collecting and making of miniatures the third largest-growing hobby in the world. But along with its growth, the prices have risen so rapidly that it has become the hobby for only the most affluent.

I am an avid miniature enthusiast, but I almost gave up collecting. Notice I said "almost gave up" this hobby. I found that to be impossible. I've learned, as have so many others, that once introduced to this mini-world, no one can escape its captivating charm.

But what is so irresistibly attractive about the diminutive? What is the captivating charm of miniatures? There seem to be no words to adequately describe the elusive seduction of things small. In *The Book of the Queen's Dolls' House*, written in 1924 by A. C. Benson, is possibly the most beautiful explanation.

> There is great beauty in smallness. One gets all the charm of design and colour and effect, because you can see so much more in combination and juxtaposition. And then, too, the blemishes and small deformities which are so inseparable from seeing things life-size all disappear; the result is a closeness and fineness of texture which pleases both eye and mind. One realizes in reading the travels of Gulliver how dainty and beautiful the folk and buildings of Lilliput were, and on the other hand, how coarse and hideous the magnifying effect of Brobdingnag was.

Miniatures may be old or new but all are an illustration of life, past or present. In short—and in little—anything a full-size house contains a microphile collects in the diminutive.

What is meant by a microphile? A microphile is a lover, devotee, and collector of miniatures. And, although the hobby of collecting and making miniatures may be the third largest, its membership is comparatively small. This is because the prices rank very close to those of the hobby of coin collecting.

Entering the enchanting world of miniatures, you will find yourself part of a most prestigious and selective group. Prestigious because microphiles include royalty, famous personages, and many who gained fame from their handsome collections. The list of famous microphiles includes Queen Mary, Alice Longworth Roosevelt, actress Colleen Moore, Helena Rubinstein, Fanny Hayes—daughter of President Rutherford B., King Chulalongkorn (immortalized in *Anna and the King of Siam*), and Sir Nevile Wilkinson who built Titania's Palace.

The selective group of microphiles includes the most affluent who collect only antiques. Some enthusiasts travel the world over to complete a special collection, even something as small as one china plate for a china service. Antiques are the epitome of the collection, but are limited to a wealthy few. Another elite group has craftsmen handcraft everything from dollhouse to furnishings to accessories. This is also most expensive.

But do not be frightened away from this fascinating hobby because you believe the expense is too great. There are many ways to circumvent the high costs involved in miniature collecting. I know, because many people, including myself, are doing it.

My moment of truth came after my husband and I had finished and furnished a nine-room Victorian manor. It shocked me when I tabulated the cost. We had invested almost $2,000 in one dollhouse!

I wanted more than one dollhouse, but knew I could not afford even a small one . . . four or five rooms. But by using items on hand, inexpensive and even free materials, I built and furnished a nine-room dollhouse for less than $100.

Sounds impossible? Well, it's not. And that's what this book is all about.

GETTING STARTED

Before we begin our dollhouse, let's review some of the materials and tools used for making dollhouses.

If you have ever checked a book of dollhouse plans or bought the plans for a dollhouse, you will have found that the basic material was plywood. Recently a new product known as foam core board was introduced for building dollhouses.

The plans in this book use neither of these products, although you may substitute either of them for the material our dollhouse calls for. And what material are we going to use? Corrugated cardboard.

I'd better stop right here. You're, no doubt, belittling the use of such a lowly material as cardboard. I, for one, do not consider it a cheap, shoddy material. If you use the right kind of cardboard and finish it with the same care you'd give expensive material, no one will ever suspect that you made a house out of cardboard. Even the Big, Bad Wolf won't be able to huff or puff it down.

The dollhouse pictured, with variations to suit your individual preferences, is made of corrugated cardboard. Let me interject a word of caution at this point. There are many kinds of cardboard. Some will make a shoddy dollhouse. I am not talking about the cardboard boxes one gets from the grocery store to pack things for moving, storage, or mailing. I am referring to the corrugated cardboard used for shipping large appliances. There is a world of difference between the two.

Let's compare the three materials mentioned: plywood, foam core board, and corrugated cardboard. I have no doubt I'll be able to change your mind as to the merits and advantages of using corrugated cardboard.

The plywood called for in most dollhouse plans is ½" fir plywood, double-A grade, faced exterior, finished both sides. This is an expensive hardwood and most difficult to work with . . . unless you have the tools and skill of a carpenter or cabinetmaker. There is a pine plywood of the same quality, but pine is a soft wood and slightly easier to work with, but it is more expensive than fir. Foam core board is very easy to work with but is quite costly.

Let's compare prices and see how much each would cost if used in our house.

½" fir plywood, double-A grade, 4′ × 8′ sheet @ $18 per sheet
　2½ sheets for shell of house　　　　　　　　　　Cost . . . $45
⅜" fir plywood, double-A grade, 4′ × 8′ sheet at $16 per sheet
　2½ sheets for shell of house　　　　　　　　　　Cost . . . $40
½" pine plywood, double-A grade, 4′ × 8′ sheet @ $22 per sheet
　2½ sheets for shell of house　　　　　　　　　　Cost . . . $55
⅜" pine plywood, double-A grade, 4′ × 8′ sheet @ $20 per sheet
　2½ sheets for shell of house　　　　　　　　　　Cost . . . $50
½" foam core board, 24″ × 40″ @ $3.35 per sheet and
¼" foam core board, 24″ × 36″ @ $2.45 per sheet (both sizes used for house)
　8 sheets of ½"　　　　　　　　　　　　　　Cost . . . $26.80
　2 sheets of ¼"　　　　　　　　　　　　　　Cost . . . $4.90
　Total cost of 10 sheets　　　　　　　　　　　　. . . $31.70
Corrugated cardboard—limitless amount　　　　　　Cost . . . free

No need to ask which price appeals to you the most.

Tools required for each of the materials are the next consideration . . . and they can be considerable.

The plywoods, fir or pine, require a complete home workshop of tools. Power circular saw, saber/jig saw or keyhole saw, drill, hammer, screwdriver, carpenter's square, razor, saw, miter box with saw, long and short blade heavy-duty knives, metal ruler, sander, clamps and/or vise, glue, and sharp pencils.

The foam core board needs nothing in the way of heavy power tools. Tools for this material are a utility knife, metal square, metal ruler, miniature miter box, miniature jigsaw (or coping saw), hot glue gun with glue sticks, craft glue, contact cement (optional), and sharp pencils.

And what do you need for corrugated cardboard? Utility knife, metal square, metal ruler, craft glue, and pencils.

Now do you want to spend hundreds of dollars for a complete home workshop, less than a hundred dollars for a miniature workshop, or less than ten dollars for all tools (assuming you haven't the simplest of tools on hand right now) needed to build a dollhouse? Again there is no need to ask which you prefer.

There is another drawback to power-tool equipment. Most women do not care to work with these tools. Even if she, or her husband, doesn't mind, the tools can only be used in basement or garage. Who would ever dare to use these power tools on the kitchen table? But both the foam core board and corrugated cardboard dollhouse can be built on the kitchen table.

Take another look at our corrugated cardboard dollhouse. It defies anyone, even on the closest inspection, to tell it from a dollhouse made of plywood or foam core board. I admit there are a couple of giveaways. Plywood and foam core board will warp; corrugated cardboard will not. The dollhouse made of plywood is so heavy it is a struggle for one person to carry it (even two can have a difficult time); one person can easily carry a foam core board or corrugated cardboard dollhouse from place to place.

So far we've only discussed the cost of materials and tools needed to build the dollhouse shell. Let's go a step further and quickly cover the materials needed and the cost of a finished dollhouse.

To buy one ready-made, completely finished, can cost from $200 all the way up to $3,000 to $4,000 and, yes, even into 5-digit figures. Now you're saying you know where to buy a dollhouse for $40. You can, but is it finished and, if so, how is it finished? Is it sturdy? And how many rooms does it have? When I'm comparing prices, I'm talking about a well-finished, sturdy nine-room dollhouse. You aren't going to buy a dollhouse like that for $40. If you can, I'll take a dozen and resell them overnight for twice the price.

I'll cover all this in depth later, but here are some of the items you'll need to finish a dollhouse. If you go the expensive way, the materials for siding, windows, doors, interior trim (wallpaper, flooring, moldings, painting, fireplaces, stairways, etc.) can cost you well over $100 and more likely $500 or more. But all the above materials for our Corrugated Dollhouse will cost you as little as twenty dollars and no more than forty dollars.

Still skeptical? Well, there's only one way to make a believer out of you. Go to an appliance store. The proprietor will gladly give you all the corrugated boxes you want . . . free. And you're ready to start building your dollhouse. What do you have to lose except the price of some craft glue . . . about $3?

So, without further ado, let's get building.

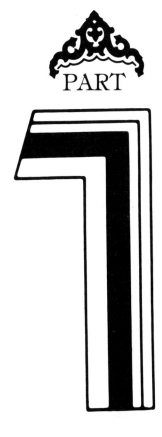

PART

THE DOLLHOUSE SHELL

1
BUILDING THE DOLLHOUSE SHELL

Materials for Shell

CORRUGATED CARDBOARD. Do not confuse this with the cardboard used in boxes you get from the grocery store. Corrugated cardboard is used for shipping large appliances. Almost any appliance dealer will let you have as many shipping boxes as you want.

WOOD STRIPS. The wood strips needed are part of the appliance packing boxes. If not, any 1″ × ½″ strips of wood will do just fine. These are optional, as I'll explain later.

NAILS. For wood strips. About 3 dozen 6-penny nails are sufficient.

GLUE. SOBO, TACKY, or any white resin glue is recommended. These glues set up quickly, dry clear, and have good bonding strength. You can also use hot glue that is applied with a hot glue gun. Use hot glue only if you intend to build more than one dollhouse. Otherwise, the expense of buying a glue gun and the sticks has defeated the purpose of this book, which is to build a dollhouse at a price anyone can afford. And, unless you have four hands or a proficient helper, hot glue can be difficult to handle. It has a quick set-up time, 60 seconds or less, and it is bonded permanently. And I mean permanent. Mistakes must be cut apart with care and difficulty, and sometimes whole sections of a dollhouse must be done over.

TOOLS FOR SHELL

Utility knife and razor-blade refills
Metal square 6″ × 12″
Metal ruler (optional)
Sharp pencils
Hammer (optional)

Building a Dollhouse

On the next several pages are the complete plans for our Corrugated Cardboard Dollhouse. Read them over carefully until you understand how the pieces fit together. The scale is ¼″ = 1″.

To save time and frustration, let's cover some important points before we begin constructing.

1. Cut 2 of each piece unless otherwise noted.

2. Make certain the corrugated cardboard you are using is of uniform thickness. From manufacturer to manufacturer, appliance to appliance, the thickness varies. You will want your corrugated cardboard, when laminated, to be either ⅜″ or ½″ thick but never a combination.

3. Laminate all pieces, unless otherwise noted. Glue the two pieces of each part together for strength and proper thickness as one would if making a dollhouse of plywood or foam core board.

4. When laminating, glue printed sides together. Paint and/or wallpaper will not always cover the heavy print on your corrugated boxes.

5. Check plans with picture on the back cover before cutting. If you want a different floor plan, choose one of the alternate floor plans.

6. Windows in the basic plan can also be changed to suit your taste. Window treatment should be decided before the holes are cut. Refer to the section on windows before making your first cut and select the ones you want.

7. The stairway in the basic plan is the easiest to make but here, again, you might have other ideas. Changes in the various stairways are included in the section on stairways.

8. Floor plans, window sizes, and stairways can be changed even after the dollhouse is constructed, but you will save time if you do the desired modifications at the beginning.

9. Check all measurements before and after you cut any piece. You may cut both pieces together of parts that are to be laminated if you carefully keep printed sides together.

10. Pre-assemble each floor as you go along. Do not glue until you know exactly where the pieces go. Although you can cut out a glued-in piece, it will save time and keep your blood pressure down if you're not gluing and re-gluing, cutting and recutting, because of a foolish mistake.

11. Above all: take your time and never—I repeat—never make a cut without a square or straight edge.

12. Review all the points covered and you will be ready to build your dollhouse with the minimum amount of errors.

Before Laminating

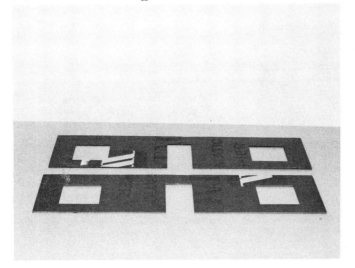

After Laminating

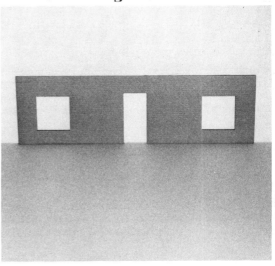

Dollhouse Plans

BASIC PLAN

The basic plan of our dollhouse has front porch, living room, dining room, and kitchen on first floor. There is a second floor overhang above the porch. On the second floor, the middle room is a library or den with a bedroom on each side, one bedroom for the lady of the dollhouse and the other for the master of the house. On the third floor is the roof extension overhang. The three rooms on this floor are a playroom, bedroom and/or storage over the master's bedroom, a child's room in the center and bathroom over the lady's bedroom.

One does not have to feel restricted to follow the basic plan as suggested. One could have three bedrooms on the second floor, eliminating the library or den. And should you wish to set your dollhouse in the time before plumbing, the bathroom could become a storage room or an extra bedroom.

All plans from the basic through alternate plan D are merely ideas to help you create your own dollhouse. Much of the joy in building a dollhouse is in making it truly your own creation.

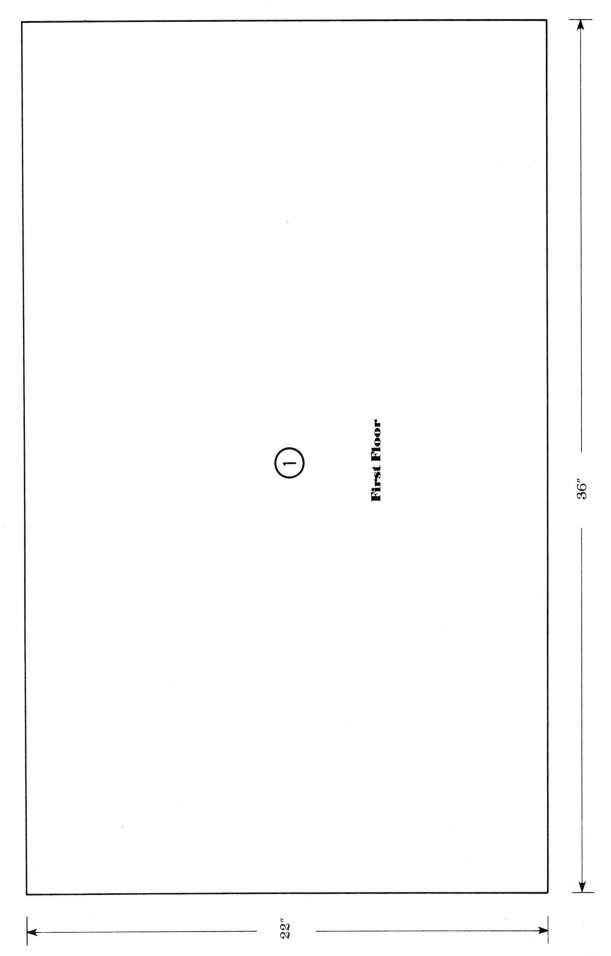

First Floor

(1)

36"

22"

5

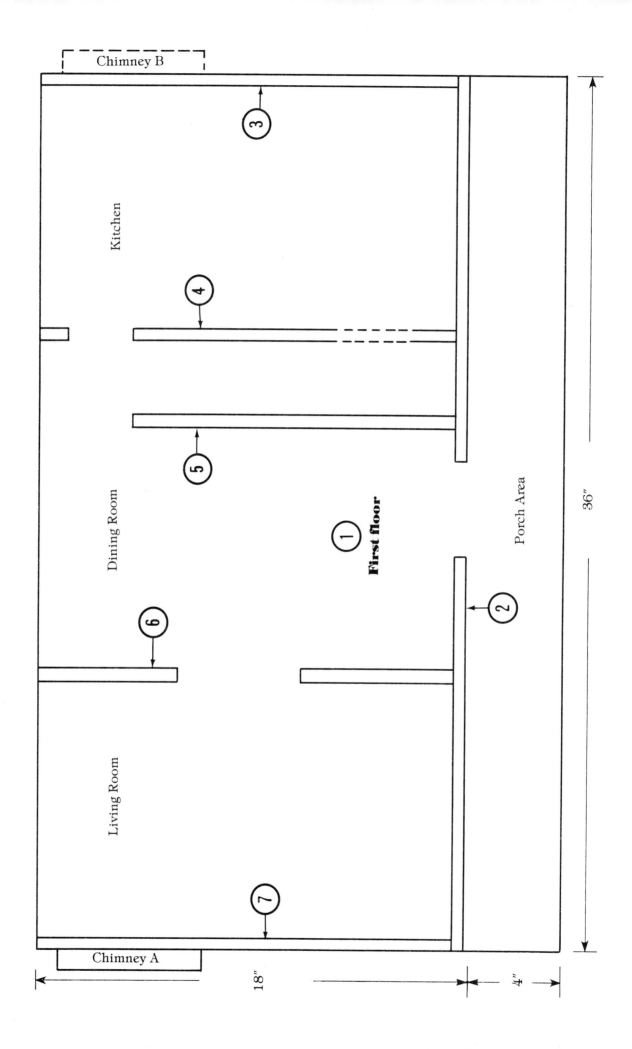

Chimney B

3

Kitchen

4

5

Dining Room

1 **First floor**

Porch Area

36"

Living Room

6

2

7

Chimney A

18"

4"

6

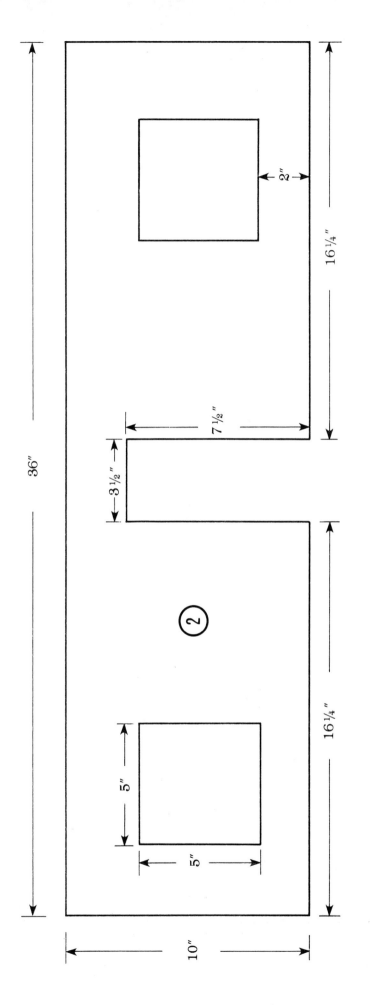

First-Floor Front

7

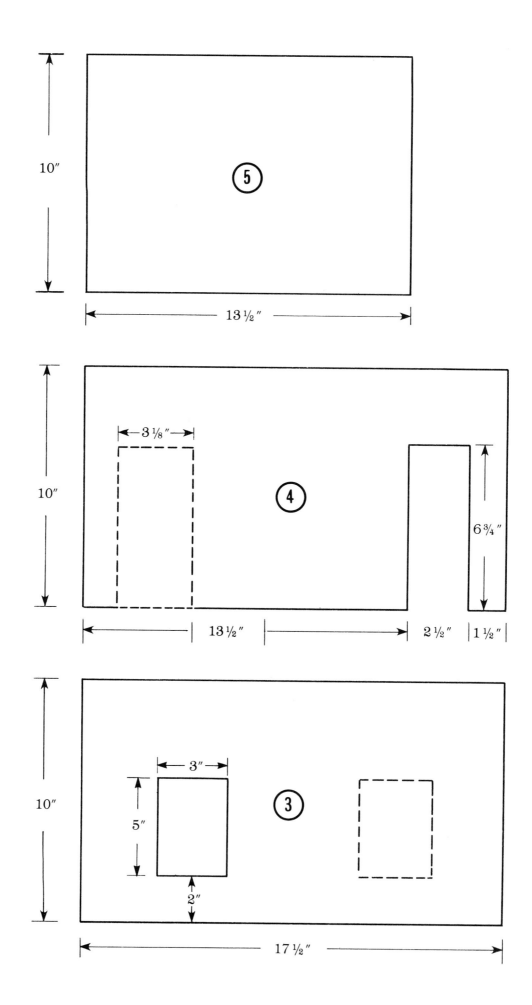

8

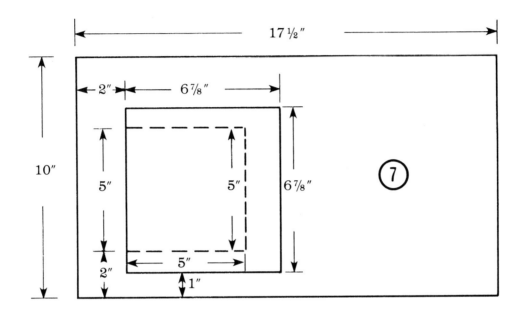

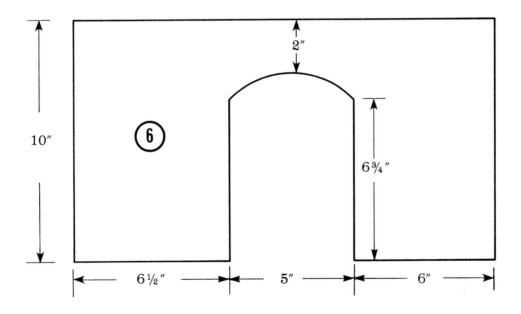

9

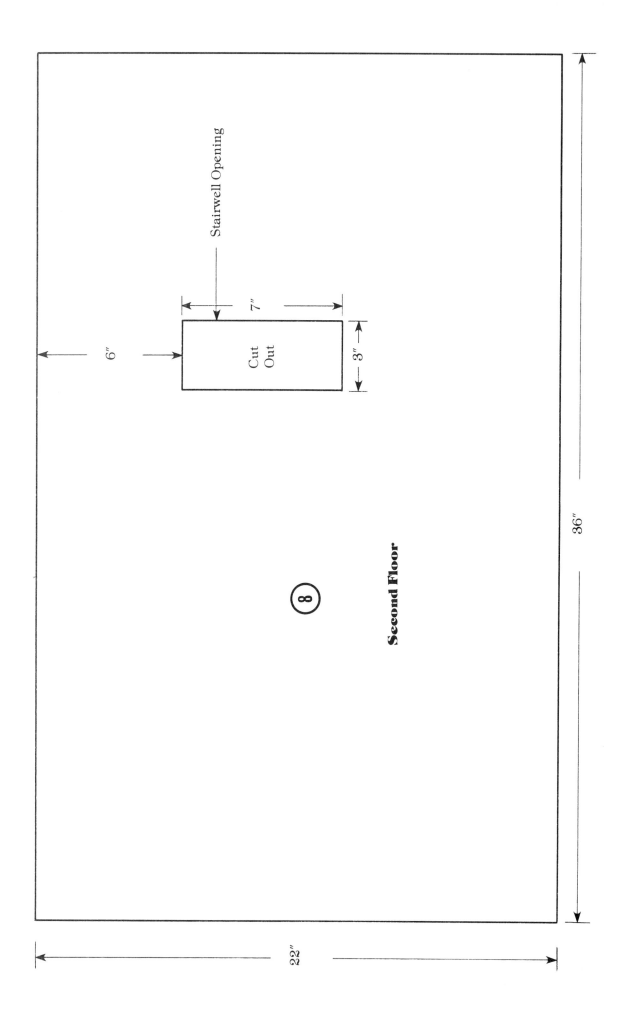

Stairwell Opening

7"

Cut
Out

3"

6"

36"

22"

Second Floor

⑧

10

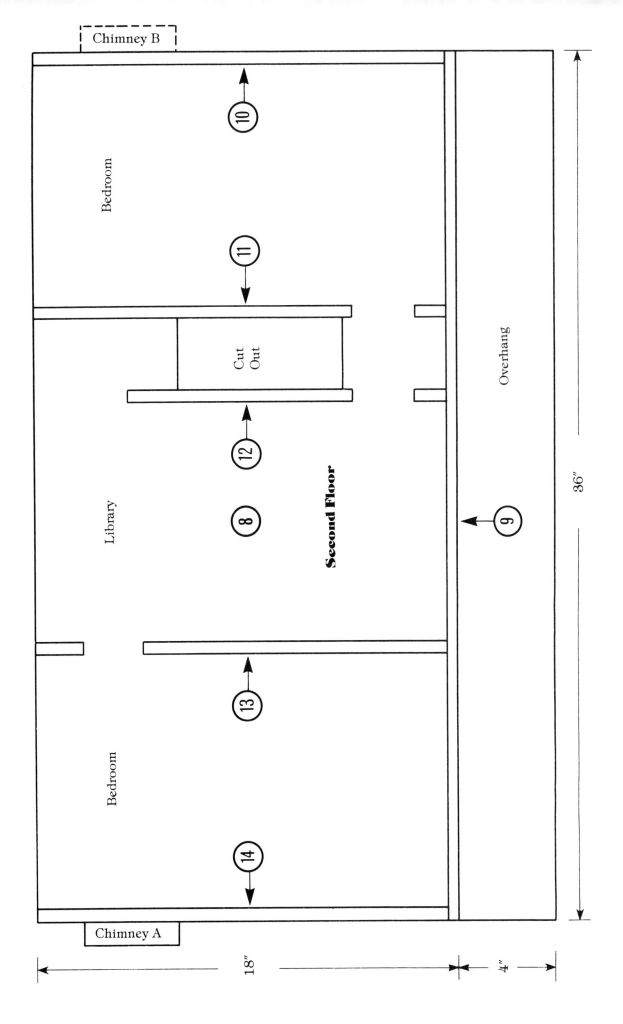

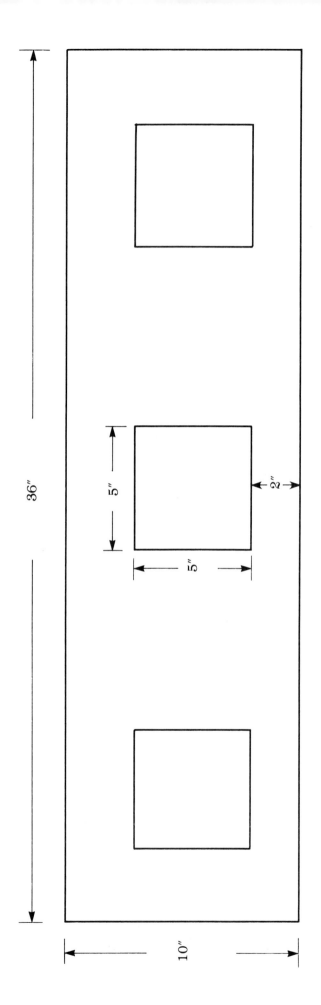

Second-Floor Front

36"

5"

5"

2"

10"

12

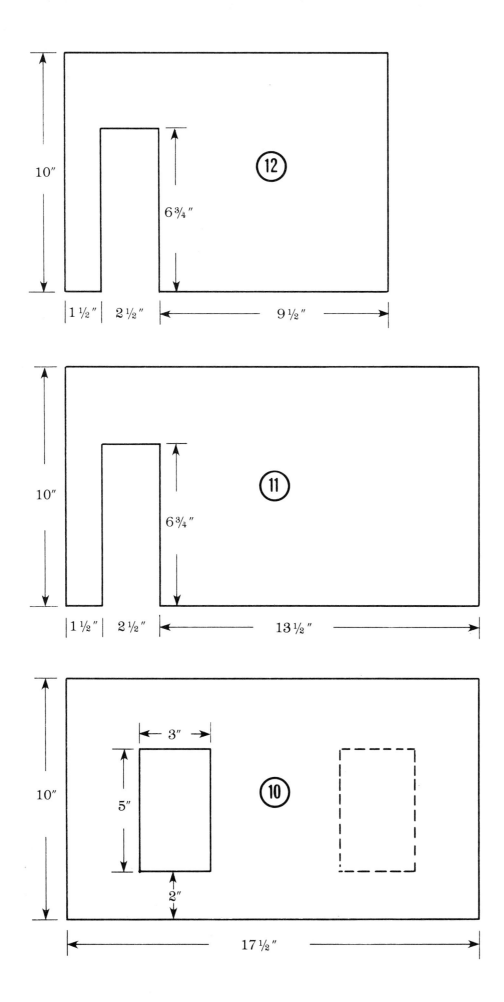

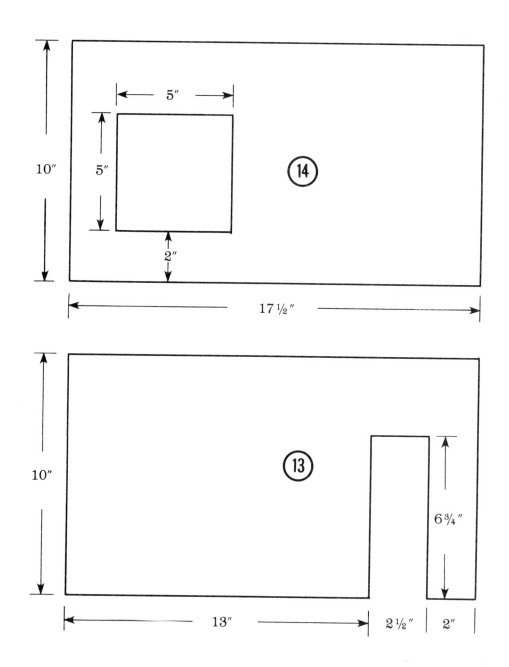

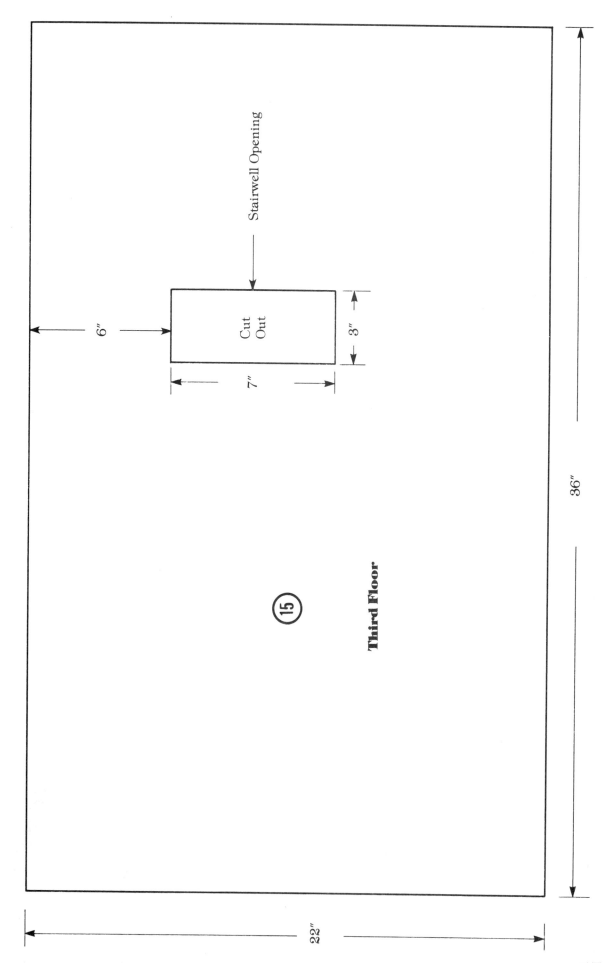

Stairwell Opening

Cut Out

6"

7"

3"

36"

22"

⑮

Third Floor

15

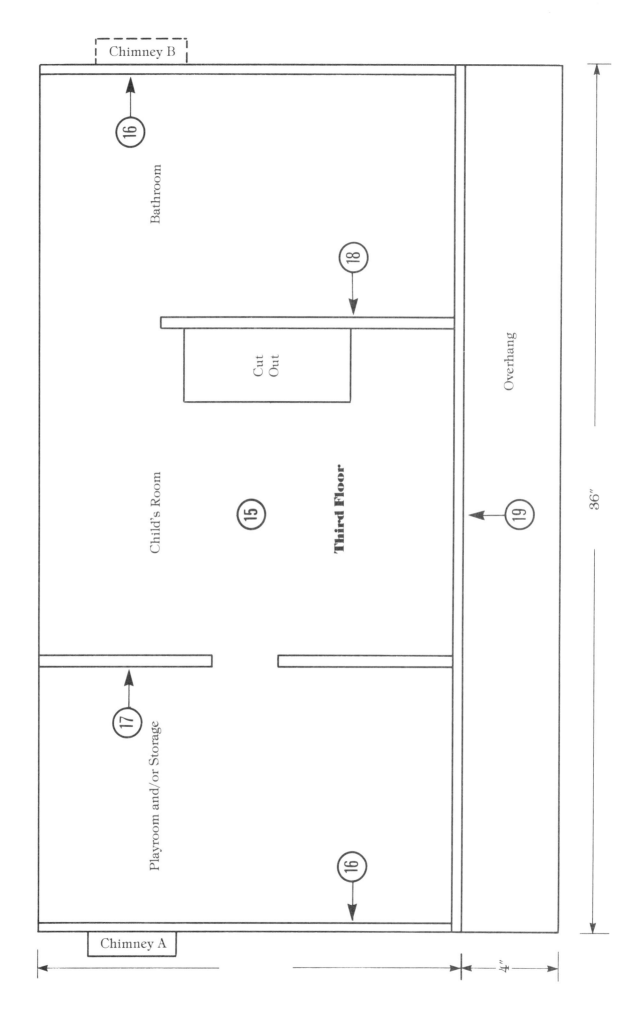

Chimney B

Bathroom

16

18

Cut
Out

Child's Room

15

Third Floor

Overhang

19

36"

Playroom and/or Storage

17

16

Chimney A

4"

16

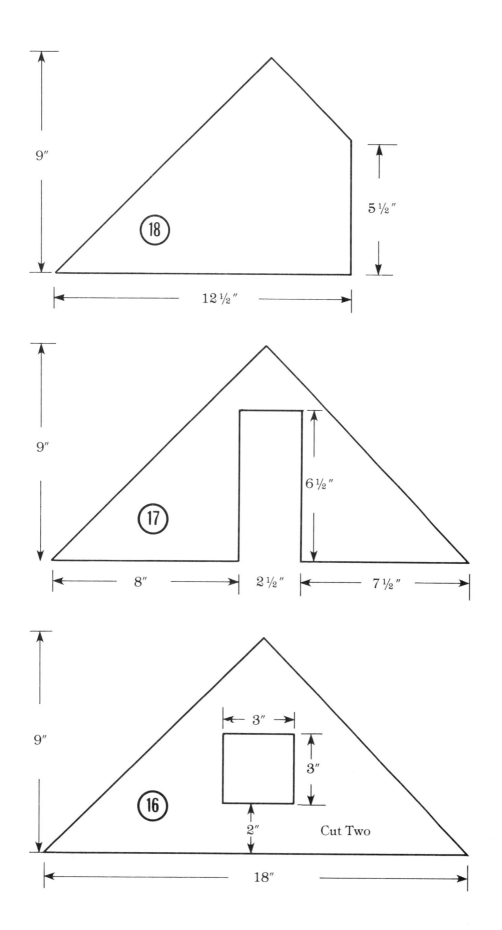

9″

5½″

12½″

⑱

9″

6½″

8″   2½″   7½″

⑰

9″

3″

3″

2″

⑯

Cut Two

18″

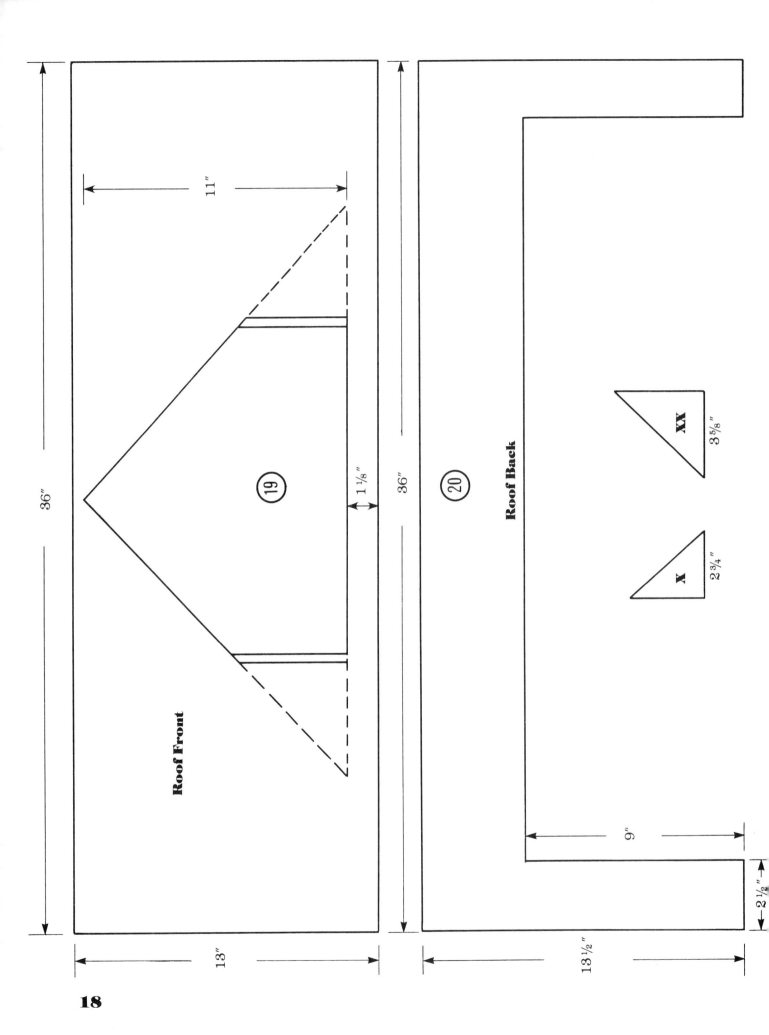

Roof Front

⑲

36"

11"

13"

1 1/8"

Roof Back

⑳

36"

13 1/2"

9"

2 1/2"

X

2 3/4"

XX

3 5/8"

18

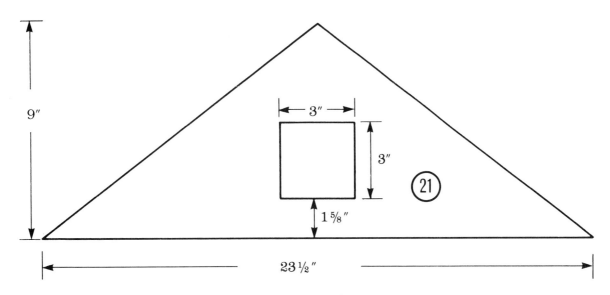

Dormer Front

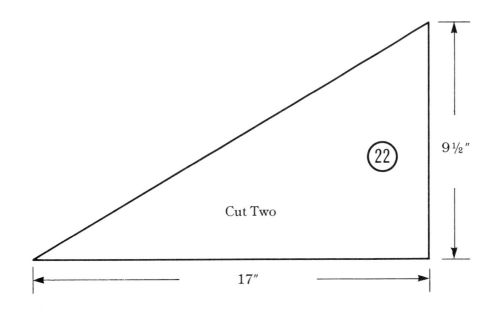

Cut Two

Dormer Roof

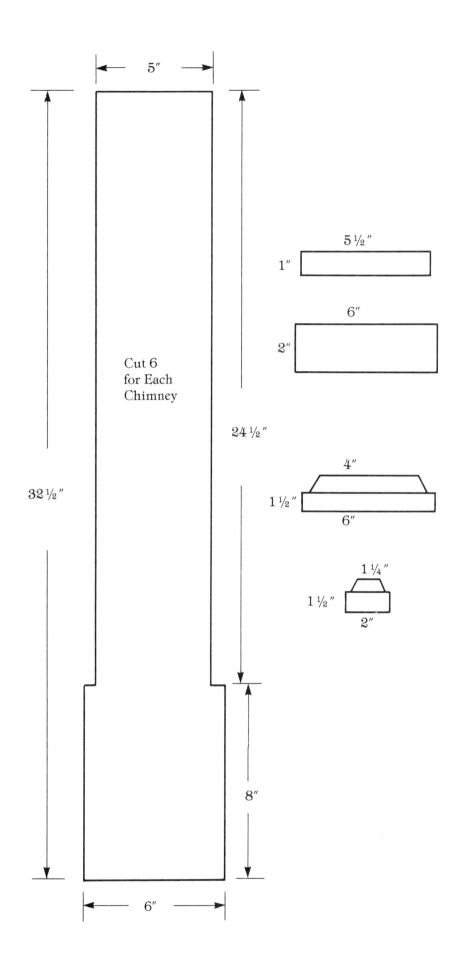

5″

5 ½″

1″

6″

2″

Cut 6
for Each
Chimney

24 ½″

4″

1 ½″

6″

32 ½″

1 ¼″

1 ½″

2″

8″

6″

ALTERNATE PLANS

In Plan A the only change is to bring walls 5 and 6 and walls 12 and 13 closer together to form a central entranceway downstairs and a hall or small sewing room/bath/hall on second floor. This hall can be furnished with a grandfather clock, table and chair, or sewing machine and cabinet. In this case you will leave the bathroom on the third floor.

In Plan B the changes are greater but no more difficult. This plan lends itself to the true Victorian. The side entrance allows for a dining room and kitchen on first floor. The second floor one has a library and living or sitting room. On the third floor are two bedrooms and one room that can be used for either a bathroom or for storage. You may exclude the bathroom from any of the plans. If you are making a period house, you will not include a bathroom, as bathrooms, as we know them, did not come into common usage until the turn of the century, and then only the wealthy had such a facility.

In Plan B do not be skeptical of the same walls used in more than one place. This is not an error on the plans. Wall 11 is used in 4 places and wall 18 is used in 2 places.

The measurements for walls and floors are the same as in the master plan. Windows are the same size or, as mentioned before, can be changed to suit your individual preference.

Plan C may be used for any of the floor plans. It is merely the elimination of the porch area and overhangs.

Plan D may also be used with any of the floor plans. It has a porch area that goes only partially across the front of the house. Over this porch area is a small roof, angled cut so snow and water will run away from the second floor. This prevents water from running back into the house, flooding walls and/or ceilings.

In Plan D the second and third floors are cut according to the floor plans in C, which eliminate the overhangs.

I could also have given an alternate Plan E, which is to build your dollhouse without a dormer. This can be used with any of the plans detailed. But as I will cover the dormer when we get our house built to that point, I will not detail it here.

Now that you have several floor plans and front-view plans, or have other ideas of your own, we'll get down to building our dollhouse.

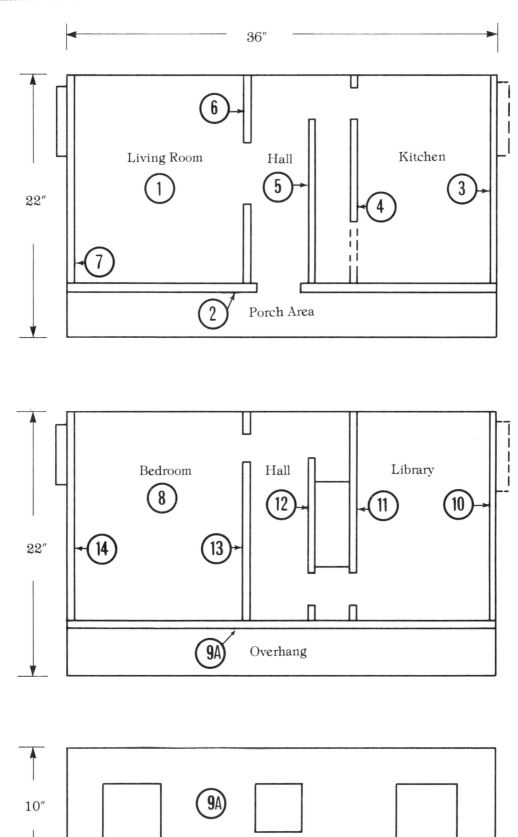

Alternate Plan B

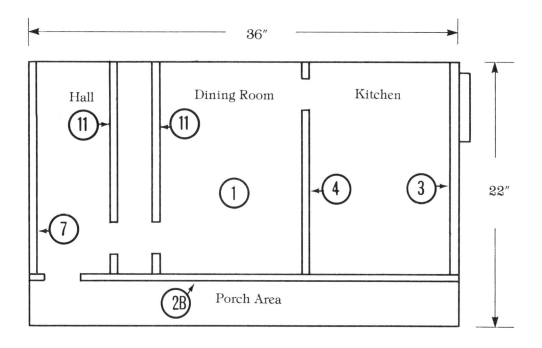

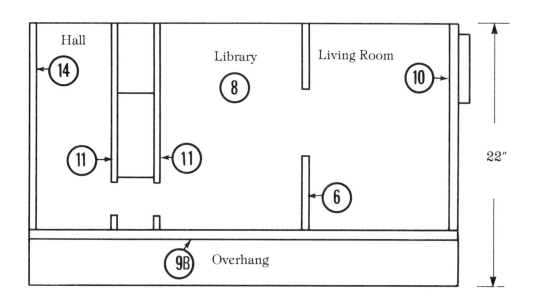

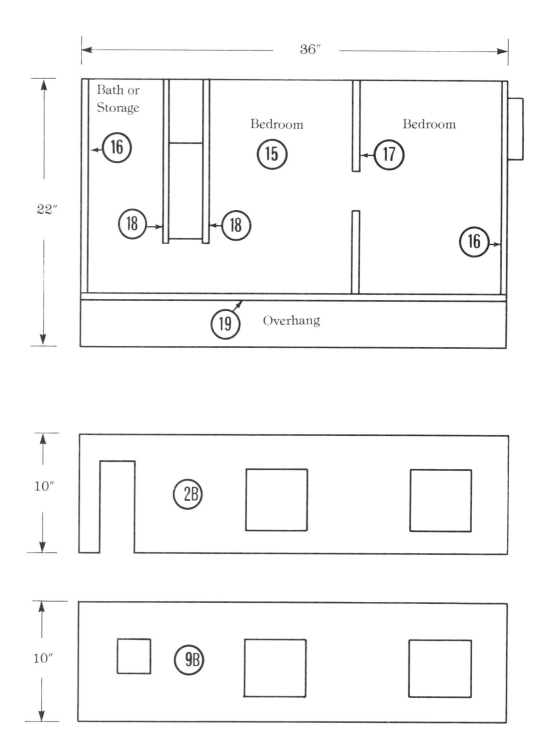

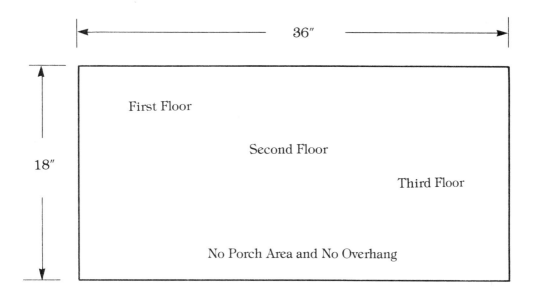

First Floor

Second Floor

Third Floor

No Porch Area and No Overhang

36″

18″

Alternate Plan C

Alternate Plan D

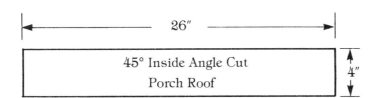

26″

4″

45° Inside Angle Cut
Porch Roof

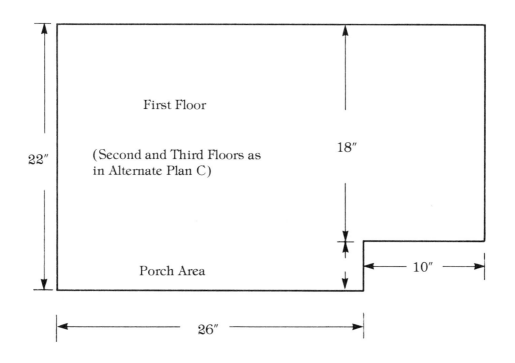

First Floor

(Second and Third Floors as
in Alternate Plan C)

Porch Area

22″

18″

10″

26″

Order of Construction

1. The base of your dollhouse may be made in one of two ways. You can use the wood that comes as tie-downs in appliance shipping boxes for base as shown in picture. Make certain the outside measurements of the base are the same as those of the first floor of your dollhouse. Nail and glue strips together. If no wood tie-downs came with your corrugated boxes, any 1″ × ½″ wood stripping will do.

Or you may laminate sheets of corrugated cardboard together until approximately 1″ thick, remembering to keep measurements of base the same as those of the first floor of your dollhouse.

2. Cut and laminate all pieces for the first floor. Check any changes to be made before cutting. If you use only one fireplace (one chimney), cut second window along dotted lines in piece #3. If you plan to use pantry, cut hole for same along dotted lines in piece #4. If not using a bay window, make smaller window opening along dotted lines in piece #7.

3. Glue and/or nail laminated floor to base.

4. Mark placement of all partitions on laminated first floor. Mark placement of same partitions on inside first floor front.

5. Glue front as indicated on porch line. At same time glue at least two of the inner walls or both side walls to keep front square.

6. Glue remaining first-floor partitions in place on placement lines. Let this assembly dry. While waiting, cut and pre-assemble second floor.

Mark first floor as shown. No need to mark the outside wall placement as these will line up automatically. Also, no need to mark door and/or archway openings. These lines are only guides to line up all partitions to keep your rooms square.

(See detailed sketch page 27)

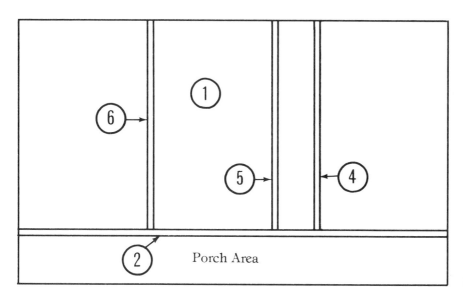

First Floor

Mark inside first floor front as shown.

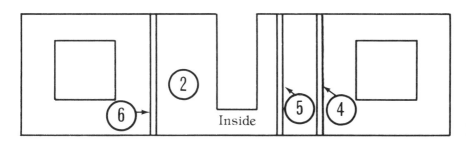

Inside

First Floor Front

Front View

7. On underside of second floor (first-floor ceilings) mark placement of all first-floor partitions. On top of second floor mark placement of all second-floor partitions. Check floor plan you are using. Avoid mistakes.

8. Glue laminated second floor in place along front, sides, and partitions, carefully aligning with all markings.

9. Mark second-floor partitions on second-floor front. Glue second-floor partitions on placement lines in same manner as was done on first floor. Check floor plan and all changes you are making.

10. On underside of third floor (second-floor ceilings), mark placement of second-floor partitions. On top side of third floor mark placement for third-floor partitions. Again be sure to check the floor plan you have selected.

11. Glue third floor in place in same manner as second floor.

12. Glue third-floor partitions in place. Keep each partition on third floor square while drying. You have no front lines to keep the triangular-shaped partitions of third floor level and square. Once again check your floor plan for proper placement.

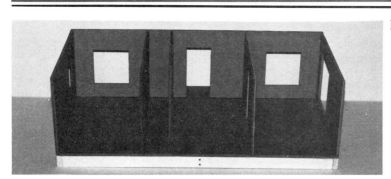

Back View

Front View

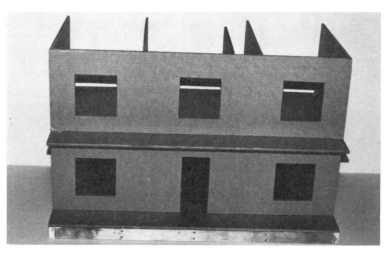

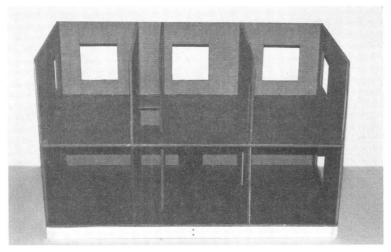

Front View

Front View

Back View

13. On underside of roof front mark placement of third-floor partitions. Check your selected floor plan. Glue along front edge of third floor and front edges of all partitions. Carefully align roof front.

(If electing not to have a dormer on your dollhouse, skip steps 14–17.)

14. Cut out dormer section in front roof between walls 17 and 18. Dormer peak should be ½″ from top edge of roof and dormer bottom approximately 1½″ up from bottom roof edge. (See plans.) Do *not* cut out the X and XX dotted-line sections.

15. Tack dormer along lower roof cut straight with dollhouse fronts.

16. Now carefully cut and angle X and XX spacers 45° to hold dormer front upright and straight. Use your square. Glue X and XX to roof and dormer. Glue dormer front along bottom at same time.

17. Line up dormer-roof sections with taper as shown in drawing. Glue to roof, edges of dormer front, and together at center.

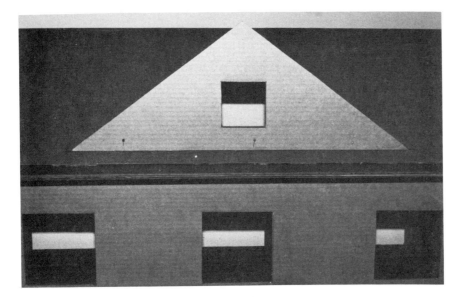

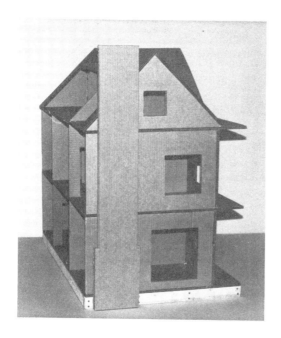

18. Before gluing back roof in place, paint the inside white (or whatever color you have chosen for the ceilings of your dollhouse). You can paint the ceilings of the third floor after back roof is in place, but it is easier to do it now than later. (See Painting, page 33). After painting with two coats, glue along back edge of partitions 17 and 18 only as far down as roof covers. Glue along both outside side edges, top edge (where roof sections are cut to fit with the 45° cut), and along third-floor-edge width of lower roof edge.

19. Laminate six pieces of corrugated cardboard for each chimney. Glue to side(s) of dollhouse shell flush with bottom of base and approximately 1½″ from dollhouse back at wider, lower edge and 1¾″ along long narrow edge. Chimney tops will be installed later as part of the finishing work. This is because we will be standing the dollhouse on its roof when doing some of the finishing, and the chimney tops, being higher than the roof, will prevent the dollhouse from being kept level.

The shell is completed. Now comes the creative, fun part. We are going to finish and decorate step by step. Each step will be explained in its proper order. You may vary ideas, but never the order of finishing . . . unless you enjoy doing things the difficult way.

2 FINISHING

Your shell is completed. Note that the bay window was not included as part of the basic shell. The bay window, if you have elected to use it, will be made and installed along with the other windows.

Finish the dollhouse, step by step, in the order given. Do not skip around when finishing your dollhouse. This will only cause problems.

Painting—Interior

One quart white latex semi-gloss or alkyd paint.

Small vials of tints to mix with white paint as base. (Do not buy small jars or cans of colors you wish to use. This is not only expensive, it can be wasteful.)

Before buying any paint, check any leftover paint you might have on hand from some painting done in and around your "real" house.

Never use a flat latex. It has a tendency to leave brush marks even after two or three carefully applied coats of paint.

Paint ceilings first. Stand the dollhouse on its roof and paint all the ceilings with two coats of paint (color a matter of choice). Do not paint any ceilings you intend to wallpaper. In my dollhouse I painted all the ceilings white except the slanted ones on the third floor. There one ceiling was painted a light peach, the other two wallpapered.

The next step is to paint all the walls you do not intend to paper.

When all the ceilings and walls have been painted, with the exception of walls you will wallpaper, decide how you want to finish the floors. The simplest way is to paint them with a coat of clear polyurethane and, because your floors already are a light brown, you will have plain varnished floors. Don't worry about the floors being too plain. Scatter rugs can take care of this.

You can buy paper flooring, such as those shown on page 34. After these floors are cut and laid, give them a coat of clear polyurethane for that light varnished luster. (For laying floor see Wallpapering, page 35).

If you cannot find the design of flooring you wish, you can draw patterns on stiff shelf paper. Use a fine, felt-tip colored pen for marking patterns. This is time-consuming, but if you are artistic, your floors will be most beautiful.

One idea you will not find in the floor patterns on page 34 is marbleizing. This effect is used in entranceway, kitchen, and bath. First paint the floor with a high-gloss paint. When still wet swirl in two or three colors with a toothpick. Experiment on a piece of scrap cardboard until you get the desired effect. It may sound difficult, but it is really quite easy and makes a beautiful floor.

A quick review of the order of painting:

1. All ceilings not to be wallpapered.
2. All walls not to be wallpapered.
3. All floors and this includes floors you paper and "varnish" with a coat of clear polyurethane.

WOOD

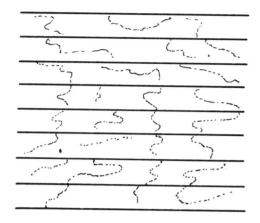

Pine

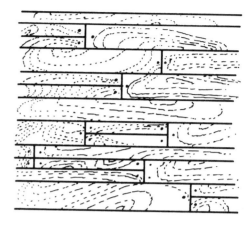

Random

Parquet

All flooring patterns are actual size. Using anything larger is not following the 1″ to 1′ scale. After flooring has been marked in pattern chosen, brush on a clear coat of polyurethane for a varnished look.

LINOLEUM, TILE

Linoleum and/or tile can be done in any color of your choosing. Use the marbleized effect, as explained before, or checkerboard squares or squares with your own individual designs.

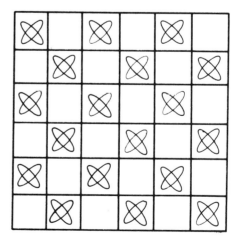

Wallpapering

Do not size walls before wallpapering the corrugated cardboard walls of your dollhouse, such as you must do if making a dollhouse of plywood.

Use regular wallpaper paste for applying wallpaper to walls and/or ceilings and floors. If you do not wish to buy wallpaper paste, you can make your own with flour and water. Some recommend using craft glue, mixed half-and-half with water for wallpapering, but I strongly advise against this. It sets up so fast you have little time to place the wallpaper properly. You must be accurate the first time in placing and matching each piece of wallpaper. One mistake and you must peel or scrape off the paper, taking some of the corrugated backing with the paper.

There are many types of paper to use for wallpapering. The most beautiful are the miniature wallpapers, but these can be expensive, so shop around for bargains. You don't have to buy the most expensive. You'd be surprised how lovely the least expensive of the miniature wallpapers can look when a room is finished and furnished. I, for one, prefer a quiet wallpaper so as not to detract from the furnishings and accessories.

Wallpaper-sample books of regular-size patterns can, at times, be a way to get free wall coverings for your dollhouse. But two notes of caution: (1) Patterns usually are too large for miniature rooms and (2) You might not have enough of one wallpaper sample to do a complete room. But it is worth a try and the price—free—can't be beat.

Small-print gift-wrapping paper also can be used for wallpaper. But care must be taken when using this kind of paper. Some paper is too flimsy, will not hold the paste without "bleeding," and can tear easily when being applied to walls. Select a stiff paper with small print. There are also some small-patterned flocked gift wraps that are heavy enough, but unless you're very careful not to have the paste too thin, these flocked papers will "run."

There are several ways to apply wallpaper. But the most satisfactory and easiest is the procedure suggested by Garth Close of Handley House Miniatures.

First cut and match paper for each wall of a room. I usually cut the front wall first, matching side walls at the front corners. Do *not* cut out for doors or windows. Wallpaper over all openings. Do not worry as openings will be taken care of when wallpaper is dry. For ease of handling, cut paper about ¼″ less than height of your room. Paper stretches when wet, and if cut exact you could have an "overlap." And if paper doesn't stretch, you have a ½″ baseboard and ½″ ceiling molding to cover the gap. If you are using a wallpaper with a border, fit it along ceiling edge, leaving gap at baseboard.

After cutting the pieces for your walls, cut vertical strips of wallpaper 1½″ to 2″ wide and the height of room less ¼″. Fold in half, pattern inside. Lay strips face down on a clean surface (never use newspaper as the print will adhere to your wallpaper) and brush with your choice of wallpaper paste. Place these strips vertically in each corner. Press paper into corner with half on each side of corner. Crease into corner. Smooth out wrinkles with clean fingers or soft cloth.

Now lay wallpaper for front wall on clean surface, brushing on a generous but not watery coat of paste. Line up on front wall, smoothing out wrinkles with hand or soft cloth. Massage toward corners and edges until all large wrinkles and bubbles are eliminated.

Do the same with paper cut for side walls. Match the pattern at front corners. If you cut and matched carefully before pasting this should be no problem.

When paper is thoroughly dry and brittle, cut out window and door holes with your utility knife.

When all the walls are painted and/or papered, you can paper the floors with random, parquet, pine, or linoleum printed miniature paper flooring. The "grain" of paper can go across or from front to back of room. A change in pattern direction can be most attractive and sometimes can save you one or more sheets of paper flooring. But do not mix the direction of pattern in a room, only in different rooms. And do not cut out for stairway openings.

Cut paper to fit floor of each room. Some floors will be cut to cover area under door cutouts. With paper flooring you do not have to come right to walls but the gap cannot be as great as that allowed on walls. You have $\frac{1}{8}$" all around the base that will be covered with baseboard.

Paste and smooth as you did for walls. When thoroughly dry, you may give all the floors a light coat of clear polyurethane for varnished or waxed luster.

Diagram for Placement of Wallpaper Strips in Corners

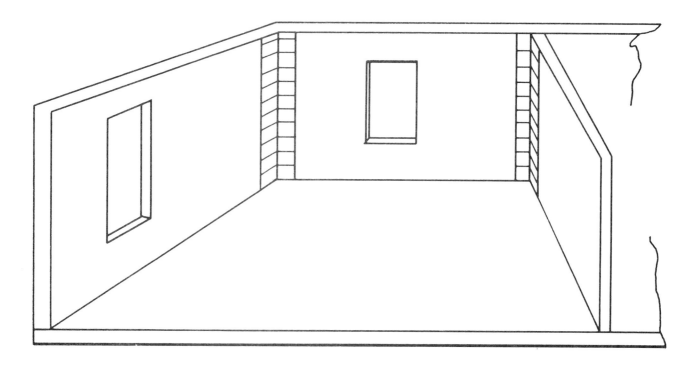

If you have a dormer on your dollhouse, note that there are no straight walls as shown in diagram for placement of strips in corners (above). The corners in the dormer room are inside and outside corners, all on a slant. You will also have a rough section where all pieces of dormer and roof come together. You can overcome this roughness with a piece of wide baseboard. Use $\frac{1}{16}$" poster board for this baseboard. If your wallpaper is not flimsy, it will cover this rough seam very nicely.

For this dormer room the paper should be an allover print that requires no matching. Cut strips for both inside and outside corners, folding in half with the pattern facing in on inside corners and out on outside corners. Once these strips are in place, cut triangular pieces to fit along slope of dormer roof. You might find it easier to cut the side walls from the patterns for these walls.

All this might look and sound difficult, but I assure you it is not. Do not select a pattern that has to be carefully matched.

Now it's back to the exterior.

Siding

You have three options in finishing the exterior of your dollhouse. You can paint, using a semi-gloss; you can "stucco"; or you can use siding.

If you choose to paint, avoid using a flat water-base paint. This paint sometimes crinkles corrugated cardboard. And never use a gloss paint of any kind. The exterior of real houses, except for trim, is never painted with high-gloss enamel. And as a dollhouse is a replica of the real, we will paint as in a real house.

Use a semi-gloss latex or alkyd paint. The color is your decision, but for authenticity check with the period of your house. You will find that most houses, until the 1930s, were painted in muted colors. White, yellow, and gray were the most popular.

Should you want to "stucco," add a textured paint product to your paint. Or you may use sand—white or light colored—for the texture. Because textured paint is thick, apply it with a trowel or piece of heavy cardboard. Your stucco can be smooth or swirled with circular motions of trowel or cardboard. Again, check the period of your house for the use of stucco. Always apply stucco with the color already added to your paint.

The most popular way to finish the exterior of a dollhouse is with siding. This takes a little more time, but the results are well worth the time and effort.

Begin by cutting several strips of $\frac{1}{16}$" illustration board (poster board and mat board are the same and the $\frac{1}{16}$" is sometimes just called light-weight) $\frac{3}{8}$" wide. I used a rough-textured illustration board, but there is nothing to prevent you from using the smooth. The rough comes in a light yellow on one side and white on the other. If you wish your dollhouse to be yellow, you can eliminate painting the siding. That also holds true if you want your house to be white. I prefer to paint it, no matter which side I use, as it gives it more depth and covers all seams and cut lines. Siding is painted with semi-gloss after it has all been glued to the exterior of your dollhouse.

Starting at lower edge, even with top of wood or laminated base, glue on a "starter" piece, a $\frac{1}{16}$" illustration board $\frac{1}{8}$" wide. This sets up the proper angle to match overlapping of siding as you work upward. Overlap the second piece ($\frac{1}{16}$" $\times$ $\frac{3}{8}$") and all pieces thereafter $\frac{1}{8}$". Marking the correct distance of $\frac{1}{4}$" for top line of each piece of siding at edges and centers, along with having your square and ruler handy, will keep all pieces lined up and straight. We don't want to end up with the last, or any piece, at a slant.

Using white craft glue, such as Sobo, you have time to move and align each piece as you go along. But don't be in a hurry. Wait until each piece sets up before going on to the next. This only takes a couple of minutes, so there isn't much delay. If you use hot glue, you have to work faster and with complete accuracy, but there is no waiting for glue to dry or set.

Cut several pieces of siding before you begin to side. All siding is $\frac{1}{16}$" $\times$ $\frac{3}{8}$" strips. The length of the strips may vary. Stopping to cut each individual piece is time-consuming. I usually have enough pieces cut to do at least one side of my dollhouse. If one has 10 to 12 strips of various lengths cut ahead, that is usually a sufficient quantity. If you have a helper, one can cut while the other glues. Four hands are better than two, but they are not always available.

Any piece of siding that slightly overlaps door or window openings can be trimmed later, after the whole house is sided and the glue thoroughly dry. But at corners and back edges come as evenly as possible. This will help when trimming outside edges with moldings. But you do *not* have to come right up to window or door holes. Work just close enough so the window or door frame will cover any such gaps . . . $\frac{1}{4}$" to $\frac{1}{2}$". Once door and window frames are installed, you'll never see any of these small gaps. (See Windows and Doors, page 38, for frame sizes.) (Picture on siding installation, page 38.)

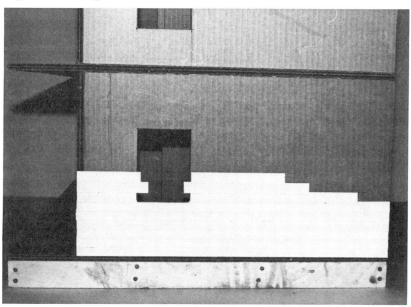

Windows and Doors

After you have selected the windows you wish to use in your dollhouse, and have cut proper-size hole openings for each, you are now ready to make your windows and doors.

I am going under the assumption you have chosen the windows as shown in the basic plan. For any change in window size, if you have not already done so, now is the time to make any adjustments. You can still go by plans and instructions for the windows in corrugated dollhouse pictured on the front cover by adjusting size of openings and frames. Remember to keep the windows a uniform height *down* from the top of each room not up from the bottom (floor).

The easiest window to change is the 16-sectioned large window. You can make it a 12-sectioned window (4 across and 3 down, or 3 across and 4 down), an 8-sectioned window (2 across and 4 down), or a 9-sectioned window (3 across and 3 down).

WINDOW A. Cut entire frame in one piece from ⅛" illustration board as shown in full-scale drawing. (⅛" is sometimes called heavyweight.)

Now check the thickness of your corrugated openings. If they are of uniform thickness as advised earlier you will have simplified making the window and door opening trims. You should have a ⅜" thickness, as this is the usual thickness of laminated corrugated cardboard.

Now cut several long strips of ⅛" illustration board ⅝" wide for all door and window opening trims; ¼" wide strips for crossbars.

Yes, I said ⅝" wide. That was neither an error in drawing, planning, or printing. Your trim must be ⅝" wide. But how do we get this figure when we are talking about ⅜" thick laminated corrugated cardboard?

Let's add it up. First we have the ⅜" thick laminated cardboard; then we have 1/16" siding with overlap making this ⅛"; then we add the inside window trim of ⅛" (this trim comes after all windows are glued in place). Add these all together: ⅜" laminated corrugated cardboard, ⅛" siding, and ⅛" inside trim and what do you have? ⅝".

But check the thickness of your laminated corrugated cardboard. It might vary. Whatever the thickness is, add ¼" and you have the size you must make all your window and door opening trims.

Window A

16-Sectioned Window Frame—Full-Size Pattern with Shutter Area

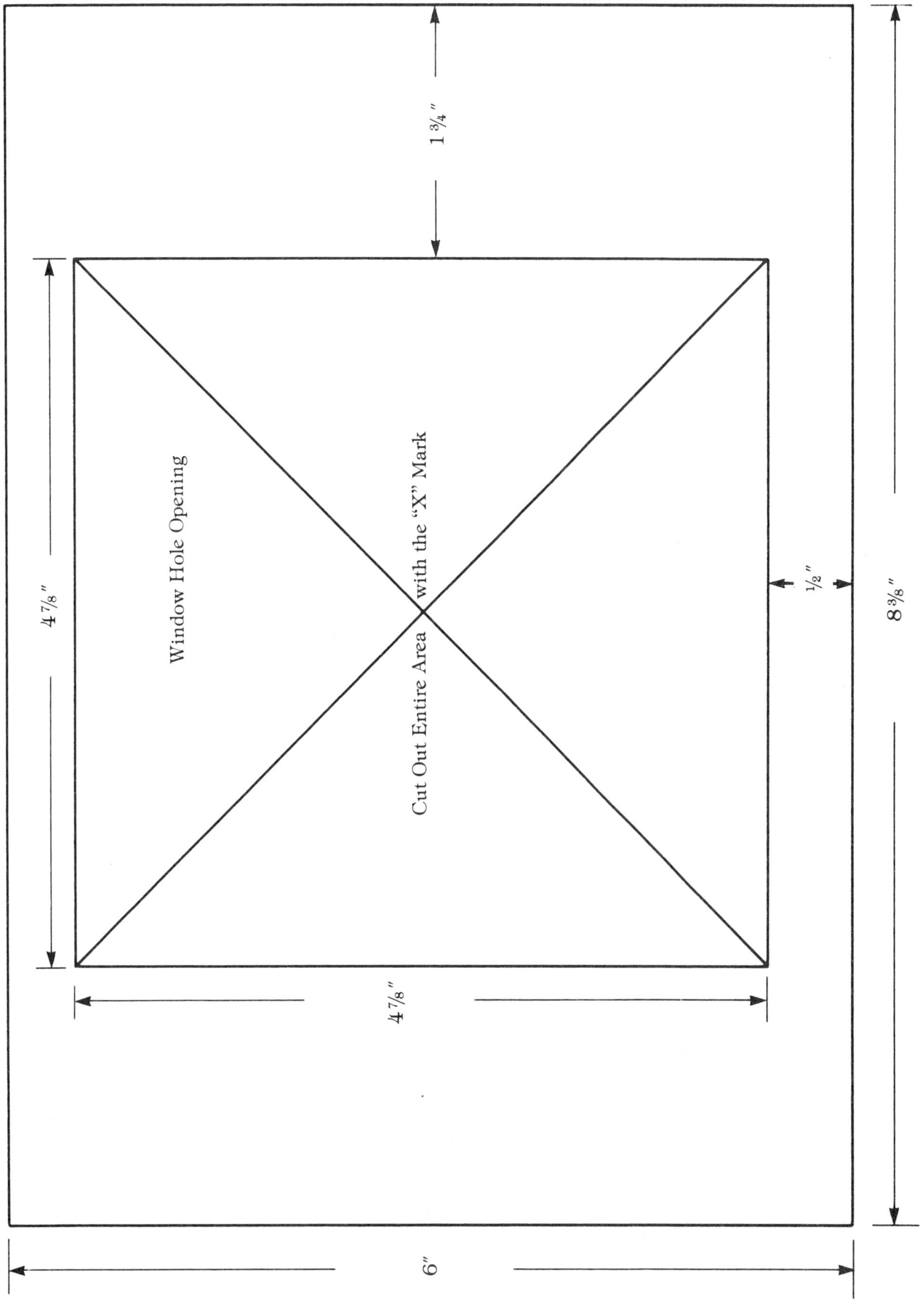
1 3/4″
Window Hole Opening
Cut Out Entire Area with the "X" Mark
4 7/8″
4 7/8″
1/2″
8 3/8″
6″

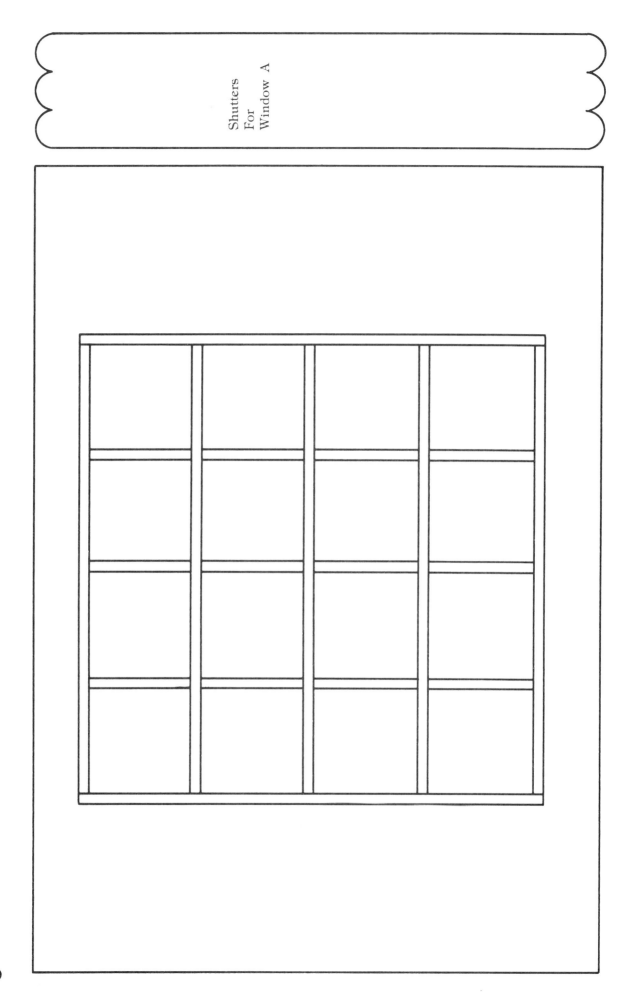

Shutters
For
Window A

Cut side opening trim and glue in place. Next measure and cut top and bottom window opening trim and glue both in place. Follow complete Window Pattern A and you should have no problems.

For window mullions (crossbars), cut 3 pieces of $\frac{1}{8}'' \times \frac{1}{4}'' \times 4\frac{11}{16}''$. Using the full-size pattern for a guide, mark and glue these pieces from top to bottom of window opening trim. (The mullions are not as deep as the opening trims.) Next, cut 12 pieces of $\frac{1}{8}'' \times \frac{1}{4}'' \times 1\frac{1}{8}''$ and glue in place as shown on full-scale 16-mullion window plan. (Apply glue with a toothpick, wiping off excess. Keep entire piece on flat surface over wax paper. Never on newspaper unless you want the daily news emblazoned across your window.)

Cut shutters of $\frac{1}{8}''$ illustration board or use 3 ice cream pop sticks glued together. Do *not* glue shutters in place until all windows are painted and shutters painted and/or decorated. We handle that part of the finishing when we come to it.

WINDOW B. Cut entire frame in 1 piece from $\frac{1}{8}''$ illustration board as shown in full-scale drawing. (See page 44 for drawing WINDOW B—DETAILED.)

Window B—Full-Size Pattern

Next cut 2 pieces $\frac{1}{8}'' \times \frac{5}{8}'' \times 2\frac{1}{2}''$ for top and bottom window opening trims. Glue in place. Cut 2 pieces $\frac{1}{8}'' \times \frac{5}{8}'' \times 3\frac{3}{4}''$ for window side trims. Glue in place.

Cut 1 piece $\frac{1}{8}'' \times \frac{1}{4}'' \times 3\frac{1}{2}''$ for long center section. Cut 2 pieces $\frac{1}{8}'' \times \frac{1}{4}'' \times 1\frac{3}{16}''$ for small cross sections. Line up all 3 pieces and glue in place.

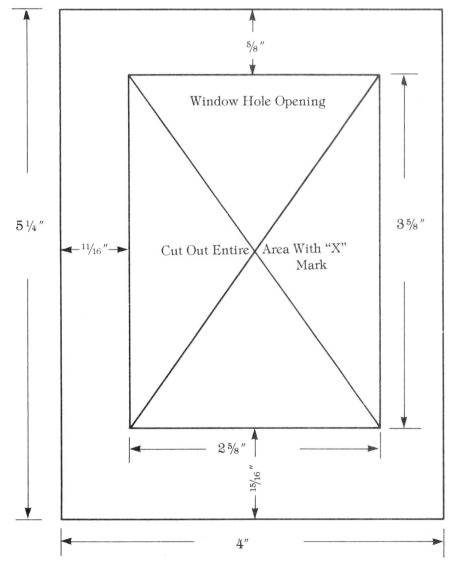

WINDOW C. Cut entire frame in 1 piece from ⅛″ illustration board as shown in full-scale drawing.

Window C—Full-Size Pattern

Next cut 4 pieces ⅛″ × ⅝″ × 1″ for top and bottom window opening trims. Glue in place. Cut 4 pieces ⅛″ × ⅝″ × 4½″ for side window opening trims. Glue in place.

Cut 2 pieces ⅛″ × ¹³⁄₁₆″ for center crossbars. Glue in place checking with pattern.

(See page 45 for drawing WINDOW C—DETAILED.)

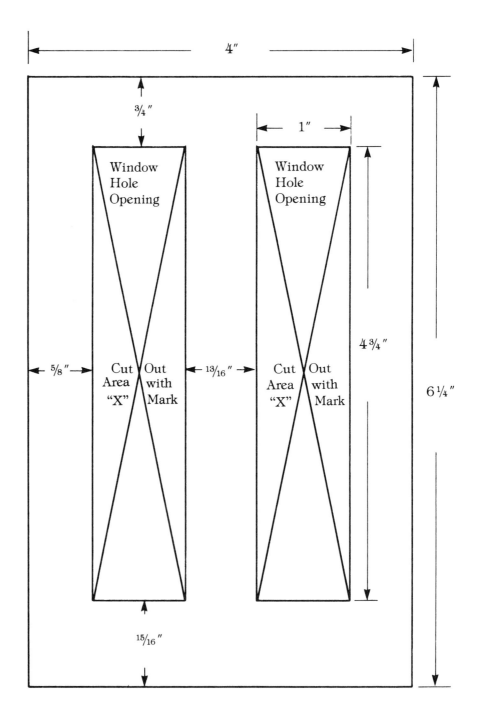

Now for the dormer and third-floor windows—small and the most intricate. Difficult, to some extent, but then is anything really easy in this Lilliputian world of dollhouse building? I think you will find, as I do, that the more challenging the project, the more rewarding the finished results.

WINDOW D.   Cut entire frame in 1 piece from ⅛″ illustration board as shown in full-scale drawing.

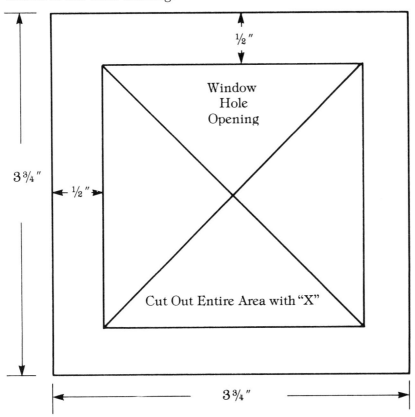

3¾″

½″

½″

Window
Hole
Opening

Cut Out Entire Area with "X"

3¾″

Window D—Detailed

Window B—Detailed

Cut 2 pieces ⅛″ × ⅝″ × 2¾″ for side window opening trims. Glue in place. Cut 2 pieces ⅛″ × ⅝″ × 2½″ for top and bottom window opening trims. Glue in place.

Cut 1 piece ⅛″ × ¼″ × 3⅝″. Fit into corners by cutting each end to a slight point. Glue in place. Cut 2 pieces ⅛″ × ¼″ × 1¾″ and fit in corners as with first piece. Glue in place.

Cut 8 pieces ⅛″ × ¼″ × ⅞″, mitering one edge of each piece as shown in detailed drawing. Glue each piece in place as you go along.

A lot of cutting and fitting, but isn't the final result worth the little extra time spent on this window? I think now you deserve a 5-minute break (at least) to admire your beautiful handiwork.

DOOR. Cut door frame from ⅛″ illustration board 7″ × 9⅜″. Cut top of door according to full-size pattern or to a design of your preference. Cut hole opening for door 3″ × 7″. If cut carefully, this can be retained for door. Then cut one more piece, door size, and laminate for ¼″ thick door. You might have to sand door slightly smaller than the opening to allow for ease of opening and closing.

Cut 8 pieces of 1/16″ illustration board ⅝″ × ⅝″ for door trim. Glue in place as indicated. (I repeat, this is also left to your own discretion. Make trims in manner pleasing to you.)

Cut 3 pieces ⅝″ × ⅝″ × 3″. Laminate 2 pieces for threshold. Glue in place at bottom edges of door frame. Glue other piece to top of door opening. Cut 2 pieces ⅛″ × ⅝″ × 6¾″ for side-door facings. Glue in place.

Pin door through threshold and top door frame ¼″ from either side for left- or right-door opening.

Cut out door trims as shown or design trims to suit your taste and/or style of house. Do *not* glue in place until door frame and trims are painted.

Cut 2 pieces ⅛″ × ½″ × 4¼″ and glue to top of door frame as indicated by dotted lines on detailed drawing of door. This may be painted before or after glued in place. It should match the color of door trim.

While on the subject of painting the door and door frame, let's detail how door and frames are painted. The outside of the door and door frame should match the main color of your windows. The threshold, door opening trims, and inside of door should be the color of the trim of interior room where door is installed. If you plan to stain the trim of this interior room, I advise staining all parts of door before painting. One can paint over stain, but it is almost impossible to stain over paint.

(DOOR FRAME - FULL-SIZE PATTERN page 47)
(DOOR FRAME - DETAILED page 48)
(DOOR and TRIMS - page 49)

Door Frame—Full-Size Pattern

9 ⅜ "

7"

Door Opening

Cut Out

2"

3"

2"

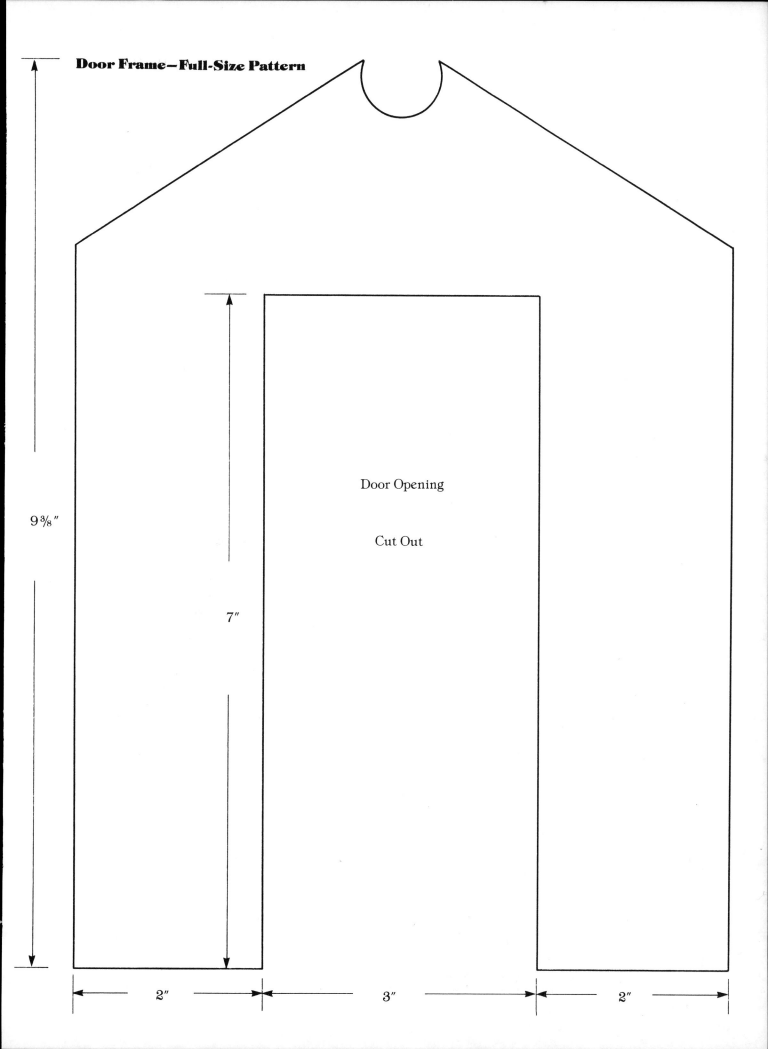

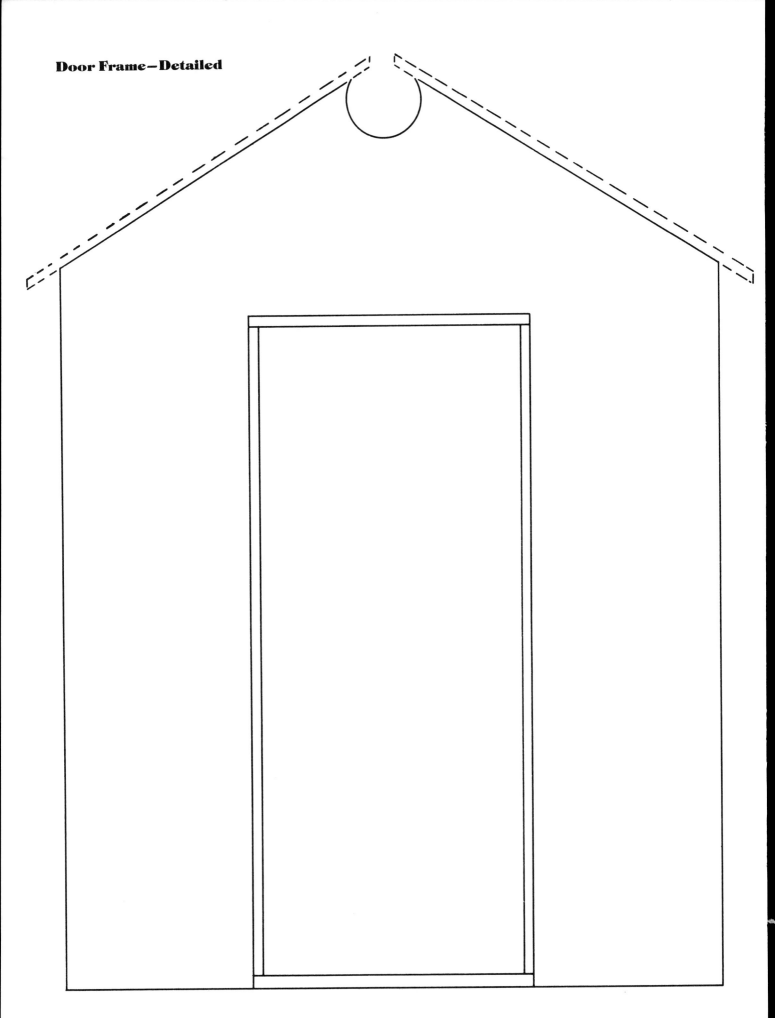

Door Frame—Detailed

Door and Trims

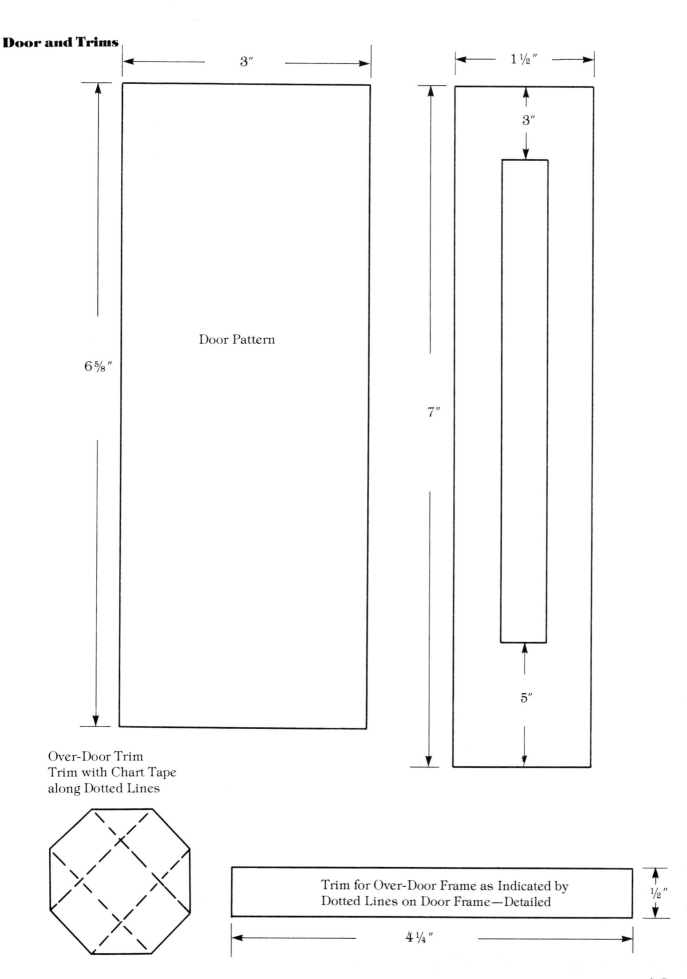

3"

1½"

3"

6⅝"

7"

Door Pattern

5"

Over-Door Trim
Trim with Chart Tape
along Dotted Lines

Trim for Over-Door Frame as Indicated by
Dotted Lines on Door Frame—Detailed

½"

4¼"

BAY WINDOW. You may have a little difficulty with the bay-window assembly, but if you follow the full-size plans, instructions, and pictures, you should have no serious problems. But should you make a mistake, you won't be out any money as most of the difficult work of the bay window is made with the *free* corrugated cardboard. (Plans: pages 51, 52, & 53)

**Bay Window
Exterior
Front View**

**Bay Window
Exterior
Side View**

**Bay Window
Interior
View**

We will start with the window sections of the bay window. Cut 2 pieces of ⅛″ illustration board the size of the full-size drawing for each window (a total of 6 pieces). Later these will be laminated for each window. Cut window-hole opening in all 6 pieces. Cut with straight cuts—the angle cuts will come later when assembling window sections.

Cut 3 pieces of thin plastic for windows. With ¹⁄₁₆″ white chart tape, outline each window frame on plastic, aligning with inside edge of hole opening. In case you don't know what chart tape is, call any drafting-supply store and they'll not only tell you what it is, but they'll sell it to you at about a dollar a roll . . . which goes a long, long way. Then carefully, with chart tape, crisscross from corner to corner. Next go diagonally from center top to center sides, center bottom to center sides. Then diagonally between the long and short diagonal strips. Then between short diagonal strips and corners. All this might sound complicated, but once you get started, it will be self-explanatory. And if you make a mistake with the chart tape, you can peel off and start over. Chart tape comes with a self-adhesive backing that never seems to lose its adhesive no matter how many times it is peeled off and replaced.

If you do not wish to buy the chart tape, you can mark the lines with a fine brush. But this takes more time and patience than most people have.

You do not have to buy chart tape or mark with a fine brush. You can save this expense and work by using the plastic trays from store-bought cookies and some candies. The ones I found have diamond markings, but any type markings will do and will serve the purpose just as well. And again going this route is free.

When windows have been marked, glue to one window frame with chart-taped or painted-side facing toward exterior of bay window. Now laminate each window with second window frame, plastic window between window-framing sections.

Cut out bay-window ceiling and floor for bay window interior. Cut 2 of each and laminate.

Bay Window—Full-Size Pattern

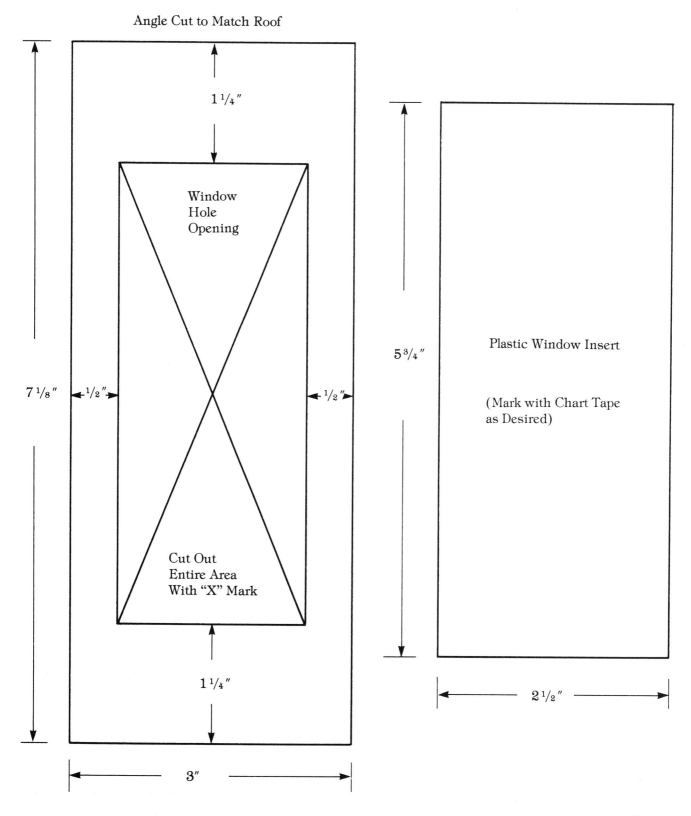

Angle Cut to Match Roof

1¼″

Window
Hole
Opening

7⅛″   ←½″→   ←½″

Cut Out
Entire Area
With "X" Mark

1¼″

3″

5¾″

Plastic Window Insert

(Mark with Chart Tape
as Desired)

2½″

Now it is time to angle-cut windows so they will not only fit together but along ceiling and floor as well. Glue window units together once they have been angle-cut to fit. Glue ceiling and floor inside window-unit frame, flush with top and bottom of assembled 3-unit window.

Cut out roof sides, center, exterior flat roof, and interior flat roof. Cut 2 of each piece and laminate.

Glue interior flat roof back flush with long straight edge of exterior flat roof.

Angle-cut roof sides, and center with cuts as shown. Fit to interior back roof and exterior flat roof. If this does not come out perfect, cut and reshape but be sure roof is not lopsided. If you make a major mistake, start over. As stated before, you won't be wasting money, only a little of your time.

Following plans, instructions, and pictures and taking your time should allow you to assemble this bay window with not too much difficulty. The pictures of the different views do not have the windows included and are painted white on flat surfaces. Making the bay window as a guide and taking pictures in this unfinished manner should make it clearer how each part is assembled.

Bay-Window Sections

Trace for exact measurements.

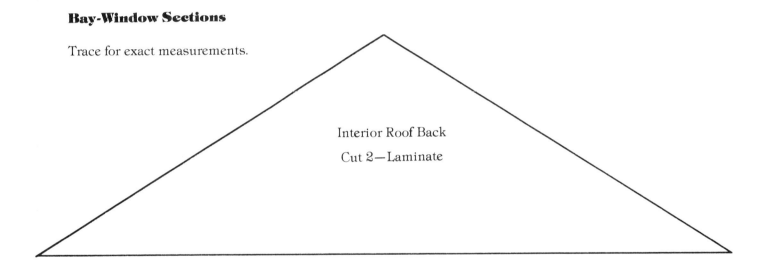

Interior Roof Back
Cut 2—Laminate

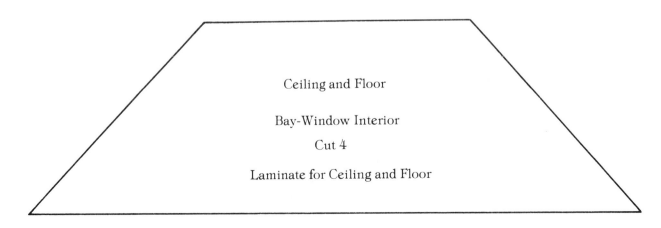

Ceiling and Floor

Bay-Window Interior

Cut 4

Laminate for Ceiling and Floor

Bay-Window Sections

Trace for exact measurements.

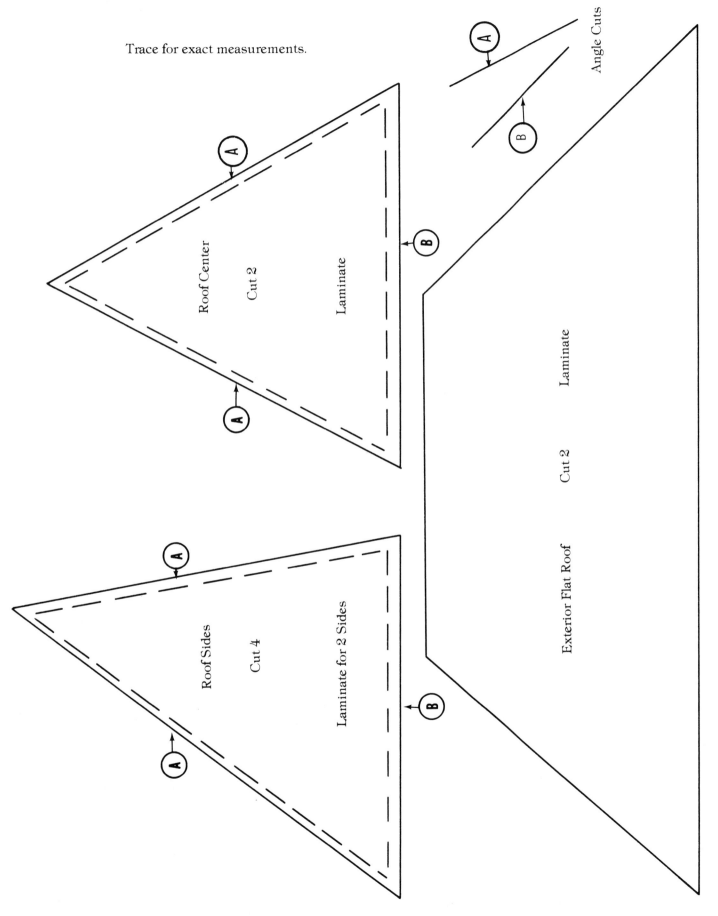

Roof Center

Cut 2

Laminate

Angle Cuts

Exterior Flat Roof   Cut 2   Laminate

Roof Sides

Cut 4

Laminate for 2 Sides

We will leave the exterior and return to more finishing work in the interior. No, I have not ignored the painting and installation of the windows. All this will be taken care of in the proper sequence. You will understand when we come to the order of final painting.

Fireplaces

There are many ways to make a fireplace. One can buy prefinished fireplaces, but these are too expensive for the purpose and premise on which this book is based—how to save money when building and furnishing a dollhouse.

I used one pre-formed, styrene fireplace in my dollhouse. It is beautifully detailed, costs only a dollar, and needs only to be painted. (See picture, page 55.) This fireplace was dry-brush painted to give it an antique appearance. A mirror was glued in the recess over the mantel. You can also decorate this recess with a picture, but I had a mirror the right size, which I did not need, so I used it. But if you want to buy a small mirror, it can be purchased for less than a dollar, and that still keeps us well within our budget.

The other fireplaces pictured, in the bedrooms and kitchen, were made of a high-density urethane. This is a Styrofoam product, not to be confused with the spongy and crumbly Styrofoam used for packing. We need something hard and firm. A piece of high-density urethane comes $1'' \times 12'' \times 16''$ and costs $3.50. This might sound expensive, but it is not. You'll get three fireplaces and the fourth for the living room if you choose not to use the preformed white styrene. Now tell me, where can you buy four miniature fireplaces for $3.50? You can't even buy one for that price.

The fireplaces can be made from illustration board or a block of wood. There are some drawbacks using either of these materials. Illustration board is too flimsy, unless laminated to $1''$ thickness, and the block of wood involves use of a power saw.

But the choice of materials, I will leave up to you. The full-size plans detailed for the fireplaces can be made of urethane, illustration board, or wood. The choice of material is not as important as to how these materials are handled.

If you make a fireplace "shell" of illustration board, it will not be sturdy and you will not be able to score brick lines as described in making the fireplaces. You will have to paint the bricks with marking pen or paint. Or you can cover your fireplace with "paper" brick (similar to paper flooring and/or wallpaper).

To make a solid fireplace of illustration board, you must laminate 8 pieces of the body of fireplace for each fireplace. Then you will be able to score with bricklike markings.

Making your fireplace of a solid piece of wood, also makes brick-scoring difficult. You will need to saw the long lines and deep-cut the smaller markings with a very sharp, heavy utility knife. Of course, you can also paint or "paper" the brick markings on wood.

The plans for the fireplaces, including the cook-stove fireplace for the kitchen, are all full-size. All parts of the fireplaces are made of the urethane, except the mantels, which are made of $1/8''$ illustration board laminated for proper thickness.

From the urethane cut all pieces you have chosen to use. By this I mean, cut the parts for all 3 or 4 fireplaces at the same time. By getting one step done for all the fireplaces instead of cutting for one, marking, painting, installing mantel, cutting backer and hearth; then repeating all this for the next fireplace and the next, you'll find you'll save time. Skipping around never gets the job done as satisfactorily.

So, first we cut all the pieces of the urethane. After these pieces are cut mark, with your square, every quarter-inch down both sides of the front. Holding metal ruler from mark to mark, score lightly with a narrow, blunt tool (such as a small, thin screwdriver) across face of fireplaces. If using the cook-stove fireplace for the kitchen, mark the hearth and chimney facing in like manner. Score sides of all pieces to match lines on front.

Then stagger-score the brick markings as shown.

Before gluing together, paint the fireplaces, hearth, and chimney with a flat white latex paint. Then for a realistic-looking brick, dry-brush surfaces lightly with a red latex paint. Next dry-brush a coat of yellow latex and finally a dry-brushed coat of brown latex.

Now cut mantels from ⅛″ illustration board, laminate and paint with semi-gloss or high-gloss white latex.

Glue mantels to chimney tops flush with back edge and ¼″ overhang on front and side edges. For cook-stove kitchen fireplace, glue fireplace to hearth, mantel to fireplace as described, and chimney facing to top of mantel flush with back edges.

For hearths in bedroom fireplaces, cut a piece of black construction paper 1″ × 4½″ and glue to bottom of fireplace. Using the same black construction paper, cut pieces 4½″ × 3½″ for inside backs of fireplaces. Glue in place along top and inside edges of fireplaces.

Glue completed fireplaces to walls of rooms in which you are using them. Check to see that they are lined up with the outside chimney. Fireplaces not lined up with an outside chimney would look ludicrous, but you'd be surprised how many forget this simple detail.

High Density Urethane Fireplace— 1″ Thick

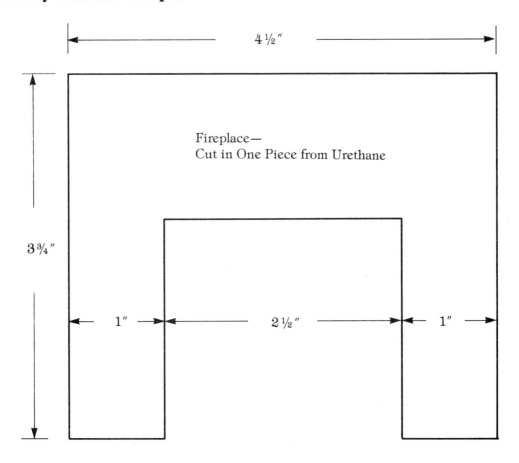

4½″

3¾″

Fireplace—
Cut in One Piece from Urethane

1″   2½″   1″

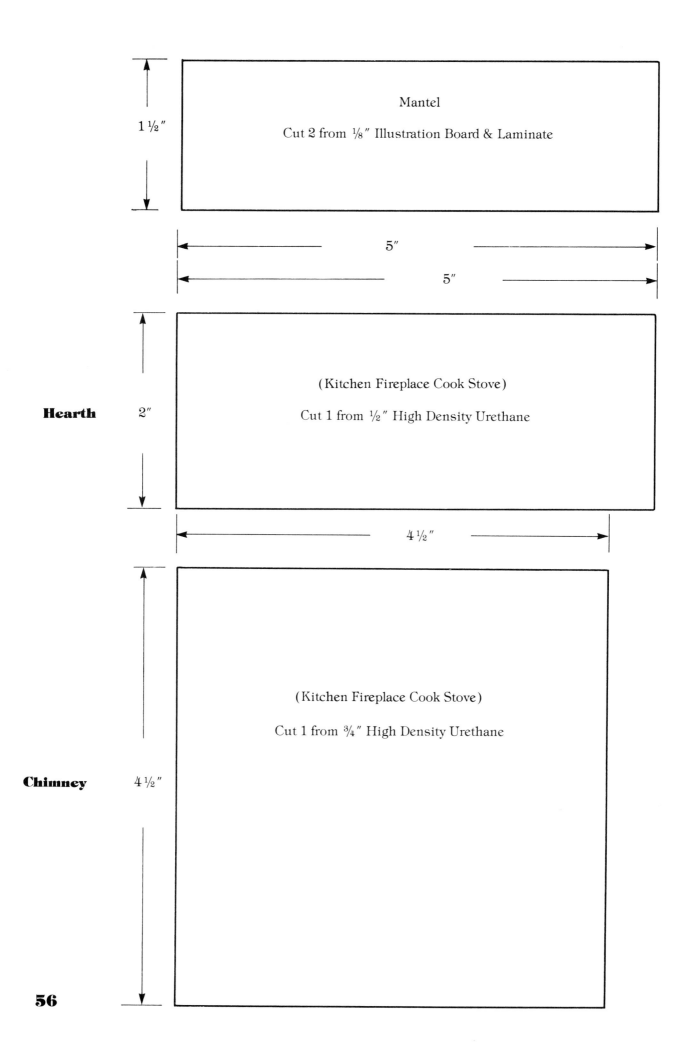

Mantel

Cut 2 from ⅛″ Illustration Board & Laminate

1½″

5″

5″

Hearth

2″

(Kitchen Fireplace Cook Stove)

Cut 1 from ½″ High Density Urethane

4½″

Chimney

4½″

(Kitchen Fireplace Cook Stove)

Cut 1 from ¾″ High Density Urethane

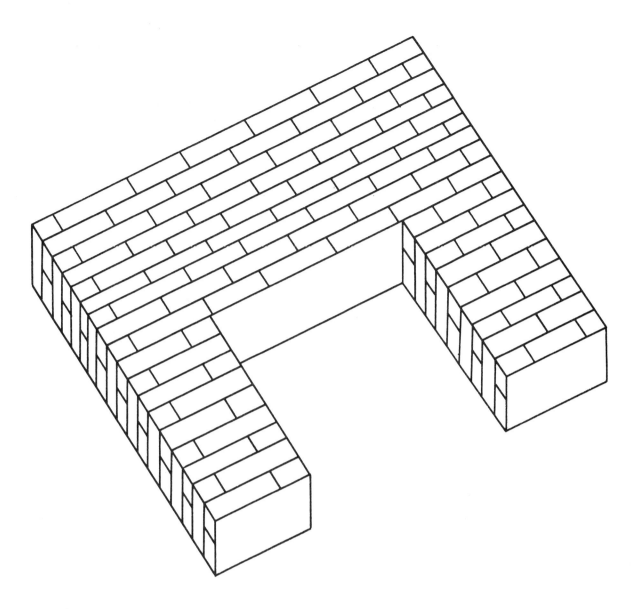

Fireplace shown is not to scale and is not full size. It merely shows you how to mark for bricks. Places not marked are to be left plain as they are in a "real" fireplace.

But you need not follow this brick marking. You can also make stone-like markings. As with most decorations in a dollhouse, it is all a matter of preference.

Stairways: Full-Size Pattern

STAIRWAY: BASIC INSTRUCTIONS

Cut 2 stringers of full-size pattern.
Cut 12 risers of full-size pattern.
Cut 12 treads of full-size pattern.
Glue top and bottom risers in place inside stringers, flush with front edge.
Glue remaining risers in place.
Glue treads in place from edge to edge of stringer against risers.

(See page 60 for detailed assembly drawings.)

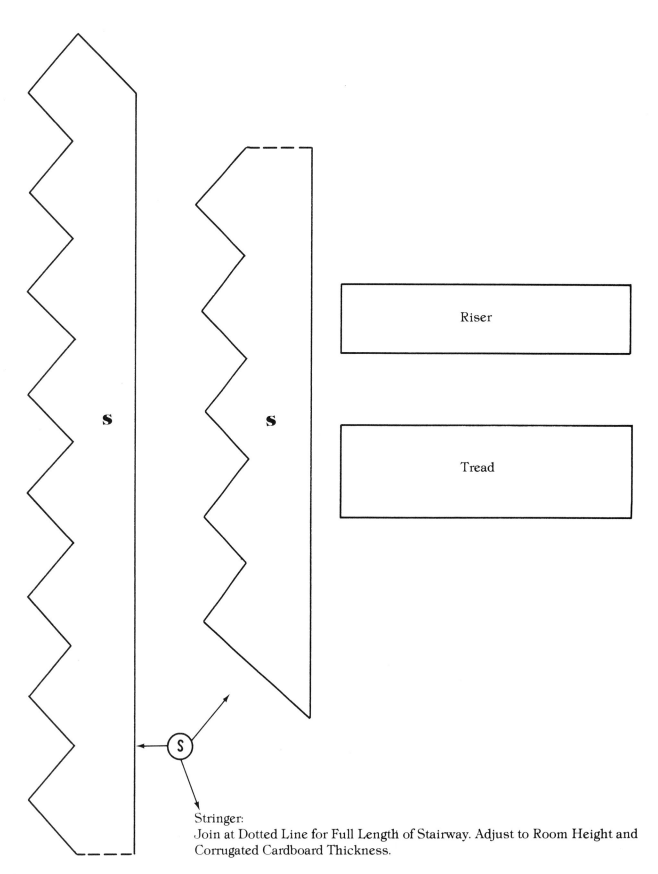

Riser

Tread

S

Stringer:
Join at Dotted Line for Full Length of Stairway. Adjust to Room Height and
Corrugated Cardboard Thickness.

If you plan to combine painting and staining on you stairway, stain and finish treads before gluing in place. Stain has a tendency to splatter, and if done after glued in, you will have to repaint risers and stringers. Paint stringers and risers after assembled and then install the stained treads.

Paint and/or stain before installing in dollhouse.

This assembly will fit between walls 4 and 5 on first floor and 11 and 12 on second floor in master plan. It will also fit between similar walls on alternate plans.

There are many ways to make and install stairways. You may prefer an open stairway, an open stairway above a paneled wall, or wall with closet, or a partially open stairway.

The basic procedure for an open stairway is the same as detailed with two exceptions: (1) Cut stair risers ⅛″ shorter in length. Install treads with overhang on side of stairway not against a wall; and (2) open stairways have newel posts, balusters, and a handrail. All these are shown on open stairway plan.

ASSEMBLY OF BASIC STAIRWAY

For an open stairway above a paneled, plain or wall with closet, cut walls 5 and 12 as shown in pattern AA. Trim as indicated, leave plain or design trim uniquely yours. If pantry in kitchen is omitted, you may cut a closet in the alternate wall section #5. Glue basic stairway along edge of wall cut, or cover with piece of wide trim as indicated in diagram with the - - - - lines.

Follow pattern BB for a partially open stairway.

You may purchase top and bottom newel posts, but these are expensive (50ᶜ each at this writing). It is not too difficult to make newel posts for only a few cents. Cut 4 pieces of ⅛″ illustration board ½″ × 3½″ and laminate for each newel post. You may leave newel posts square and top with square or round piece of illustration board or wooden bead. However you make the newel posts, keep the total height no more than 3½″. (See drawings of various newel post treatments.)

Balusters for open stairways may be made of lollipop sticks cut 2″ long but no larger than 3/16″. Doweling, 3/16″, may also be used or illustration board cut 3/16″ square (⅛″ × 3/16″ laminated to 1/16″ × 3/16″ for those who have elected not to use 3/16″ illustration board). Make handrails as follows:

Cut 1 piece ⅛″ × ⅜″ the length from newel post to newel post, angle cutting ends to fit on flat surface of newel post (as shown in the drawings). Cut 2 pieces of 1/16″ × ⅛″ the same length. Glue the 1/16″ edge to underside of ⅜″ wide top railing so posts will fit securely between handrail sides as shown.

For finished look on handrailing and/or newel posts made of illustration board, sand edges to a slight round. Once painted, with the "professionally" rounded edges, your post will be indistinguishable from factory-made wood-turned and -carved newel post balusters and handrails.

Should you elect not to build a dormer on your dollhouse, then you will have to make a different-style stairway to get to the third floor. As plans are now, without a dormer, you would "hit" your head on the ceiling as you came up the stairs to the third-floor landing. So follow the "turned" stair plans as shown with dormer eliminated.

These turned stairways may also be used for first- to second-floor stairs. But make certain they do not take up valuable floor space needed for furniture. In central entrance and side entrance hallways, stairs add a touch of elegance.

The third-floor landing will not be diagrammed as I believe you can make this simple project from the picture of the middle room on the third floor of the dollhouse. (See back cover.) (Page 61 - OPEN STAIRWAY) (Page 62 - 65 - PATTERN AA) (Page 66 - 67 - PATTERN BB) (Page 68 - NEWEL AND BALUSTER POSTS DETAILED) (Page 70 - 72 - TURNED STAIRWAYS)

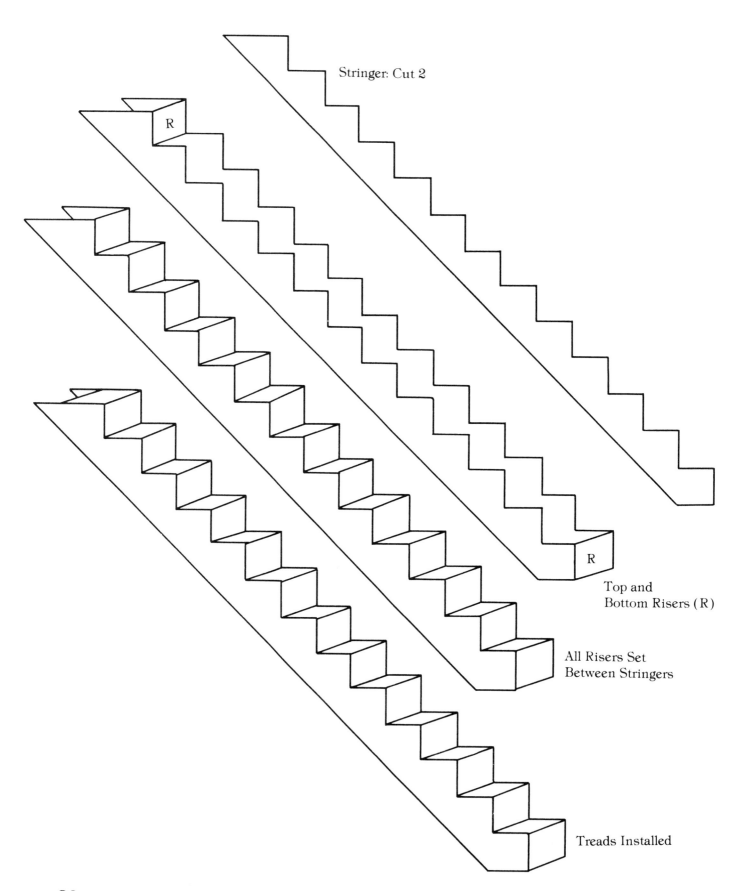

Stringer: Cut 2

R

R

Top and
Bottom Risers (R)

All Risers Set
Between Stringers

Treads Installed

Open Stairway

Newel posts shown plain. Choose your own design for finishing. Newel posts shown only for placement.

The underside of an open stairway, when left open, shows all the risers and treads. For a more finished look, when stairway is assembled and fit into opening, cover the open back with a piece of ⅛″ illustration board between the two stringers from floor to ceiling of room.

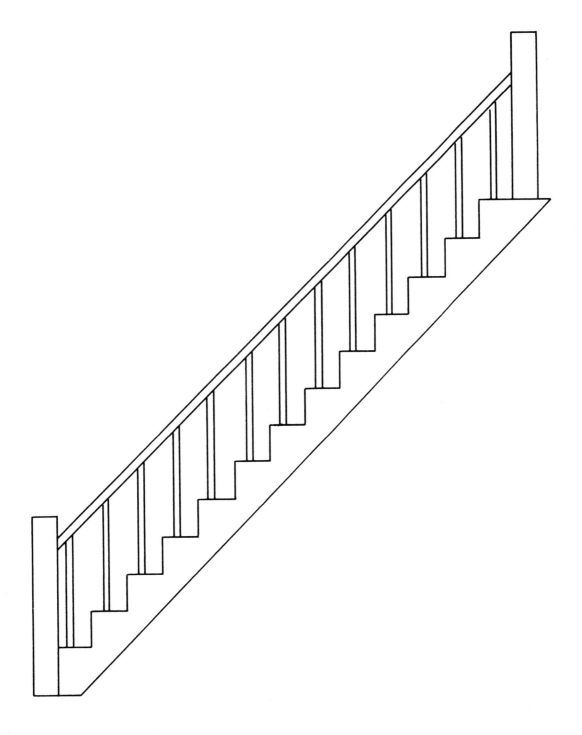

Pattern AA

When using an open stairway in the master plan, cut walls 5 and 12 (or similar walls on alternate plans), according to Pattern AA.

Scale: $\frac{1}{2}'' = 1''$

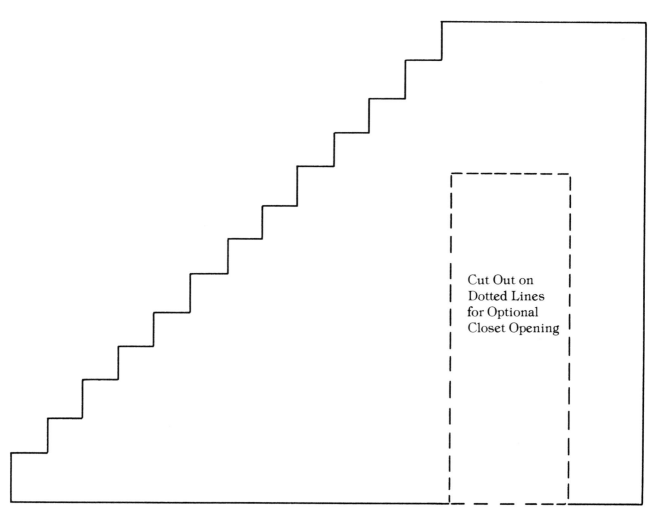

Cut Out on
Dotted Lines
for Optional
Closet Opening

Pattern AA (continued)

Walls 5 and 12 cut to accommodate open stairway with stairway installed.
   Scale: ½″ = 1″
   Wall is plain; to be painted or papered.

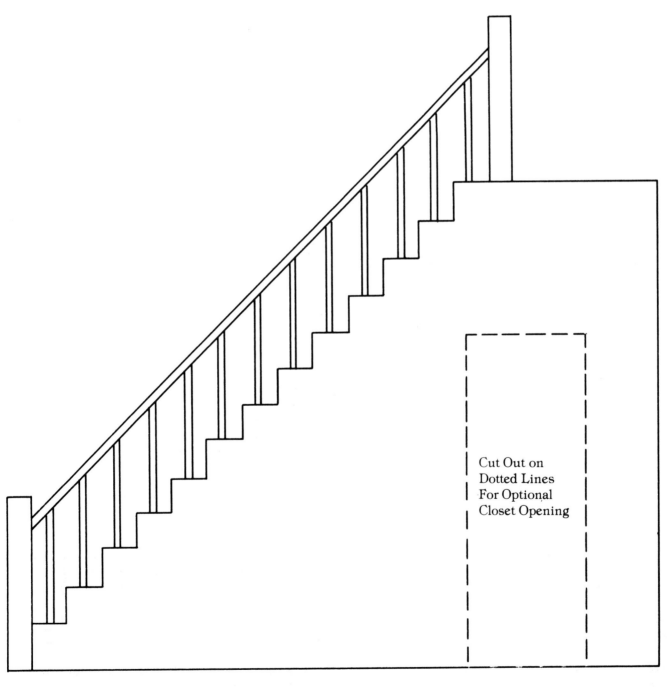

Cut Out on
Dotted Lines
For Optional
Closet Opening

Pattern AA (continued)

Cut strips of ⅙″ × ¹⁄₁₆″ illustration board for paneling, or use a simulated panel miniature wallpaper (1).

Cut piece of ⅛″ illustration board length of stair stringer, width ½″ to 1″ for wide trim (2).

Cut 3 pieces of ¹⁄₁₆″ illustration board, various widths and overlay for floor molding trim (3).

Cut optional closet door opening if pantry not used and a closet is wanted (4).

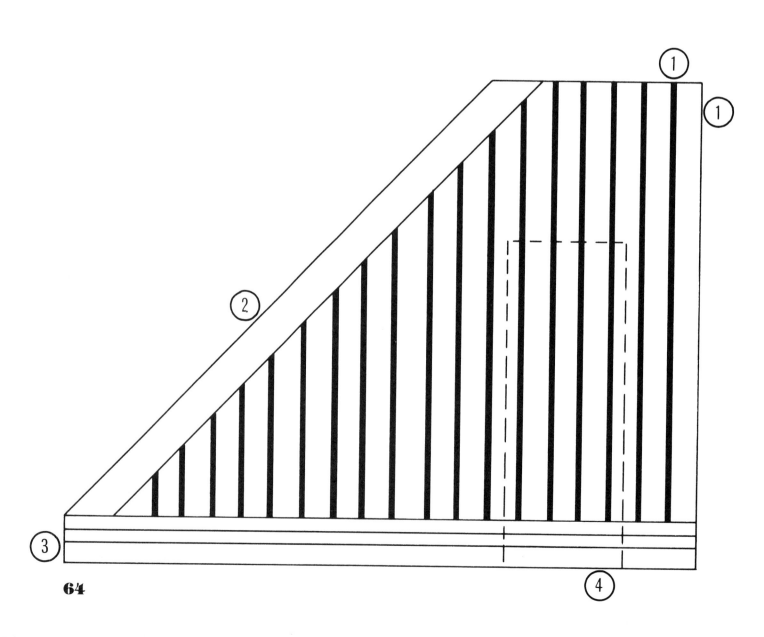

Pattern AA (continued)

Detailed sketch showing how trim covers stringers, risers, and treads.

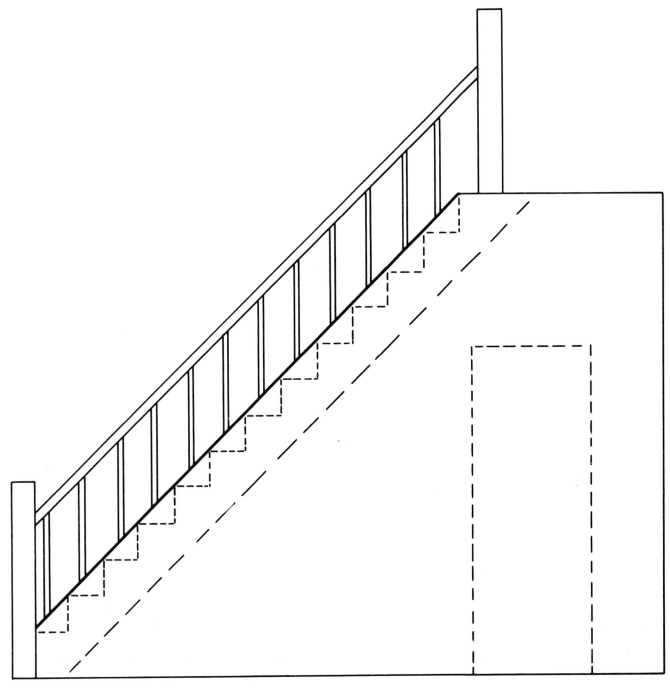

Pattern BB

When using a partially open stairway in master plan, cut walls 5 and 12 (or similar walls on alternate plans), according to PATTERN BB.
Scale: ½″ = 1″

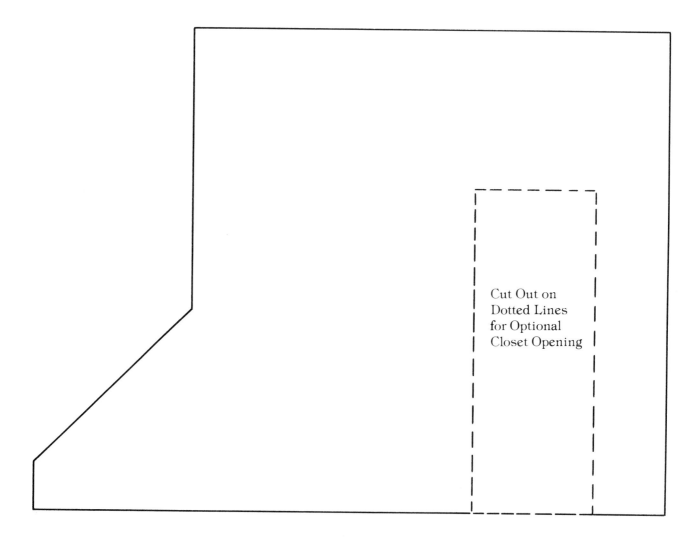

Cut Out on
Dotted Lines
for Optional
Closet Opening

Pattern BB (continued)

Scale: $\frac{1}{2}'' = 1''$

   Cut strips of $\frac{1}{8}''$ illustration board ($\frac{1}{2}''$- $\frac{3}{4}''$ W) for random-design as shown. You may leave this wall plain or decorate in manner pleasing to you. You *must* cut a piece of molding to cover stringer, risers, and treads in area of partially exposed stairway.

   On stairway section covered by the wall, you will not use balusters but you may use a top newel post, which is optional, depending on your landing.

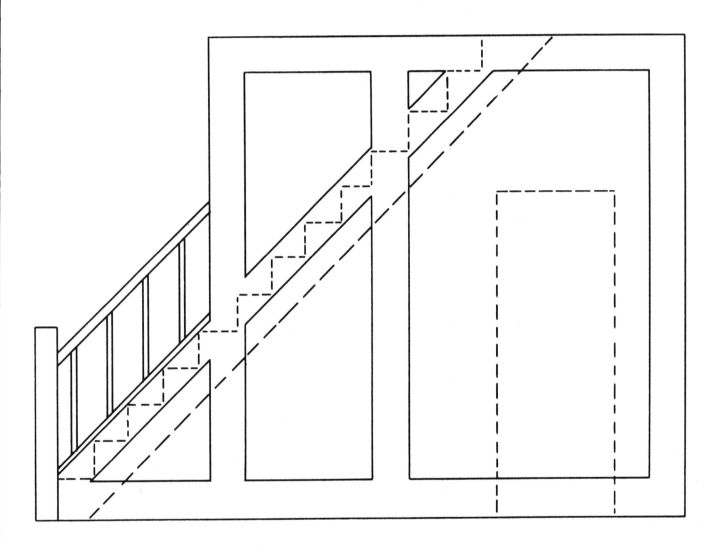

Newel Posts and Balusters

There is no "must" newel-post shape. It can be square with no trim, round with no trim, or ornately trimmed with hand carving or wood beads. The only dimension that is standard for the miniature is 3½″ high.

The same is true for balusters. These can be round or square, plain or fancy. Keep the length of balusters close to 2″. You can purchase these posts, as mentioned previously about newel posts, but they cost 10¢ to 15¢ each. I might also add, one can purchase handrails, but these are also too expensive for our dollhouse.

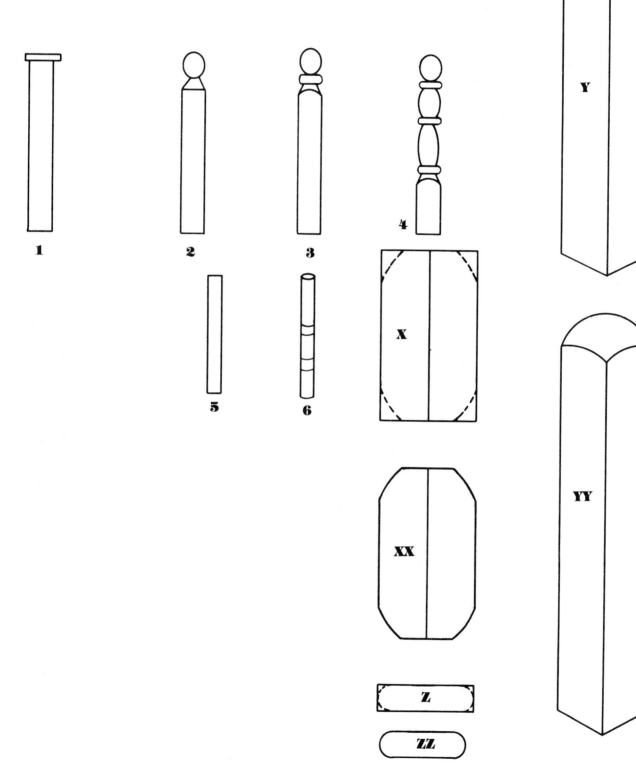

POSTS:

1. Square post cut of illustration board with $\frac{1}{16}$" square piece cut to have $\frac{1}{16}$" overhang on all 4 sides. (Check page 59 for size of newel posts.)

2. Square post with small square topped with round wood bead.

3. Fancier post with cut as diagrammed in large drawings Y and YY with piece cut as in drawings Z and ZZ, topped with round bead.

4. Super-fancy post using all cuts as diagrammed in larger drawings and large and small wood beads.

5. Square baluster cut from $\frac{1}{8}$" × $\frac{1}{8}$" illustration board.

6. Round baluster cut from lollipop stick or $\frac{1}{8}$" doweling. This can be "roll" scored with knife, if desired. To "roll" score: Place dowel on hard surface and, while holding knife tightly against dowel, roll the dowel full circle to make a cut. It is not necessary, but it does add a nice touch after the baluster is stained or painted.

X and XX. Marking square of illustration board for center newel post trim. Make shorter or longer as desired.

Y and YY. Marking and carving newel post full-length or shorter for using only as part of post.

Z and ZZ. Marking and carving small trims on newel posts.

NOTE: Patterns are not scale. Only detailed to show various styles and how to make.

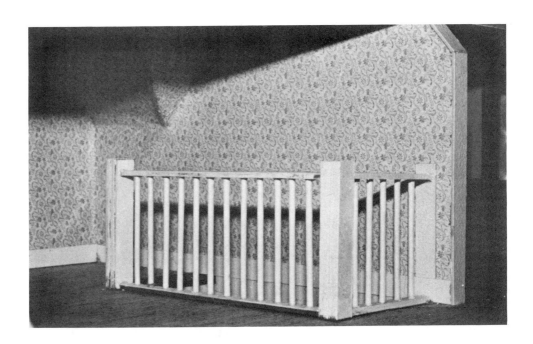

Turned or Change of Direction Stairs
(First stair may be rounded as shown for formal setting.)

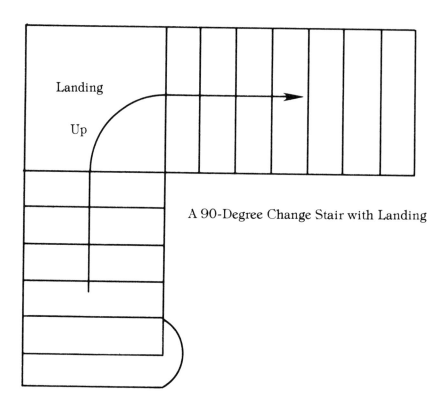

A 90-Degree Change Stair with Landing

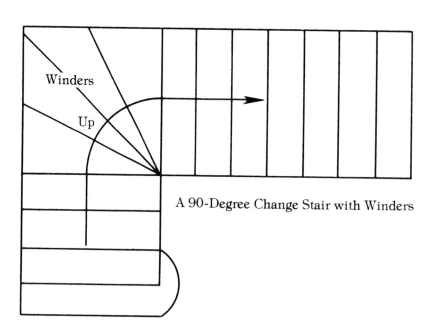

A 90-Degree Change Stair with Winders

90-Degree Change Stair with Landing

You may use closed or open stringers. This is matter of choice and positioning of stairs. Use newel posts, balusters, and handrails as shown for straight-flight stairs.

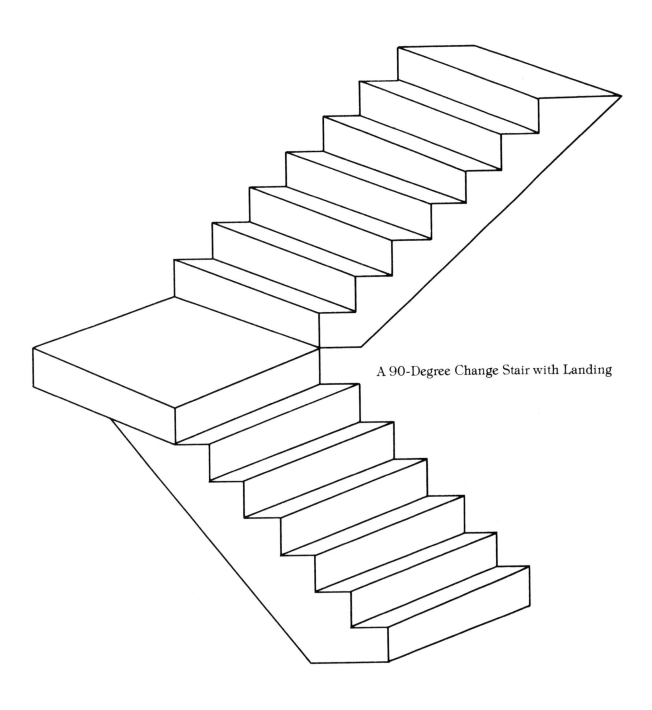

A 90-Degree Change Stair with Landing

90-Degree Change Stair with Winders

You may use closed or open stringers. This is a matter of choice and positioning of stairs. Use newel posts, balusters and handrails as shown for straight-flight stairs.

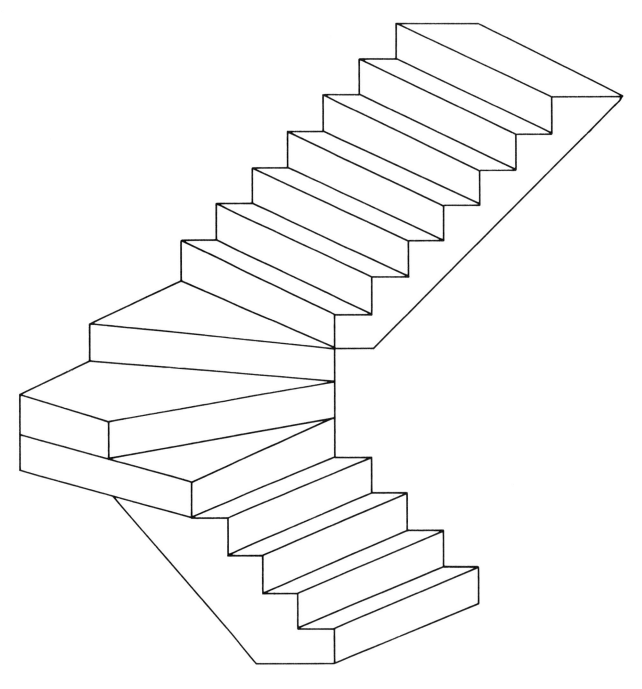

Pantry (Optional)

MATERIALS

$\frac{1}{8}''$ illustration board
$\frac{1}{16}''$ illustration board
1 piece of plastic $2'' \times 6''$
2 straight pins or small nails

1 large-headed pin
Sobo glue
Paint
Chart tape (optional)

ASSEMBLY

Glue back inside sides as indicated by dotted lines. Glue top and base to back and sides as indicated by dotted lines. Glue shelves to back and sides as indicated by dotted lines.

Trim plastic with two strips of $1/16''$ chart-tape, vertically to form 3 long panes for door opening; or trim as desired.

Glue plastic to one side of door frame. Laminate door frames with plastic between.

Pin door with straight pins through base and top, $3/8''$ in from side edge.

Glue top and side door trims to front edges of sides and pantry top.

Paint entire unit.

Push in round-headed pin where indicated by dot on door frame.

Slide entire unit into wall opening in kitchen wall of dollhouse.

Pantry (Optional)

Cut all pieces from full-size pattern.

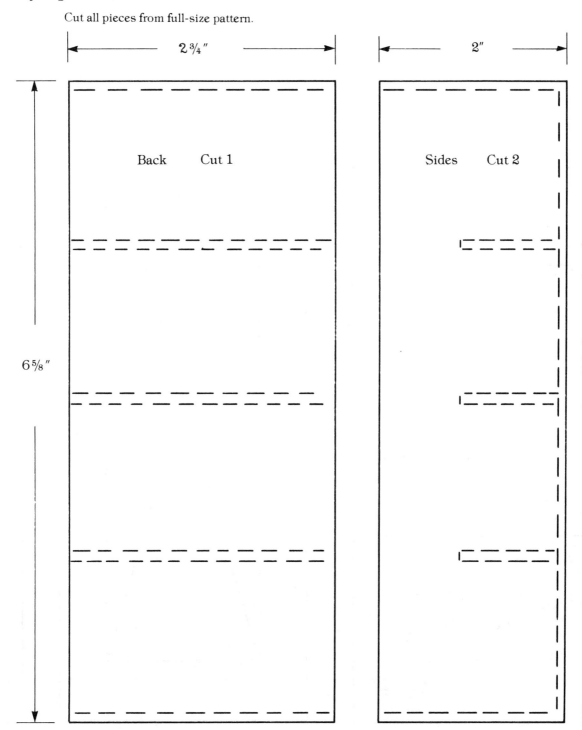

All pattern pieces for pantry are full-size and cut from $1/8''$ illustration board unless otherwise indicated.

Pantry (continued)

All pattern pieces for pantry are full-size and cut from ⅛" illustration board unless otherwise indicated.

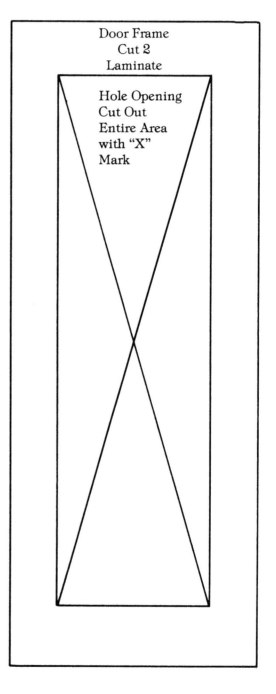

Top Door Trim
Cut 1 from ¹⁄₁₆"

Shelves   Cut 3

Top   Cut 1

Base   Cut 1

Door Frame
Cut 2
Laminate

Hole Opening
Cut Out
Entire Area
with "X"
Mark

Side Door Trim   Cut 2 from ¹⁄₁₆" (Right & Left)

Inside Door and Window Trim, Base and Ceiling Moldings

Cut several strips of $\frac{1}{16}'' \times \frac{1}{2}''$ illustration board. These will be used for all trims and moldings for entire interior of dollhouse so cut 10 to 12 long strips. You may need more, but this will give you a good start.

Now comes another decision-making time. How do you want to finish the trims and moldings for each room? You will want to stain some and paint others to match or contrast with painted or wallpapered rooms.

Rooms selected for staining should be done first. Measure trim needed for base, ceiling, doors, and windows. Let's say you'll need 12 feet. Stain at least that much. It may sound like a lot but when you start trimming, you'll find it is, most likely, an underestimation. Now slip window(s) into room(s) that will have a stained molding. Slip window(s) out. Stain the *inside* edges of window opening trims of these windows.

Measure trims for all other rooms. Paint insides as desired. Repeat same process for all the windows as you did for the stained trim.

Set painted trims aside.

Now comes the time to paint the exteriors of all the windows. When windows have been painted, glue in place in proper rooms. We've simplified some of the painting: No reaching into rooms to try painting the small edges of window-opening trims. You may also, at this time, paint, trim, and glue shutters in place.

When cutting door and window trims and some of the moldings, you will have several angle-cuts to make. If you find you are within your budget, it might be a good idea to buy a miniature miter box and saw combination. The price, at this writing, is $6. You might have some trouble when first using it, as, for some unknown reason, the rip saw with the miter box can only cut in one direction. But it is handy for those 45° and even straight 90° cuts.

Should you not wish to invest in this tool (which will also come in handy when making the miniature furniture), you can make a miter box in one of two ways.

The easiest way to make one is to use a piece of wood $\frac{1}{2}''$ thick $\times$ 4" long $\times$ 2" wide. With saw, cut on lines as indicated for guide lines when you are cutting 45° and 90° cuts.

This is the easiest miter box to make, but it is not the easiest to use because being flat, with no sides to hold the small trim, it is difficult to hold trim in place while cutting angles.

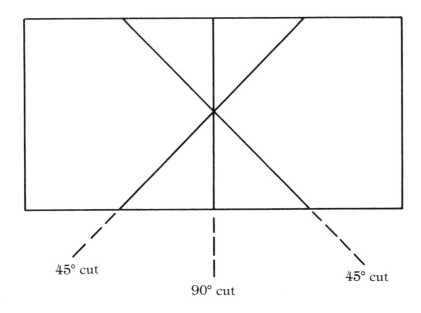

45° cut   90° cut   45° cut

This is a low-cost box-type wood miter box—to be used with coping saw and/or utility knife.

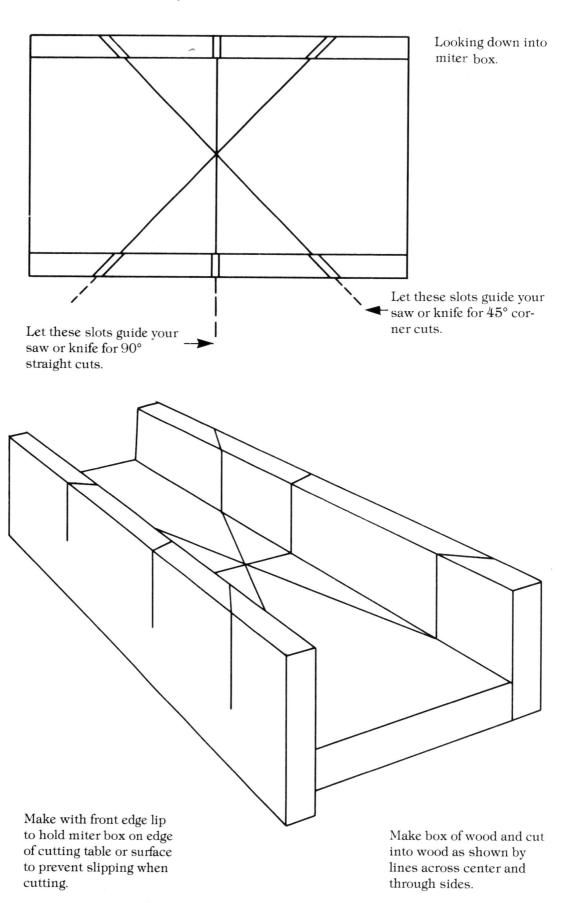

Looking down into miter box.

Let these slots guide your saw or knife for 45° corner cuts.

Let these slots guide your saw or knife for 90° straight cuts.

Make with front edge lip to hold miter box on edge of cutting table or surface to prevent slipping when cutting.

Make box of wood and cut into wood as shown by lines across center and through sides.

Now that you have bought or made a miter box, you are ready to cut interior door casings, door and window trims, base and ceiling moldings.

Each room will be trimmed in this order:

1. Door casing
2. Door and window trim
3. Base and ceiling moldings. Ceiling molding is not necessary if wallpaper with border is used.

First check thickness of the laminated cardboard door openings. If the normal ⅜", cut several (about 6) strips of ¹⁄₁₆" × ⅜" illustration board for door casing. Paint to match trim in room. If going from one room to another that is painted or stained differently, you may use the color from either room for this casing. Now cut and install as shown in diagrams.

Window casings are already in windows. Bring trim up to window casings, and glue in place as shown in diagram for window trim.

If you do not have the patience to cut 45° corners for window and door trims, you may cut them straight across. But the 45° angles give a more professional look.

Base and ceiling moldings may or may not be angle-cut at corners where they meet. If you do angle-cut, stand molding up in miter box and 45° down the ½" width of moldings.

Once all doors and windows are trimmed, and base and ceiling moldings glued in every room, it's back to more exterior finishing.

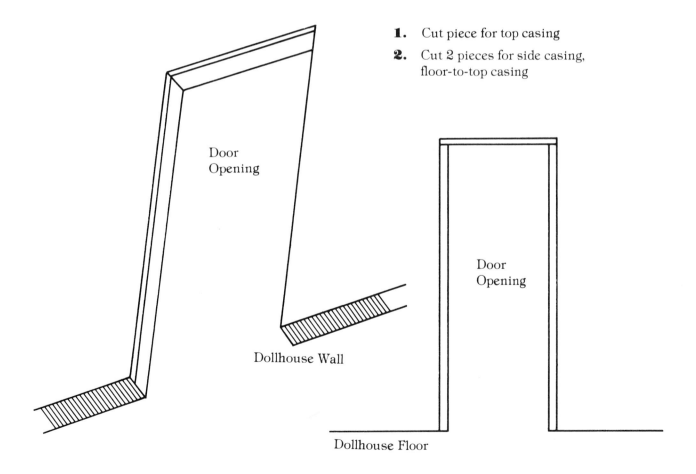

1. Cut piece for top casing
2. Cut 2 pieces for side casing, floor-to-top casing

Door Opening

Dollhouse Wall

Door Opening

Dollhouse Floor

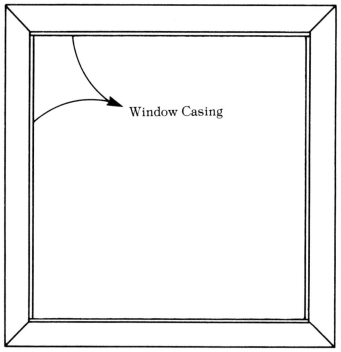

Window Casing

45° corners

Outside Posts and Filigree

If using porch and overhangs as in master plan or alternate plans, you have several ways to make the posts. (You can buy ready-made wood turned posts but these cost $2 or more apiece. And as we need eight posts, this in itself could be so costly as to defeat the purpose of the book—how to build and furnish a dollhouse for $100 or less.)

The least expensive way to make the posts is to laminate ⅛″ × ½″ × 10″ lengths of illustration board together for each post. Four pieces laminated together should make perfect square posts. And there is nothing wrong with square posts. We see them in "real" houses and dollhouses of all kinds. If you think they are too plain, you can trim them with pieces of filigree (See Filigree, pages 103-104).

For my Corrugated Cardboard Dollhouse, I used ⅝″ round doweling for the posts. Doweling comes in 36″ lengths. Out of each dowel you will get three posts, so you will need to purchase three pieces of doweling. This leaves an excess of 28″, but this will be put to good use when furnishing our dollhouse. It can be used for table bases, plant stands, and many other accessories. And the cost? About 55ᶜ to 70ᶜ a 36″ length.

After posts are in, make porch railing of ice-cream sticks and handrails in the same manner as you made the handrails as described in the section on stairways (page 59). Leave section open for entrance to dollhouse. Cut sticks or ⅛″ × ⅛″ illustration board into 2″ pieces and set on a long piece of ⅛″ × ¼″ illustration board. Mark another piece of ¼″ illustration board and glue posts to second piece. This unit of bottom rail, 2″ high posts, and handrail will be glued to posts ½″ above porch floor. Decorate between tall posts with filigree, detailed next.

78

FILIGREE

This can be purchased, as pictured, in most miniature and/or crafts stores. It comes in 12″ × 12″ sheets and the price varies from $1.35 to $1.50. You can sometimes get what lumber stores call "scrap pieces" for much less and some times even for free.

The detailed drawing of the filigree pattern must be cut from one continuous length of filigree board to fit securely between large porch posts.

Cut 3 pieces of A-B and 2 pieces of C. The dark area is the pattern for the filigree you will use. Or you can create your own pattern. Once your design is determined, place the board in a horizontal position slightly overhanging the edge of your worktable. Place a piece of corrugated cardboard under the filigree to prevent bottom edges of filigree from tearing during cutting. Saw through both the filigree and corrugated cardboard with downward stroke of coping saw or utility knife. Rough edges may be sanded later or trimmed with utility knife.

Sheet of Uncut Filigree

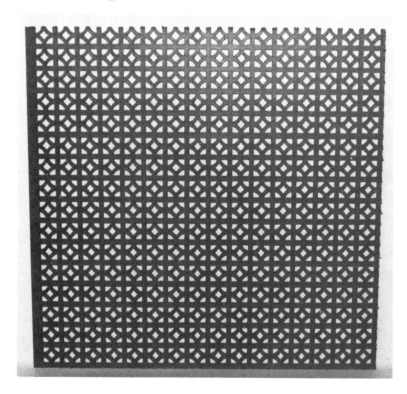

A Front trim between posts (continued and joining to **B** at arrows)

C Side trim

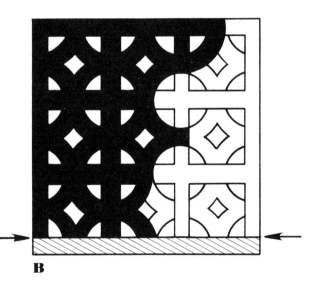

B

Roof

There are several ways to finish the roof, listed in order of difficulty:

a. Paint in color desired
b. Texture-paint (as on dollhouse pictured)
c. Use sandpaper for simulated roofing, tab-cut as shown in drawing
d. Cut individual shingles as shown and explained in drawing

One can also buy roofing, but this is expensive. Minimum cost for the entire roof is $20 for individual shingles and $15 for tab-cut strip shingles. Deep-formed shingle styrene panel roof would cost about $18.

Tab-Cut Roofing: Cut in lengths desired but only 1 ¼" wide. Cut on dark lines for tab cuts. Overlap as shown by dotted lines.

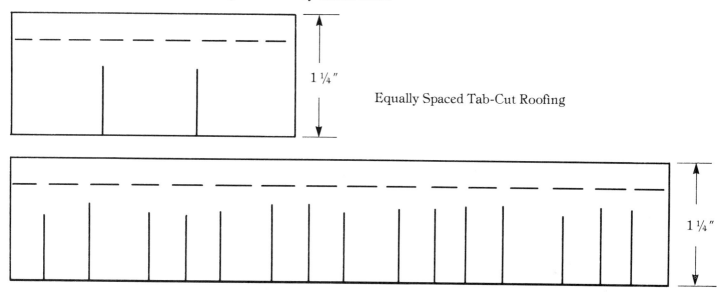

1 ¼"

Equally Spaced Tab-Cut Roofing

1 ¼"

Random-Spaced Tab-Cut Roofing

Plain Roof Shingles

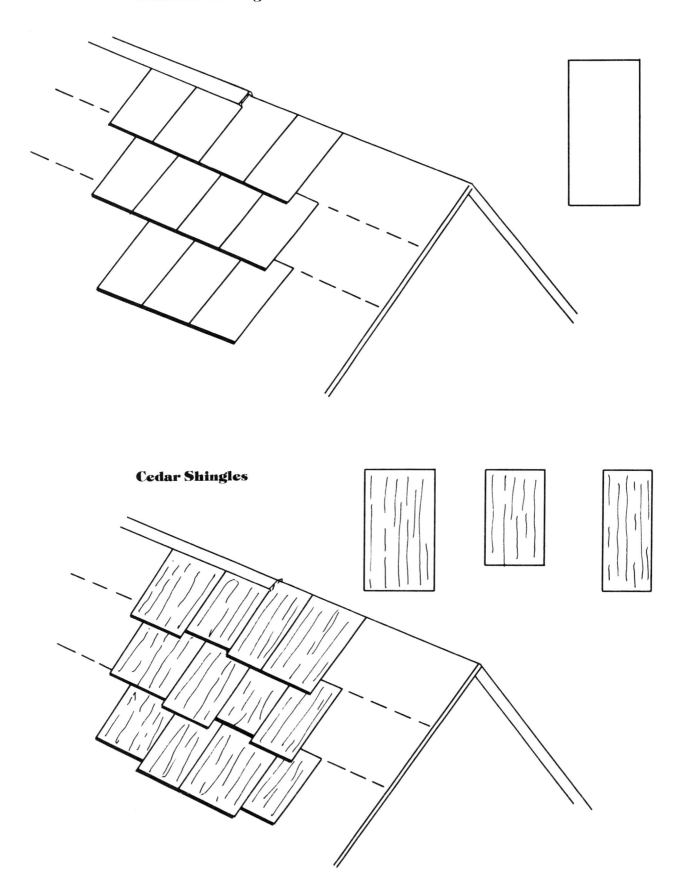

Cedar Shingles

When roofing your dollhouse with tab-cut strips or single shingles, always draw a line where tops of shingles are to be placed. Overlap ¼". Make single shingles, plain or cedar, never longer than 1¼". Plain are always cut same length. Cedar shingles are cut random lengths as shown. (Pictures of shingles and how installed on roof are not to scale.)

When cutting plain or cedar shingles of cardboard, flatten overlapping edge with rolling pin. Keep thick part of shingle, as shown by darker lines, at the bottom. Paint roof after all shingles are glued in place.

To make cardboard appear like regular cedar shakes, crinkle or mark with stiff brush (wire or vegetable brush is fine for this). After painting cedar shingled roof, use brush again to give it a weathered look.

After all shingles are glued on roof, edge top of roof with a roof ridge made of ⅛" × ¼" strips of illustration board, tapered where front and back ridge meet on roof peak.

Bay Window Finishing

Paint interior and exterior of bay-window unit before gluing to dollhouse. Make roof on bay window in same manner as used on main roof of dollhouse. Trim interior edges with ¹⁄₁₆" illustration board in same manner as for all other interior trims.

Chimney Finishing

Paint chimney. Leave plain or texture-finish. You may score brick markings as was done on inside fireplaces. Or you may score to resemble stone. Chimneys on dollhouse pictured were texture-painted without any markings.

Cut chimney tops from patterns as shown on page 20. These may be cut from pieces of soft wood or high-density urethane. Chisel out center of chimney top(s) bottom to fit down over chimney body. These may or may not be glued in place.

Chimney top—Hollowed-out bottom

Outside Moldings

Cut strips of illustration board ¹⁄₁₆″ × ¼″ to finish all exposed edges of corrugated cardboard. Trim roof edges with the same strips. Trim bay-window roof edges in like manner.

Trim house front, side and back corners with illustration-board strips. Cover entire base with ¹⁄₁₆″ × ¼″ illustration board the full height of base.

For a finer finish paint strips before gluing in place.

TRIM PICTURES

Exposed Corrugated Cardboard Edges

**Trimmed
Cardboard Edges**

Roof Trim

Dormer Roof Trim

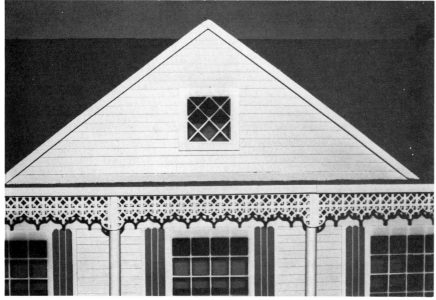

Bay-Window Trim

Front Corner Trims

Overhang Trim

Base Trim

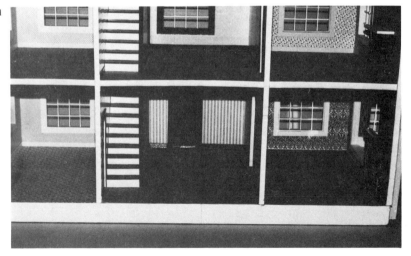

Our Dollhouse Is Finished!

It is difficult in these times of changing prices to give the exact cost of materials used (except for the corrugated cardboard, which will always be the same price—free). You will also have some material left over such as glue, paint, polyurethane, illustration board, clear plastic, chart tape, doweling, etc. These materials can all be used for making our furniture and accessories.

The exact cost of the dollhouse as I finished it came to $48.97, but it can be made as inexpensively as $15 to $20. These prices are at both ends of the cost range. Your cost will be somewhere between these figures, but never higher—if you bought with caution.

Examples: Never buy the most expensive paint and always use paint you have on hand.

Do not buy the most expensive miniature wallpapers, unless you can afford a cost overrun.

Buy slightly damaged illustration board (poster board, mat board, or whatever it is called at your crafts shop) at reduced prices. A person using this material for sign painting or artwork must have perfect sheets. You do not need flawless sheets. Our paint, wallpaper, and cutting can go around or cover any defects.

And always use what you have on hand, provided it is suitable or interchangeable.

PART

2

FURNISHINGS

3

FURNISHING OUR DOLLHOUSE

A home is not a home until comfortably furnished. The same is true with dollhouses. No matter how beautifully you may have decorated your dollhouse, it will never be complete until the furniture is in place, the curtains hung, chandeliers ready to be lighted, pictures accenting a special area, rugs on the floor. Your dollhouse must have a lived in, occupied look.

But must the dollhouses of purist microphiles be occupied? It is rare to find a miniature dollhouse with miniature occupants. Why? Most miniature dolls, or people, are not to scale and those that are sometimes look hideous. Miniature articles seem to be beautiful in everything except the people. Should you wish to have occupants in your dollhouse, that is your decision. I prefer fantasizing, being a miniature purist, imagining what my "people" look like or are doing.

Without further delay, let's begin to furnish our dollhouse. Look over the patterns for the furniture. You will find the only measurements given are the height, width, and length. All pattern pieces are full-size. Each has been checked and double-checked. To overcome errors, all furniture pieces were designed, drawn, and built. Any and all errors were noted and corrected on the original patterns *before* the final patterns were drawn. Because of this care, these patterns are as error-free as humanly possible.

There are plans, assembly instructions, and pictures for each piece of furniture. If you follow plans and instructions carefully, you should be able to assemble each piece of furniture mistake-free. For extra insurance, to guard against any mistake in cutting or assembling, I suggest you pin all pieces together before gluing. And when I say pin, I mean to lightly set pins in place. Don't "nail" parts together. Pinning is akin to basting in sewing.

Why are measurements not given for each piece of furniture? It's because it's more enjoyable spending your time making furniture, than reading and checking ruler or tape. If measurements, instead of actual size, were given, mistakes would be all too frequent. Which would you prefer? Measuring a piece of $1\frac{3}{16}'' \times 3\frac{13}{16}''$, or tracing a pattern that has already measured this piece for you? The fun and joy of making miniature furniture is lost, and there is nothing more provoking than cutting and assembling a piece of furniture, only to discover it has been measured and cut wrong.

Line up supplies before beginning to make your furniture. Don't run out and buy everything you think you'll need. Look around the house. Visualize every thing in a Lilliputian way. You'd be surprised how many things are "miniature" and you never realized it.

For example: I looked and looked for two large identical beads or round objects for pedestal bases on my dining room table (the one patterned in the section on Dining Room Furniture). One day while doing dishes, I spotted exactly what I needed—the bottle top on my dishwashing liquid. Now don't disdain this freebie or any others like it. Once stained, it took on the appearance of beautifully hand-carved wood.

You'll find buttons, beads, ribbons, lace, scraps of material, and various bottle caps and tops suitable for your miniature furniture. The same way you can get out-of-date wallpaper-pattern books, you can get upholstery sample books to use for making draperies and miniature upholstery.

Following are supplies and tools needed for your miniature furniture.

SUPPLIES

These will also be listed as needed for each piece of furniture.

ILLUSTRATION BOARD.   This may be called by other names, such as poster board, mat board, etc. And don't forget to look for bargains when buying illustration board.

$\frac{1}{8}$"—also called heavyweight—2 pieces in addition to leftovers from dollhouse

$\frac{1}{16}$"—also called lightweight—1 piece in addition to leftovers from dollhouse

PAINT.   White latex or alkyd paint left over from dollhouse as well as the tints

STAIN AND FINISHING.   One pint latex, satin-finish base coat

2 4-ounce cans of stain and glaze, one can light colored such as cedar and one can darker color such as cherry or black walnut

Polyurethane (optional) left over from dollhouse or one pint if you did not build the dollhouse

TRIMS.   Paper doilies, braid, or rickrack

GLUE.   Sobo, Tacky, or any other good white resin glue

TOOLS

Utility knife and razor blades
Metal square
Ruler
Emery boards (or #240 wet and dry sandpaper)
Jig (for squaring furniture parts—optional and explained later)
Tweezers
Toothpicks—for applying glue
Wax paper—to place under glued or painted furniture while working on each article and then allowing pieces to dry. Never use newspapers as print comes off and is not easy to cover with paint or stain.
Small paintbrush—#190, bristles $\frac{3}{4}$" long and $\frac{1}{4}$" wide at tip when spread.

OPTIONAL TOOLS

Coping saw
Jigsaw
Small table vise
Small clamps

SUGGESTIONS FOR ASSEMBLING AND FINISHING

Some pieces of furniture call for 3/16" illustration board. This is done by laminating 1/16" and 1/8" boards for two reasons: It is almost impossible to buy 3/16" board, and it is very difficult to cut.

Many instructions for staining miniature furniture, whether made of wood or illustration board, tell you to stain before assembling as stain will not cover glue. Other instructions tell you to assemble the furniture, carefully wiping off any excess glue, then stain. If you can't wipe all the glue off, you are told to sand until all traces of glue are gone. I do not recommend either method. I'll give a brief explanation why and let you judge.

STAINING BEFORE ASSEMBLING. If you use a water-base stain, all pieces must be weighted down while drying or they will warp. This can often leave unwanted marks that cannot be eliminated. Even an alkyd stain applied in this manner has the same problems.

If you stain before assembling, no matter how carefully you have cut each pattern piece, most will need sanding after assembling and there goes the depth of stain. When staining over sanded areas, you'll get overlaps and parts of your furniture will have a darker stain than others. This mars the professional look we are striving for.

STAINING AFTER ASSEMBLING. This method also has drawbacks. Even though you have wiped or sanded off glue, you'll have difficulty getting an even stain. You'll have "white" spots where the glue settled in, and there is no way that you can remove the spot it leaves.

PROPER STAINING PROCEDURE. Apply glue carefully, but it is not necessary to wipe or sand thoroughly. Paint entire assembled piece of furniture with coat of latex; stain finish base coat. Then cover with one-coat stain-and-glaze product. The base coat covers all glue spots and makes an even color over which to apply stain. And always paint the inside, backs and bottoms of all pieces.

It is most important that the base coat is thoroughly dry before the stain is applied. Let dry 3 to 4 hours and touch up any missed spots or give entire piece of furniture a second coat of base.

Apply stain with a small brush. Stain each piece of furniture in sections. You cannot stain an entire piece at one time as you have to hold on to part of it or lay it down during and after staining.

Wait 5 or 10 minutes after brushing on stain, then wipe lightly with a soft cloth or paper towel to get a wood-grain effect. Continue staining and wiping until entire piece is stained and grained.

Be sure to cover the entire piece. Who's going to see the inside, bottom, or back of a piece of furniture when it's in your dollhouse? Everyone curious enough to see how you made an item. If you haven't painted the "never-seen" areas, they'll know in an instant you've made your furniture from illustration board. But if you finish an entire piece, not even the most curious will know it is not made of wood. Even should you tell them it is made from illustration board, they will refuse to believe until they give it a very close, careful scrutiny.

DECORATING AND FINISHING. If you want fancy Baroque or Victorian trims, cut small patterns from 3 thicknesses of doilies and glue on furniture where desired before applying base coat. Paint and stain over doily trim.

After you have finished staining and wiping a piece of furniture, you may give it a coat of polyurethane. In most cases you will find this is not necessary, as the stain-and-glaze product would give you all the luster desired.

You can also use small braid or rickrack trims for your furniture, painting in same manner as doily trims.

For ornate drawer and/or door pulls, cut small patterns from gold doilies. Or you can buy a special gold paper in most crafts stores from which you can design your own patterns. There is a gold metal that comes in thin sheets which can also be used for this purpose. We will discuss this gold metal sheeting when making hinges and handles.

GLUING. Always squeeze a small dab of glue onto wax paper and then with toothpick apply glue to edges or various parts of your furniture as described in the assembly of each piece.

SANDING. Emery boards have both coarse and fine grain. I use these exclusively as they are small enough to work into all corners and cuts of miniature furniture. The #240 wet and dry sandpaper works only on the larger flat surfaces where emery boards will work just as well.

ASSEMBLY JIG. You can make or buy a jig to hold pieces square while glue is drying. To make a jig: Use small board, or top of wood worktable. Make a perfect square corner with two smaller pieces of wood about an inch high. Securely nail to surface board. When assembling furniture, line up with this squared corner and you'll never have lopsided furniture.

If you do not care to make a jig, keep your metal square handy and line up assembled pieces using your square as a guide. This takes more care and time, but again, I leave it up to you.

HINGES, HANDLES, AND KNOBS. Straight pins are used for hinging flush doors. Small gold pins inserted into sequins can be used for drawer knobs. Map pins may also be used for drawer knobs. Loops (from a card of hooks and eyes) make perfect drawer handles. Backs of screw-type earrings or men's small dress studs make beautiful Georgian and Victorian doorknobs. An upholstery twist pin is another idea for doorknobs or large dresser-drawer knobs.

Hinges can be made from small pieces of the gold-metal sheet, bent around a straight pin that in turn is bent to resemble a staple. This is for an outside butt, T, or square hinge. One can also "paint" a hinge on a flush door that has been pinned at top and bottom.

When it comes to hinges I don't try to save money. Hinges are so small and the making of them so difficult, that I buy hinges with the pins already for installation. Houseworks of Atlanta, Georgia, makes a full line of hinges and other tiny hardware. The difference in price between making the few outside hinges needed for all the pieces of furniture in this book is only about $5. And, considering the difficulty factor and time-consuming patience to make a mini-hinge, you'll be way ahead if you buy the few hinges needed.

These assembly instructions cover the main how-tos for all pieces of furniture. Any variation will be listed in the instructions for a particular piece along with the use of an optional tool.

So let's get busy and start making the furniture to furnish our dollhouse.

Be sure to read all instructions thoroughly before beginning work.

4

THE KITCHEN

Icebox
Dry Sink
Cupboard
Butcher Block
Table
Chairs

Icebox

(2⅝″ wide × 1¾″ deep × 4¼″ high)

MATERIALS

⅛″ illustration board   Latex satin base coat
1/16″ illustration board   Stain and glaze
Sobo glue   4 hinges
Aluminum foil   2 handles
Straight pins

INSTRUCTIONS

1. Trace and transfer pattern pieces onto ⅛″ illustration board.

2. Cut all pieces, laminating parts as indicated.

3. Cut aluminum foil the size of parts marked X and glue to same, dull-side out. Foil will crinkle from the glue, but this gives the appearance of the galvanized interior of iceboxes.

4. Place back (A) on flat surface.

5. Glue sides (B) flush with back edge.

6. Glue ice-section base (C) and icebox base (C) as indicated by dotted lines on sides (B) and back (A).

7. Wrap center shelf (D) with foil and glue as indicated by dotted lines on sides and back.

8. Glue ice-section front (E) flush with top and side edges.

9. Slightly cut top edge of laminated icebox drip-pan section at an angle both front and back. Use flat toothpicks for shims to hold piece slightly below icebox bottom and pin from sides with short straight pins.

10. Cut long ⅜″ wide strips from 1/16″ illustration board, then cut into smaller pieces as follows:

6 pieces for sides and front facings—4¼″ long
4 pieces for side top and bottom facings—1″ long
3 pieces for icebox front facings and bottom facing—1⅞″ long
2 pieces for icebox top (front and back) facings—2 9/16″ long
2 pieces for icebox top (sides) facings—1 1/16″ long

11. Glue side facings (front and back) flush with front and back edges.
Glue side facings (top) flush with icebox top.
Glue side facings (bottom) flush with top of icebox legs.
Glue front facings (sides) flush with edge of side facings.
Glue front top facing flush with top of icebox.
Glue bottom of icebox section front facing ⅛″ below icebox section bottom.
Glue bottom front facing ⅛″ above icebox base. Be careful not to glue to swinging drip-pan door.

12. From the ⅜″ wide strips of 1/16″ illustration board cut the following:
2 pieces for ice section door front and back facings—2 3/16″ long
2 pieces for ice section door side facings—9/16″ long
2 pieces for icebox door front sides—2⅜″ long
2 pieces for icebox door top and bottom facings—1⅜″ long

13. Glue ice-section top and icebox door facings to sections (G) and (H) with ⅜″ overhang on all sides.

14. Reinforce icebox lid with ⅛″ × ¼″ strips under facings.

15. Sand.

16. Paint entire icebox (except where foil-lined) with base coat. I used a light base coat. Allow to dry at least 3 to 4 hours.

17. Brush on stain and glaze. Let set for 5 to 10 minutes. Wipe lightly with cloth or paper towel until you have the wood-grain look you want.

18. Hinge. (See Hinges, page 195.)

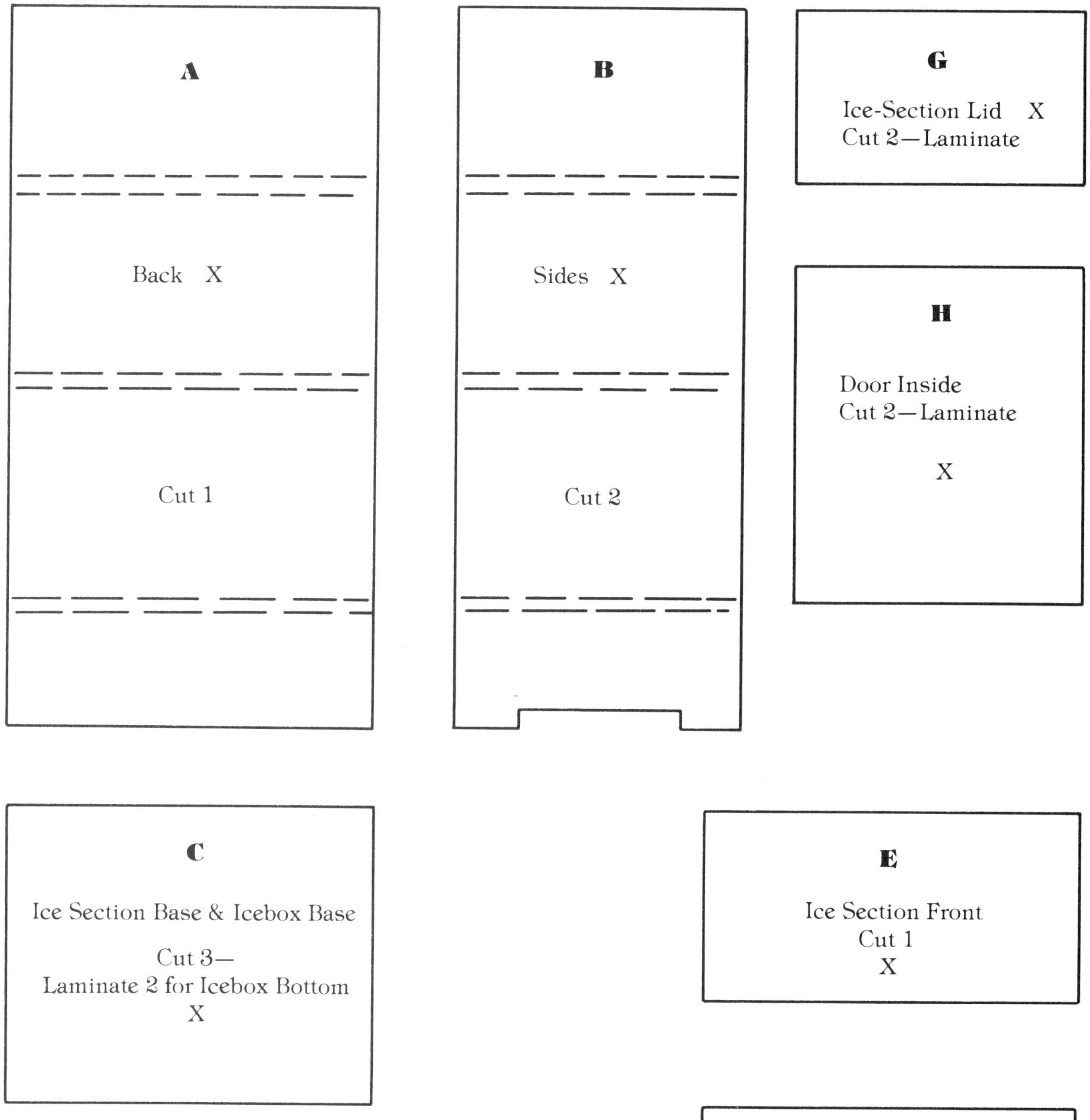

A

Back   X

Cut 1

B

Sides   X

Cut 2

G

Ice-Section Lid   X
Cut 2—Laminate

H

Door Inside
Cut 2—Laminate

X

C

Ice Section Base & Icebox Base

Cut 3—
Laminate 2 for Icebox Bottom
X

E

Ice Section Front
Cut 1
X

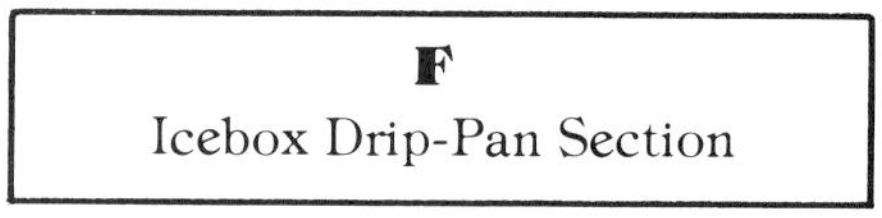

F

Icebox Drip-Pan Section

Cut 2—Laminate

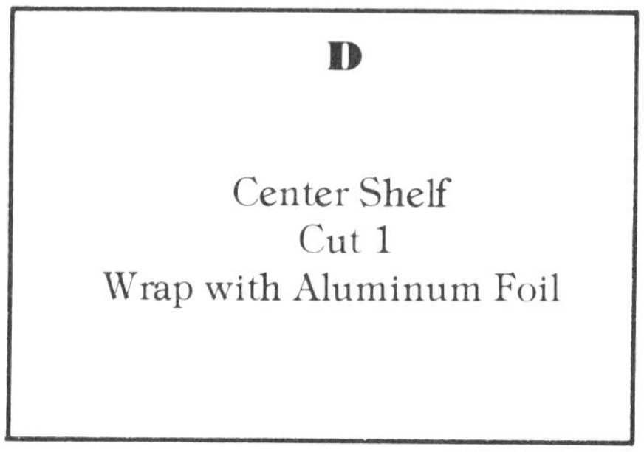

See assembly instructions for framing facings and trim, hinges and handles.

All pieces cut from ⅛″ illustration board.

D

Center Shelf
Cut 1
Wrap with Aluminum Foil

Dry Sink

(Base: 4 1/4" wide × 2 1/8" deep × 2 1/2" high)

(Sink top and backsplash: 4 5/8" wide × 2 1/4" deep × 9/16" high)

MATERIALS

1/8" illustration board
1/16" illustration board
Sobo glue
Flat black paint
Latex satin base coat
Stain and glaze
Straight pins
2 doorknobs

INSTRUCTIONS

1. Trace and transfer pattern pieces onto $1/8''$ and $1/16''$ illustration board. (The laminated top, bottom, and center framing pieces may be cut of $3/16''$, eliminating the necessity to laminate but difficult to cut.)

2. Cut all pieces, laminating parts as indicated.

3. Place back (A) on flat surface.

4. Glue sides (B) to back, outside edges even.

5. Glue base (C) to back and sides with bottom of base (C) even with dotted lines.

6. Glue door stop to sides and even with top of base.

7. Cut top, bottom, side, and center framing pieces of $1/8''$ and $1/16''$ illustration board and laminate. (Or cut from $3/16''$ illustration board without laminating.)

8. Glue $1/4''$ edge of top frame to sides even with top edge.

9. Glue $1/4''$ edge of bottom frame $1/8''$ up from lower side edge and along front edge of door stop.

10. Glue side frames along side edges (keeping pieces flush) and to top and bottom frames.

11. Glue center frame section to door stop and top and bottom frames. When framing is completed check to make certain it is flush and square.

12. Glue 1 continuous strip of $1/16'' \times 3/8''$ illustration board around sink bottom. Starting at center back glue along $1/16''$ edge of sink, curve around edge; wait until dry; continue along side and next rounded edge; wait until dry. Proceed in this manner until ends join at center back. Cut carefully with scissors and glue seam. Paint inside of sink with dull black paint.

13. Glue sink in place on underside of dry sink top.

14. Glue backsplash in place even with back edges of sink top.

15. Cut doors of $3/16''$ illustration board (or laminate $1/16''$ and $1/8''$ for each door).

16. Sand.

17. Paint all parts (except black sink) with base coat. Allow to dry for 3 to 4 hours.

18. Brush on stain and glaze. Let set for 5 to 10 minutes. Wipe lightly with cloth or paper towel until wood grained.

19. Pin doors at top and bottom side edges, $1/8''$ in from sides, through top and bottom frame. For all pinning glue along door edges first. This will eliminate any splitting of the illustration board. Don't force pins into place. Use nail or similar pointed object to make a starter hole for pins.

20. Glue sink top in place flush with back edges, overhang on front and side edges.

21. Attach door pulls. (See Handles and Pulls, page 196.)

Dry Sink

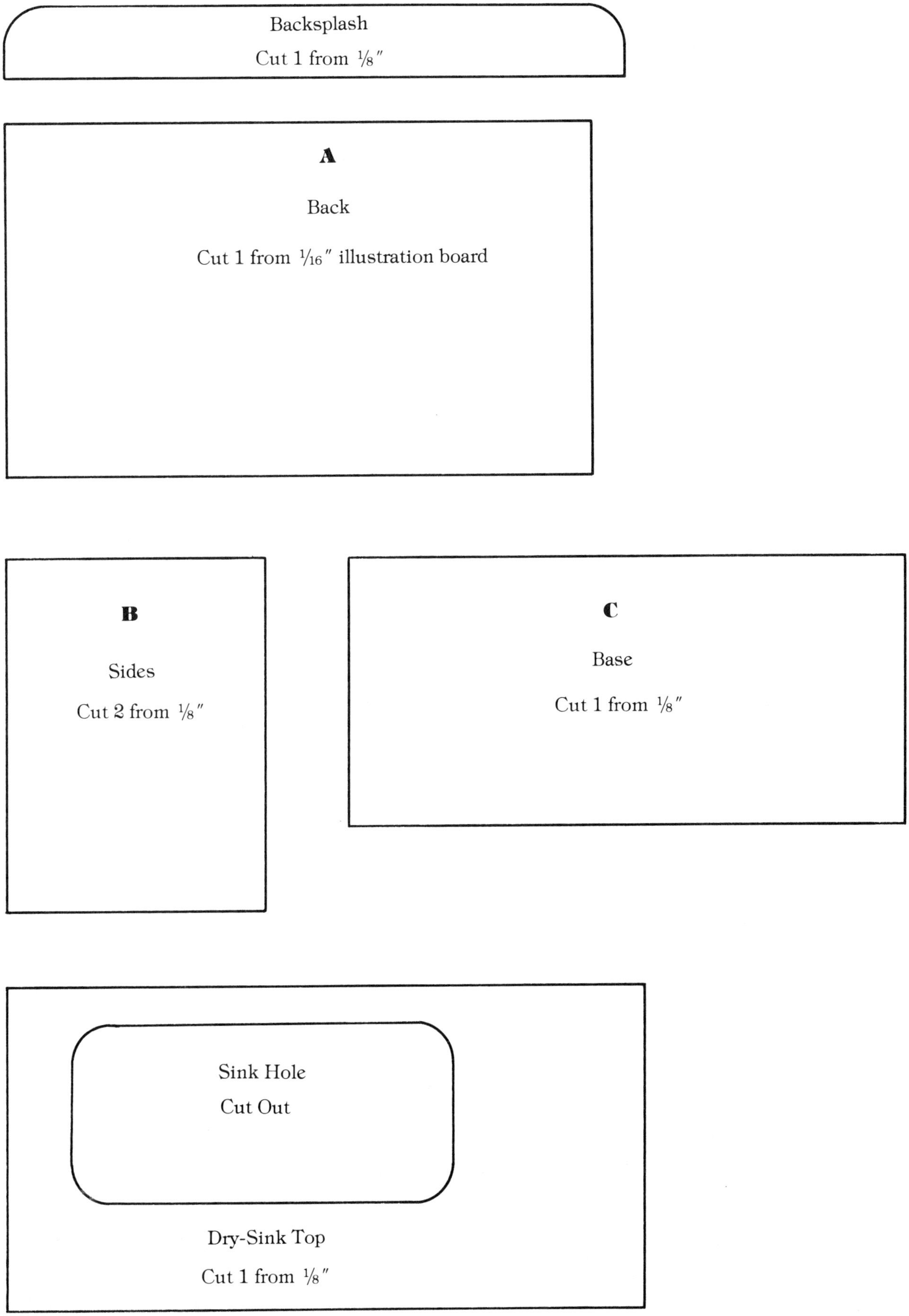

Backsplash
Cut 1 from ⅛″

A

Back

Cut 1 from ¹⁄₁₆″ illustration board

B

Sides

Cut 2 from ⅛″

C

Base

Cut 1 from ⅛″

Sink Hole
Cut Out

Dry-Sink Top

Cut 1 from ⅛″

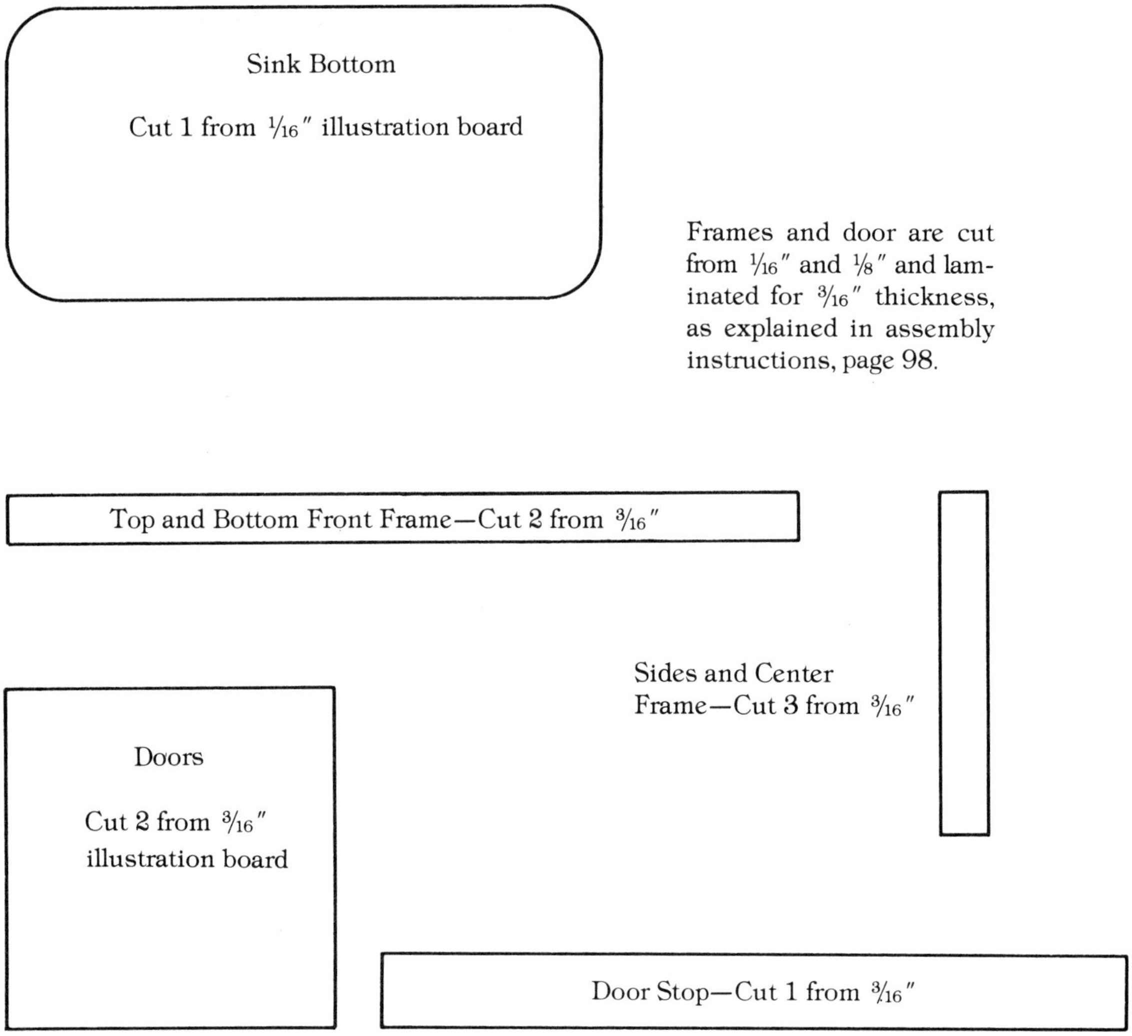

Sink Bottom

Cut 1 from ¹⁄₁₆″ illustration board

Frames and door are cut from ¹⁄₁₆″ and ¹⁄₈″ and laminated for ³⁄₁₆″ thickness, as explained in assembly instructions, page 98.

Top and Bottom Front Frame—Cut 2 from ³⁄₁₆″

Sides and Center Frame—Cut 3 from ³⁄₁₆″

Doors

Cut 2 from ³⁄₁₆″ illustration board

Door Stop—Cut 1 from ³⁄₁₆″

Cupboard

(Top Section: 3⁹⁄₁₆″ wide × 1″ deep × 3″ high)
(Lower Section: 3⁹⁄₁₆″ wide × 1⁷⁄₈″ deep × 2⁷⁄₈″ high)
(Overall Measurements: 3⁹⁄₁₆″ wide × 1⁷⁄₈″ deep × 5⁷⁄₈″ high)

MATERIALS

¹⁄₈″ illustration board
¹⁄₁₆″ illustration board   Gold straight pin
Sobo glue   4 drawer pulls
Latex satin base coat   2 hinges
Stain and glaze   Door handle

INSTRUCTIONS

1. Trace and transfer pattern pieces onto ⅛" and 1/16" illustration board.

2. Cut all pieces, laminating parts as indicated. (Do this in two steps. Cut all pieces for top section and assemble. Cut all pieces for bottom section and assemble. Then glue both sections together and finish as detailed.)

3. TOP SECTION: Place back (A) on flat surface.

4. Glue sides (B) to back flush with sides and bottom of back (A).

5. Glue laminated top (C) even with top of back and sides.

6. Glue top shelf divider centered between sides; glue shelf underneath, using your square to keep level.

7. Glue bottom shelf divider and bottom shelf in place in same manner.

8. Cut long strip of 1/16" illustration board ¼" wide.

9. Cut 4 pieces vertical side trims from the ¼" strip and glue on sides flush with front, back, and top edges.

10. Cut 6 pieces horizontal side trims from the ¼" strip and glue between vertical trims at top, center, and bottom.

Set completed top section aside.

11. LOWER SECTION: Place back (D) on flat surface.

12. Glue sides (E) to back flush with sides and bottom of back (D).

13. Glue top (F) even with top of back and sides.

14. Glue the 1/16" breadboard insert under top (F) even with front edge.

15. Glue center breadboard insert under the 1/16" breadboard insert to left side (as cupboard faces you).

16. Laminate the other 1/16" breadboard insert and ⅛" breadboard insert and glue this under breadboard center insert and to both left and right sides (E). You now have a space on the right of lower cupboard section for breadboard.

17. Glue 1 piece laminated part (H) for base ⅛"up from bottom edges of sides and back.

18. Glue the center laminated section part (H) ½" below bottom breadboard insert.

19. Glue vertical and horizontal trims to door.

20. Cut out and laminate center top and bottom dividers; set in place but do not glue until drawers are made to ensure proper placement for ease of drawers sliding in and out.

21. FOR ALL DRAWERS: Place drawer bottoms on flat surface. Frame with back, front, and sides. Inside frame, glue back and front bracing.

22. Glue drawer fronts in place with even overhang on all four sides.

23. Sand both top and bottom sections. Sand door and drawer fronts for slightly rounded edges.

24. Place top and bottom sections on their backs on flat surface. Glue top section to bottom section even with backs and sides.

25. Paint all parts with base coat. Allow to dry 3 to 4 hours.

26. Brush on stain and glaze. Let set for 5 to 10 minutes. Wipe lightly with cloth or paper towel until wood grained.

27. Hinge door. (See Hinges, page 195.)

28. Attach drawer, breadboard and door pulls or handles. (See Handles and Pulls, page 196.)

Cupboard

Top Section

A

Back

Cut 1 from ⅛″ illustration board

B

Sides

Cut 2 from ⅛″

Side trim (vertical) cut 4 from ¹⁄₁₆″

C

Top

Cut 2 from ⅛″ and laminate

Side trim (horizontal) cut 6 from ¹⁄₁₆″

D

Shelves

Cut 2 from ⅛″

Dividers—Cut 2 from ⅛″

Lower Section

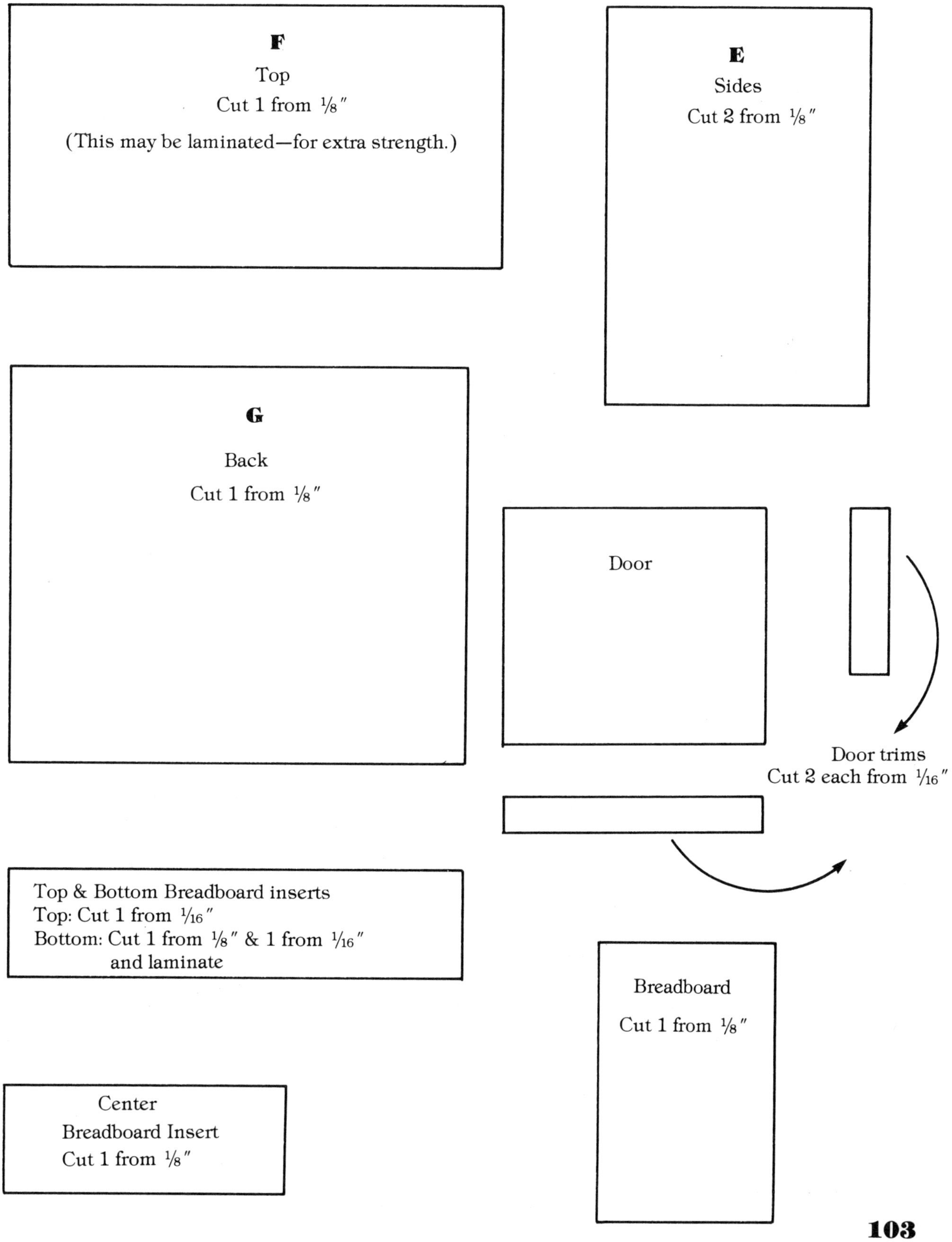

F

Top

Cut 1 from ⅛"

(This may be laminated—for extra strength.)

E

Sides

Cut 2 from ⅛"

G

Back

Cut 1 from ⅛"

Door

Door trims
Cut 2 each from ⅟₁₆"

Top & Bottom Breadboard inserts
Top: Cut 1 from ⅟₁₆"
Bottom: Cut 1 from ⅛" & 1 from ⅟₁₆"
and laminate

Breadboard

Cut 1 from ⅛"

Center
Breadboard Insert
Cut 1 from ⅛"

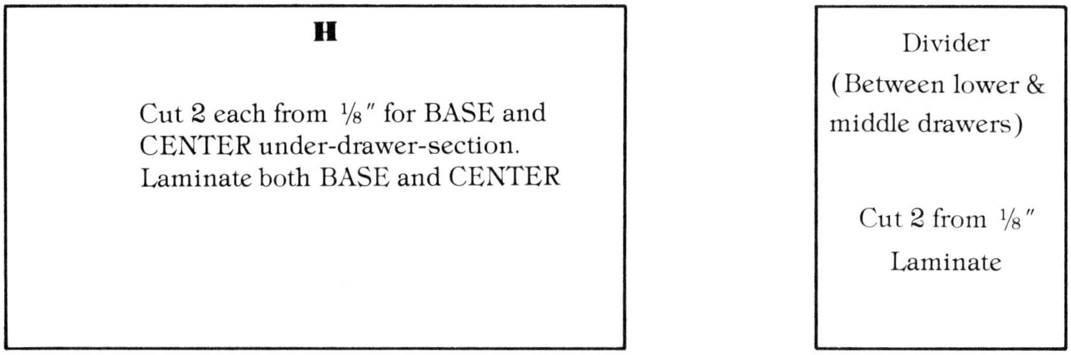

H

Cut 2 each from ⅛″ for BASE and
CENTER under-drawer-section.
Laminate both BASE and CENTER

Divider
(Between lower &
middle drawers)

Cut 2 from ⅛″
Laminate

Top and Middle Drawers   Cut parts for each drawer

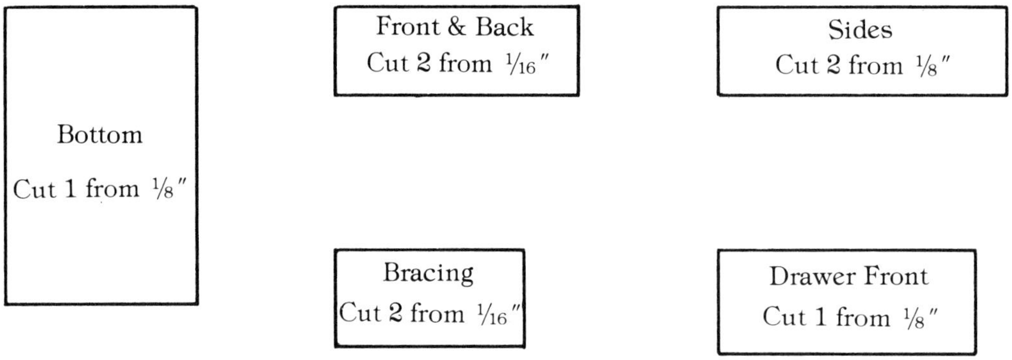

Front & Back
Cut 2 from ¹⁄₁₆″

Sides
Cut 2 from ⅛″

Bottom

Cut 1 from ⅛″

Bracing
Cut 2 from ¹⁄₁₆″

Drawer Front
Cut 1 from ⅛″

Left-Hand Top Drawer   Make bottom 1½″ × 1½″. Check for fit in
your cupboard. Then make all other parts as above to fit in space for this
drawer. (This can vary and that is why I do not give pattern. You must make
it fit your space.)

Bottom Drawer   Use pattern for top and middle drawers for BOTTOM of
this drawer.

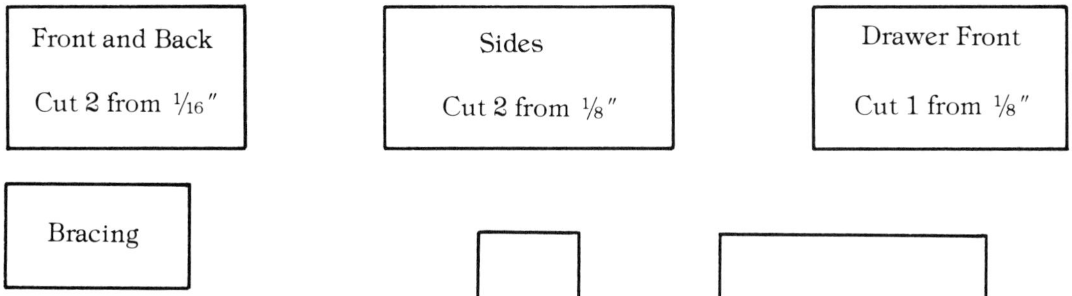

Front and Back

Cut 2 from ¹⁄₁₆″

Sides

Cut 2 from ⅛″

Drawer Front

Cut 1 from ⅛″

Bracing

Cut 2 from ¹⁄₁₆″

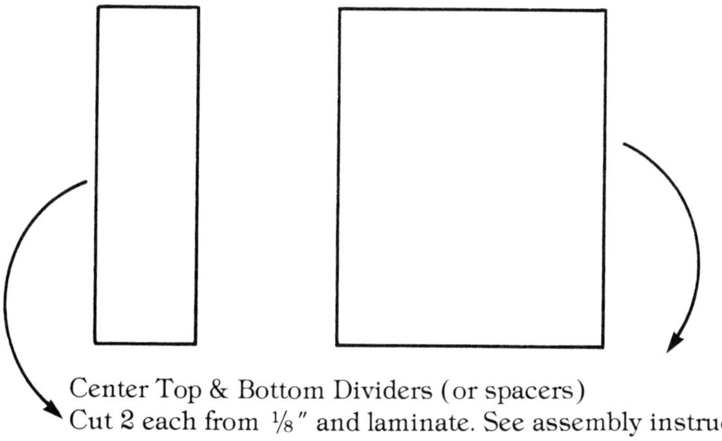

Center Top & Bottom Dividers (or spacers)
Cut 2 each from ⅛″ and laminate. See assembly instructions.

Butcher Block

($2\frac{1}{4}''$ wide $\times$ $2\frac{1}{4}''$ deep $\times$ $2\frac{1}{2}''$ high)

MATERIALS

$\frac{3}{16}''$ illustration board or
$\frac{1}{8}''$ illustration board and
$\frac{1}{16}''$ illustration board
Sobo glue
$\frac{1}{4}''$ doweling—6" long
Latex satin base coat—light and dark
Stain and glaze
$\frac{1}{8}''$ doweling—$2\frac{1}{2}''$ long
Round toothpick, blunt thin nail, or heavy wire
Silver paint
Black paint (gloss or dull)

INSTRUCTIONS

1. Trace and transfer pattern pieces onto illustration board.
2. Cut all pieces, laminating parts as indicated. (See pattern for explanation of size and lamination.) Sand with pieces held together.
3. On first and last piece for butcher block, paint outside and all edges with light base coat. Paint six more pieces on top, bottom, and side edges with light base coat.
4. Paint top, bottom, and side edges of the remaining seven pieces with dark base coat. When dry, glue all 15 pieces together, alternating light and dark.
5. Cut slot and drill or punch holes in tool holder as shown on pattern. Sand.
6. Glue tool holder to side of butcher block (on light colored plain side), centered and $\frac{1}{8}''$ down from top edge. Brace under tool holder, being careful not to cover slots or drilled holes for tools. Paint with light base.
7. From $\frac{1}{4}''$ doweling cut 4 legs $1\frac{1}{2}''$ long. Glue to bottom of butcher block $\frac{3}{16}''$ in from front, back, and side edges. Paint with light base.
8. Brush on stain and glaze. Let set for 5 to 10 minutes. Wipe lightly with cloth or paper towel until wood grained.

9.   TOOLS: Cut from patterns.

CLEAVER. Attach handle at x with pin and/or glue. Or you may cut the entire cleaver from ⅛″ illustration board and sand to right size.

KNIFE. Cut thin slot into ⅛″ doweling handle (Handle cut ½″ long). Glue knife "blade" into slot.

MEAT MALLET. Make mallet head from ⅛″ illustration board or ⅛″ doweling. Cut ⅛″ doweling ¾″ long. With point of nail make small hole in center of mallet head and center of handle. Using either ⅜″ long round toothpick, wire, or heavy pin, attach head to handle, gluing for strength.

PRONG. Cut ⅛″ doweling ⅝″ long. Cut off head of 1″ thin nail. Insert nail point into doweling and glue. (A round toothpick may also be used in place of the nail.)

Paint heads of all tools silver and all handles black. Set into holder on butcher block, handles up.

Butcher Block

Cut 15 pieces of (**A**) from ³⁄₁₆″ illustration board or
cut 15 pieces from ⅛″ and 15 pieces from ¹⁄₁₆″ and
laminate. DO NOT glue these pieces together until painted.

Tool Holder   Brace underside with ⅛″ × ⅛″ strip.

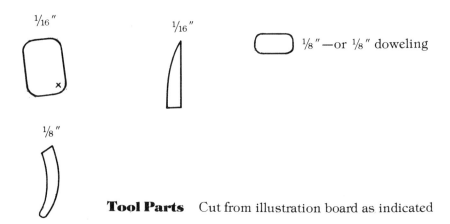

Tool Parts   Cut from illustration board as indicated

106

Table

(4" wide × 2½" deep × 2⅝" high)

MATERIALS

⅛" illustration board
Sobo glue
Latex satin base coat
Stain and glaze

INSTRUCTIONS

1. Trace and transfer pattern pieces onto ⅛" illustration board.

2. Cut all pieces, laminating parts as indicated.

3. To underside of tabletop glue under-table and upright brace ¾" from back edge and ¼" from side edges for one piece and ¾" from front edge and ¼" from side edges for the other piece.

4. Glue bottom brace to center top edges of upright base pieces.

5. Glue uprights flush with bottom of upright base against bottom brace and center of under-table and upright braces.

6. Sand lightly.

7. Paint with base coat. Allow to dry 3 to 4 hours.

8. Brush on stain and glaze. Let set 5 to 10 minutes. Wipe lightly with cloth or paper towel until wood grained.

Table

```
Table Top

Cut 1
```

```
Uprights—Cut 4
```

```
Under-Table and Upright Brace—Cut 2
```

```
Upright Base—Cut 2
```

```
Bottom Brace—Cut 1
```

All pieces cut from ⅛" illustration board

Chair

(Make at least 2 chairs for your kitchen table.)

($1\,^{3}/_{4}$ " wide $\times$ $1\,^{1}/_{2}$ " deep $\times$ $3\,^{1}/_{8}$ " high)

MATERIALS

$^{1}/_{8}$ " illustration board
$^{1}/_{16}$ " illustration board
Sobo glue
Latex satin base coat
Stain and glaze

INSTRUCTIONS

1. Trace and transfer pattern pieces onto $^{1}/_{8}$ " or $^{1}/_{16}$ " illustration board.
2. Cut all pieces, laminating parts as indicated.
3. Glue chair seat between sides $^{1}/_{16}$ " down from side seat curve.
4. Glue center $^{3}/_{4}$ " down from top of sides, centering from front to back.
5. Lightly dampen top back rest and glue to side tops resting on notches with $^{3}/_{16}$ " overhang on both sides.
6. Sand lightly.
7. Paint with base coat. Allow to dry 3 to 4 hours.
8. Brush on stain and glaze. Let set 5 to 10 minutes. Wipe lightly with cloth or paper towel until wood grained.

Chair

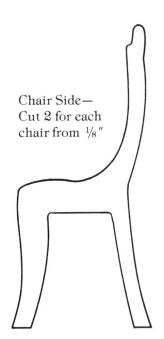

Chair Side—
Cut 2 for each
chair from $^{1}/_{8}$ "

Top Back Rest

Cut 1 from $^{1}/_{16}$ " for each chair

Center

Cut 1 from $^{1}/_{16}$ "
for each chair

Chair Seat

Chair Seat

Cut 1 from $^{1}/_{8}$ "
for each chair

5
THE BATHROOM

Bathtub
Washstand
Toilet
Flush Box
Towel Rack

Bathtub

(6⅛″ long × 3⅛″ deep × 2″ high)

MATERIALS

⅛″ illustration board
¹⁄₁₆″ illustration board
Sobo glue
White paint—gloss or satin
Latex satin base coat (I used dark base for all bathroom pieces.)
Stain and glaze (I used cherry stain for all bathroom pieces.)

INSTRUCTIONS

1. Trace and transfer pattern pieces onto ⅛″ illustration board.
2. Cut all pieces, laminating parts as indicated.
3. Glue tub front and back (B) flush with ends of sides (C).

4. Glue bottom braces (D) flush with tub bottom—one to tub front and sides; the other to tub back and sides.

5. Cut long pieces of $\frac{1}{16}'' \times 1\frac{1}{2}''$ to go around tub bottom. Starting at center round edge glue flush with tub bottom all around tub back to starting point. Cut carefully with scissors and glue seam. Paint inside of tub with white paint.

6. Cut trim pieces of $\frac{1}{16}'' \times \frac{3}{8}''$ and $\frac{1}{16}'' \times \frac{1}{4}''$. Cut these into the following sizes:

Cut $\frac{1}{16}'' \times \frac{3}{8}''$ strip into:
4 pieces 6″ long
4 pieces $\frac{3}{8}''$ long
8 pieces 1″ long
Cut $\frac{1}{16}'' \times \frac{1}{4}''$ strip into:
2 pieces $5\frac{5}{16}''$ long
2 piece $2\frac{1}{4}''$ long

7. Glue trim pieces on as follows:
Glue 6-inch-long pieces to top and bottom tub sides.
Glue $3\frac{1}{8}''$ long pieces to top and bottom tub front and back.
Glue 1″ long pieces to tub corners at sides, front, and back.
Glue $5\frac{5}{16}''$ long pieces to center of tub sides.
Glue $2\frac{1}{4}''$ long pieces to center of tub front and back.

8. Paint all pieces with base coat (except white tub). Let dry 3 to 4 hours.

9. Brush on stain and glaze (except on white tub). Let set 5 to 10 minutes. Wipe lightly with cloth or paper towel until wood grained.

10. When thoroughly dry (overnight preferably), glue tub to underside of tub top (A).

11. Glue tub top to tub sides, front, and back with a slight overhang all around.

12. Make faucets from earring backs or solder wire bent to shape.

13. Paint round gold drain in tub or use gromet or sequin/bead holder. (When sanding tub use emery board only. Sand strips before gluing in place; after painting with base coat sand edges only. Touch up if needed with base coat.)

Washstand

MATERIALS

$\frac{1}{8}''$ illustration board
$\frac{1}{16}''$ illustration board
3″ × 3″ vinyl asbestos tile (optional)
Sobo glue

White paint—gloss or satin
Latex satin base coat
Stain and glaze
Hinges or straight pins

INSTRUCTIONS

1. Trace and transfer pattern pieces to $\frac{1}{8}''$ or $\frac{1}{16}''$ illustration board and vinyl asbestos tile.

2. Cut all pieces, laminating parts as indicated.

3. Place back (C) on flat surface.

4. Glue sides (D) flush with back (C).

5. Glue top (E) and bottom (E) to back and sides flush with top, bottom, and side edges.

(3″ wide × 1¾″ deep × 3⅝″ high—
Measurements include vinyl top and backsplash.)

6. Glue bottom shelf (E) to back and sides ⅜″ up from bottom.
7. Glue top of center shelf 1⅛″ down from top ³⁄₁₆″ in from front edges to both back and side edges.
8. Glue a ¹⁄₁₆″ × ⅝″ strip around sink bottom, cutting and gluing at seam. Paint sink inside with white paint. Glue under sink cutout in washstand top.
9. Cut 4 pieces of ¹⁄₁₆″ illustration board 2″ × ³⁄₁₆″, and glue to door fronts and sides. Glue top and bottom door trims keeping small edge of trim at center fronts of doors.
10. Cut 1 piece of ¹⁄₁₆″ illustration board ⅜″ × 2 ¹³⁄₁₆″ and glue to bottom front and bottom shelf.
11. Cut long piece of ¹⁄₁₆″ illustration board ⅜″ and then cut as follows:
    4 pieces 2½″ long
    6 pieces 1″ long
12. Glue the 2½″ pieces to sides flush with front, back, top, and bottom edges. Glue the 1″ pieces to top, bottom, and center between side trims.
13. Paint with base coat (except sink). Let dry 3 to 4 hours. (Sand as for tub.)
14. Brush on stain and glaze (except on sink). Let set 5 to 10 minutes. Wipe lightly with cloth or paper towel until wood grained.
15. Hinge doors with butt hinges (Houseworks #1122) ⅛″ down from top of door frame and ⅛″ up from bottom of door frame. Or pin door at top and bottom through washstand top and bottom shelf ⅛″ in from side edges, then paint hinges on doors and side frame. (See Hinges, page 195, for alternative ideas.)
16. Glue vinyl asbestos (or any type of thin linoleum) washstand top to illustration board underlayment, flush with back and even overhang on front and sides.
17. Glue vinyl asbestos (or linoleum) backsplash to washstand top flush with back and side edges.
18. Make faucets from earring backs or solder wire bent to shape.
19. Paint round gold drain in sink or use gromet or sequin/bead holder.

Bathtub

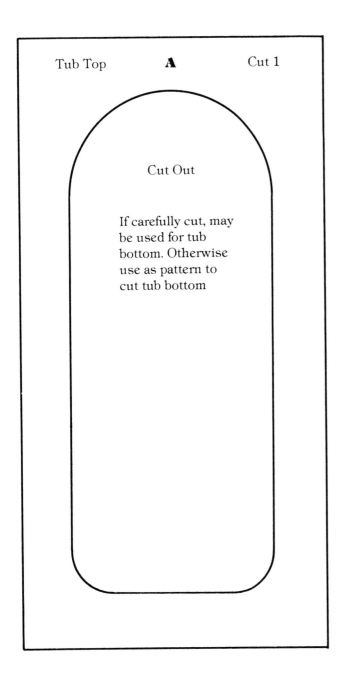

Tub Top   **A**   Cut 1

Cut Out

If carefully cut, may
be used for tub
bottom. Otherwise
use as pattern to
cut tub bottom

D

Bottom Braces   Cut 2

B

Tub Front And Back

Cut 2

All pieces cut from ⅛″ illustration board

C

Tub Sides

Cut 2

Washstand

A

Backsplash

Cut 1 from Vinyl asbestos

or ¹⁄₁₆″ illustration board

D

Sides

Cut 2 from ⅛″

B

Top

Cut Out

Cut 1 from Vinyl asbestos

or ¹⁄₁₆″ illustration board

G

Sink Bottom

Cut 1 from ⅛″

C

Back

Cut 1 from ⅛″

H

Doors

Cut 2 from ⅛″

Top & Bottom Door
Trims

Cut 4 from ¹⁄₁₆″

Cut out as indicated by dotted lines for top only.
(Sink opening)

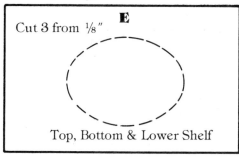

E

Cut 3 from ⅛″

Top, Bottom & Lower Shelf

F

Center Shelf

Cut 1 from ⅛″

Toilet

(1⅞″ wide × 2⅛″ deep × 1½″ high.
Measurements include toilet seat cover.)

MATERIALS

⅛″ illustration board
1 section from plastic egg carton
Sobo glue
Latex satin base coat
Stain and glaze
Hinges

INSTRUCTIONS

1. Trace and transfer pattern pieces to ⅛″ illustration board.
2. Cut all pieces, laminating as indicated.
3. Place bottom (B) on flat surface.
4. Glue sides (C) flush with bottom, even with front and back edges.
5. Glue front and back (D) flush with bottom and side edges.-
6. Cut a long piece of 1/16″ × ⅜″ illustration board and then cut as follows:
  6 pieces 1¼″ long
  4 pieces 1⅛″ long
  2 pieces 15/16″ long
7. Glue the 1¼″ pieces to side and front corners, gluing front corners last to cover seam. Glue the 1⅛″ pieces to sides at top and bottom. Glue the 15/16″ pieces to front at top and bottom.

8. Cut off egg carton section ¾″ from bottom and glue to underside of toilet top.

9. Paint with base coat including lid (E) (except white toilet bowl). Let dry 3 to 4 hours.

10. Brush on stain and glaze including lid (E) (except white toilet bowl). Let set 5 to 10 minutes. Wipe lightly with cloth or paper towel until wood grained.

11. Glue top to base flush with back, even overhang on sides and front.

12. Hinge lid (E) at back edge. (See Hinges, page 195.) (Sand as explained in sanding of tub.)

Flush Box

(1⅞″ wide × 1″ deep × 1⅛″ high)

MATERIALS

⅛″ illustration board
Sobo glue
Latex satin base coat
Stain and glaze
3″ length fine gold chain or gold thread
2 small gold straight pins
1 small black bugle bead or ¾″ length ¹⁄₁₆″ doweling or similar item
2 plain straight pins
1 piece ⅛″ copper or brass tubing (or gold-painted doweling), 4½″ long

INSTRUCTIONS

1. Trace and transfer pattern pieces to ⅛″ illustration board.

2. Cut all pieces, laminating parts as indicated.

3. Place bottom (B) on flat surface.

4. Glue sides (D) flush with bottom, even with front and back edges.

5. Glue front and back (C) flush with bottom and side edges.

6. Cut long piece of ¹⁄₁₆″ × ⅜″ illustration board and then cut as follows:
6 pieces 1″ long
4 pieces ⅜″ long
2 pieces 1¼″ long

7. Glue the 1″ pieces to side and front corners . . . gluing front corners last to cover seam. Glue the ⅜″ pieces to sides at top and bottom. Glue the 1¼″ pieces to front at top and bottom.

8. Glue flush box top (A) flush with back and even overhang on sides and front edges.

9. Sand in same manner as for tub and other bathroom pieces.

10. Pin top of small chain to side top trim of flush box, ¼″ under top. Glue or hook a pin or bead on lower end of chain.

11. Make small hole on underside of flush box and top back edge of toilet, centered ¼″ from back edges of both. Glue 1⅝″ length of round toothpicks into both holes. Cut copper or brass tubing length to fit room that will be the bathroom. Insert toothpicks (those glued to flush box and toilet) into tubing. If you are using doweling, make holes for toothpicks and glue doweling, cut to size, into holes.

12. Paint with base coat. (This may be done before Step 9, if preferred.) Brush on stain and glaze. Let set 5 to 10 minutes. Wipe lightly with cloth or paper towel until wood grained. (This may also be done before Step 9.)

Toilet　　　　　　　　　　**Flush Box**

All pieces cut from ⅛″ illustration board.

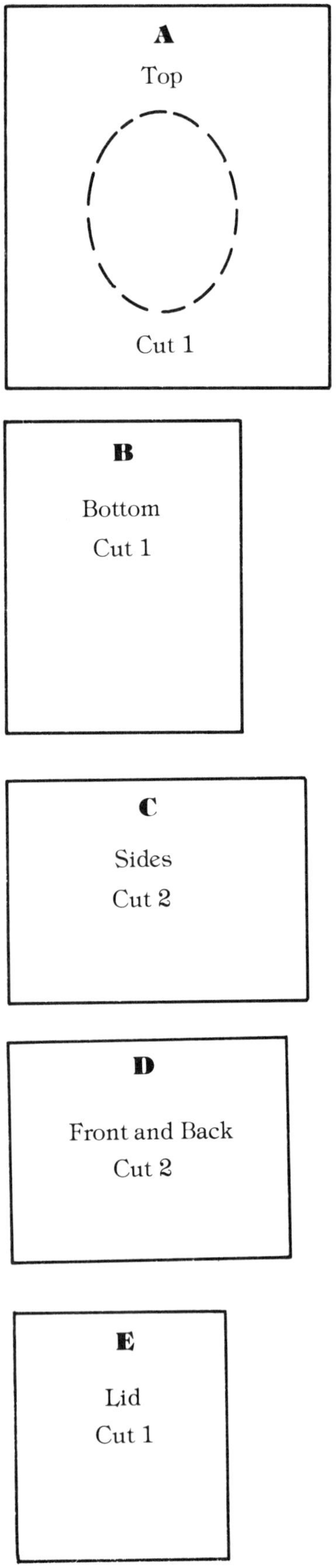

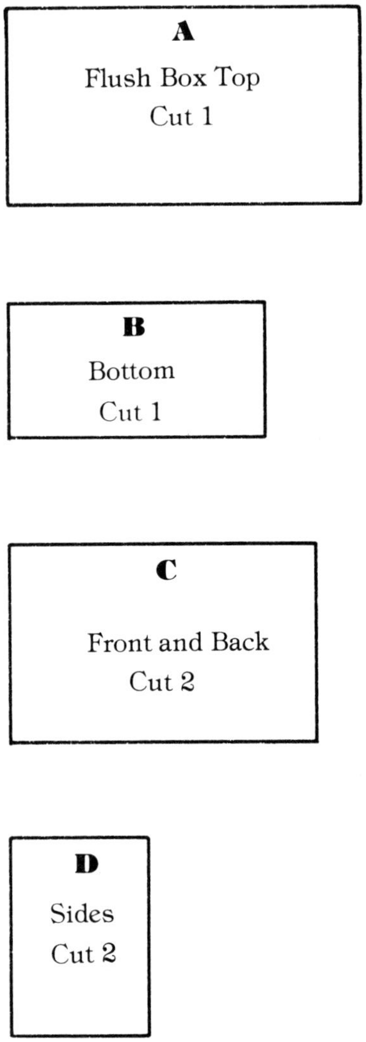

A

Top

Cut 1

A

Flush Box Top
Cut 1

B

Bottom
Cut 1

B

Bottom
Cut 1

C

Sides
Cut 2

C

Front and Back
Cut 2

D

Front and Back
Cut 2

D

Sides
Cut 2

E

Lid
Cut 1

Towel Rack

Sides
Cut 2

Bottom—Cut 1

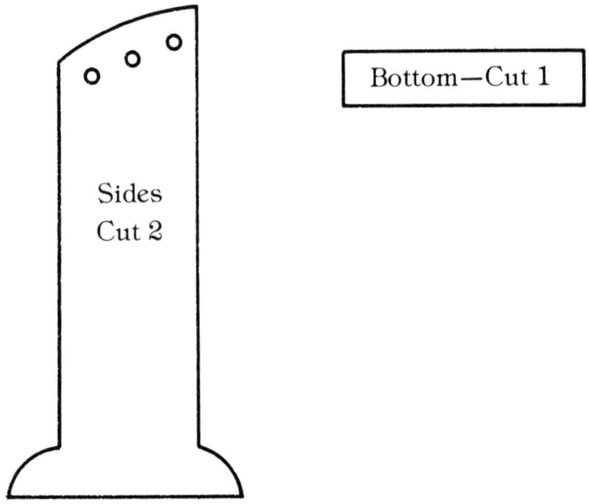

Towel Rack

(1½″ wide × 1¼″ deep × 2½″ high)

MATERIALS

⅛″ illustration board
3 round toothpicks
Sobo glue
Latex satin base coat
Stain and glaze

INSTRUCTIONS

1. Trace and transfer pattern pieces to ⅛″ illustration board.
2. Cut all pieces, laminating parts as indicated.
3. Glue bottom bracket, centering on sides flush with bottom.
4. Cut toothpicks 1½″ long and glue into holes as indicated on pattern.
5. Paint with base coat. Let dry 3 to 4 hours. Sand edges only.
6. Brush on stain and glaze. Let set 5 to 10 minutes. Wipe lightly with cloth or paper towel until wood grained. (See Accessories, page 204, for towels to hang on rack.)

6

THE BEDROOM

Basic Bed

MATERIALS

$\frac{1}{8}''$ illustration board
$\frac{1}{16}''$ illustration board
Sobo glue
Latex satin base coat
Stain and glaze

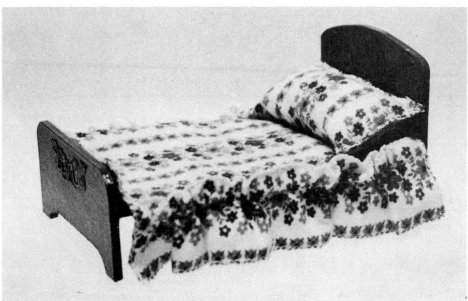

(6½" long × 3¾" wide × 3½" high.
Height measured at highest point of headboard.)

INSTRUCTIONS

1. Trace and transfer pattern pieces onto ⅛" and ¹⁄₁₆" illustration board.
2. Cut out pieces.
3. Laminate headboard (B) and foot (C).
4. Cut slots in headboard and foot as noted by dotted lines on pattern.
5. Glue bottom (A) into slots on headboard and foot.
6. Paint with base coat. (If leaving plain skip Step 7.) Sand all edges.
7. Cut designs for trim from three thicknesses of paper doilies. Glue on where desired. Paint with light covering of base coat.
8. Brush stain and glaze over entire surface including doily trim. Let set 5 to 10 minutes. Wipe lightly with cloth or paper towel until wood grained.

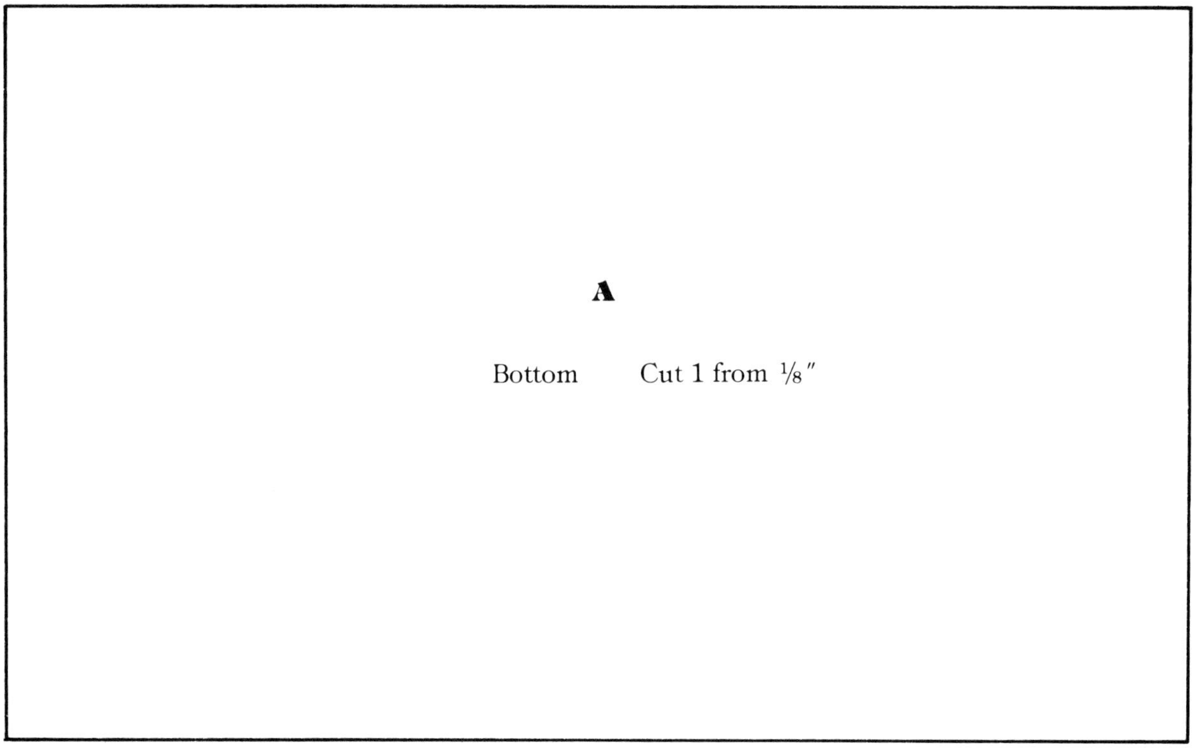

A

Bottom   Cut 1 from ⅛″

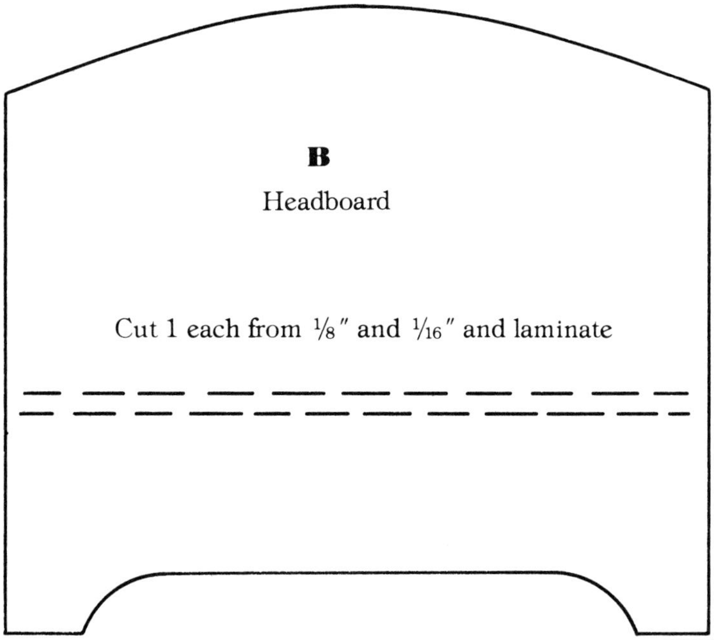

B

Headboard

Cut 1 each from ⅛″ and ¹⁄₁₆″ and laminate

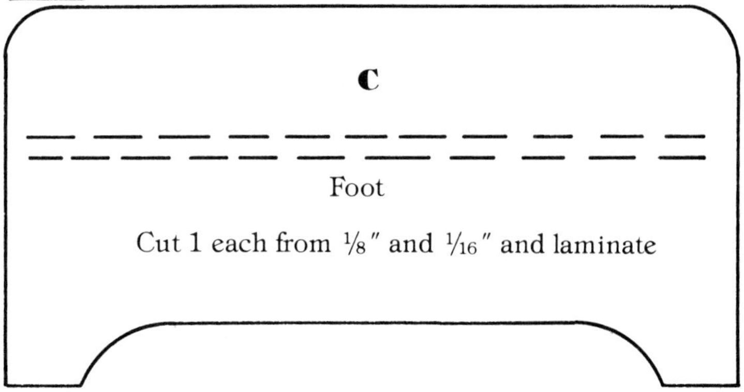

C

Foot

Cut 1 each from ⅛″ and ¹⁄₁₆″ and laminate

Four-Poster Bed

(6⅝" long × 4" wide × 3" high.
Height measured at highest point of headboard.)

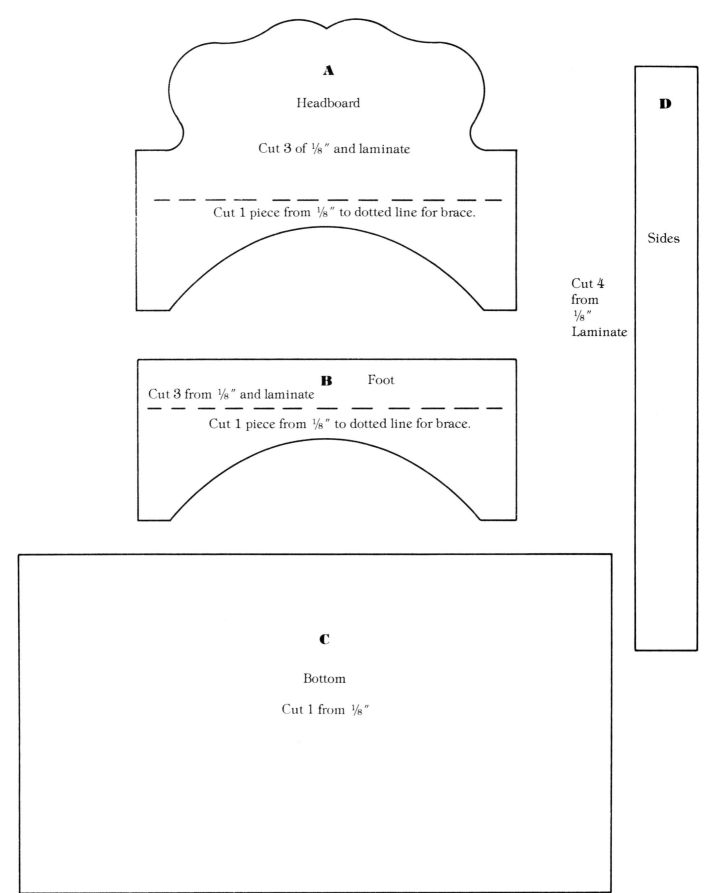

A

Headboard

Cut 3 of ⅛″ and laminate

Cut 1 piece from ⅛″ to dotted line for brace.

D

Sides

Cut 4
from
⅛″
Laminate

B   Foot

Cut 3 from ⅛″ and laminate

Cut 1 piece from ⅛″ to dotted line for brace.

C

Bottom

Cut 1 from ⅛″

MATERIALS

⅛″ illustration board
Sobo glue
Doweling and/or beads (¼″) 4 pieces 4″
    high (See instructions)
Doily or braid trim (optional)
Latex satin base coat
Stain and glaze

INSTRUCTIONS

1.   Trace and transfer pattern pieces onto ⅛″ illustration board.
2.   Cut all pieces, laminating parts as indicated.
3.   Laminate 3 pieces of headboard (A).
4.   Laminate 3 pieces of foot (B).
5.   Glue braces as indicated by dotted lines to both headboard and foot.
6.   Glue sides (D) on bottom braces flush with outside edges of foot and headboard.
7.   Glue bottom 1¾″ down from top of headboard; ⅜″ down from top of foot; ⅛″ down from top of sides.
8.   Make posts of ¼″ doweling alternating with beads in any manner you wish. For finishing top of doweling, put into pencil sharpener until slightly rounded. You may also laminate two 6″ pieces of ⅛″ × ⅛″ illustration board, leaving square or rounding at top and carving, if this is one of your artistic skills.
9.   Paint with base coat. (If leaving plain, skip Step 10.) Sand all edges.
10.   Cut designs for trim from three thicknesses of paper doilies or one piece of sewing braid. Glue on where desired. Paint with light covering of base coat unless using gold doilies or braid. Then do not apply trim until after the stain and glaze. (I did not instruct you to do this for the basic bed as a plain bed is usually used in Nanny's room and gold trim would be out of place.)
11.   Brush on stain and glaze over entire surface including doily trim, except as instructed in Step 10. Let set 5 to 10 minutes. Wipe lightly with cloth or paper towel until wood grained.

Canopy Bed

MATERIALS

⅛″ illustration board
¼″ doweling—20½″ long
⅛″ doweling—22½″ long
Sobo glue
Latex satin base coat
Stain and glaze

INSTRUCTIONS

1.   Trace and transfer pattern pieces onto ⅛″ illustration board.
2.   Cut all pieces.
3.   Laminate headboard (C) and foot (D).
4.   Laminate tester sides (E) and cut grooves through ⅛″ thickness as shown on drawing.

(6 3/16″ long × 4 5/8″ wide × 6 1/4″ high.
Height measured to highest point of tester.)

5.   Glue base to sides ⅛″ down from top long edges, flush at top and bottom edges.

6.   Glue headboard (C) to base (A) ⅞″ up from bottom edge.

7.   Glue foot (D) to base ⅛″ down from top edge.

8.   Cut 4 pieces of ¼″ doweling 5⅛″ long. Glue in plac at all 4 corners, ⅝″ below bottom of headboard and foot. [Top of side posts will be 3½″ above sides (B).]

9.   Cut 5 pieces of ⅛″ doweling 4½″ long. Glue in slots flush with top round of testers forming top of canopy bed. Glue entire top assembly at four corners to top of ¼″ doweling.

10.   Paint with base coat. Carefully sand where needed.

11.   Brush with stain and glaze. Let set 5 to 10 minutes. Wipe lightly with cloth or paper towel until wood grained.

Canopy Bed

All pieces cut from ⅛″ illustration board

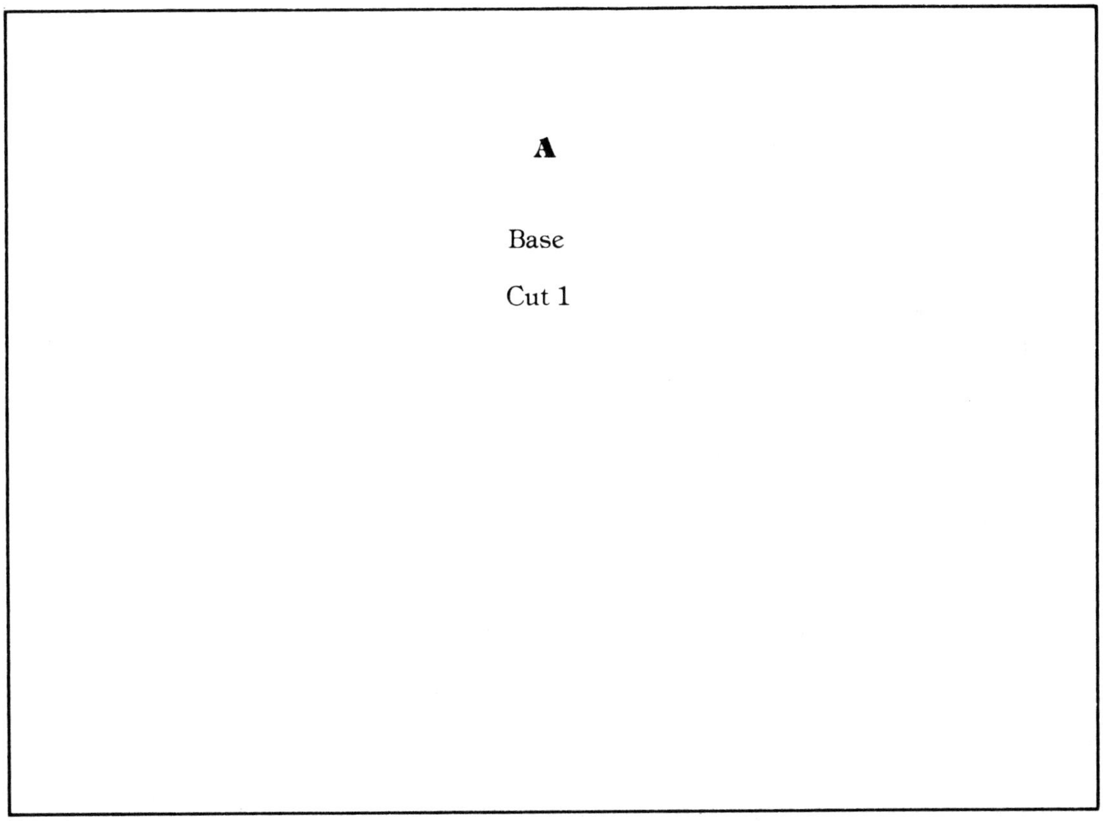

A

Base

Cut 1

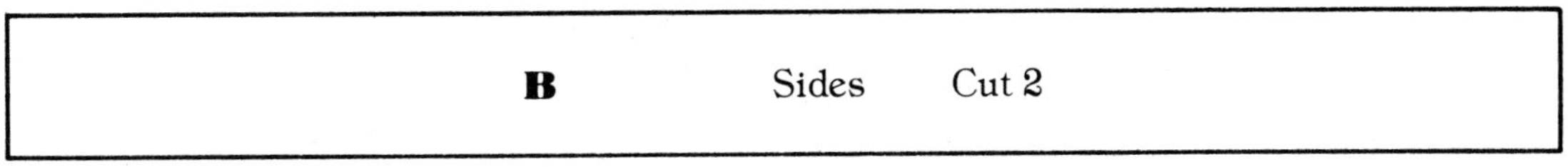

B   Sides   Cut 2

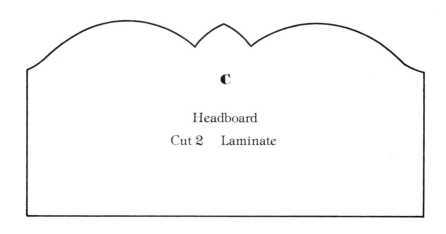

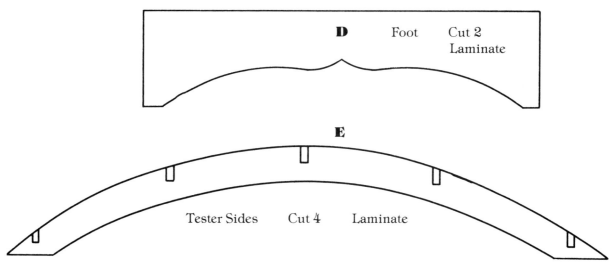

All pieces cut from ⅛″ illustration board

Privacy Bed

MATERIALS

⅛″ illustration board
Sobo glue
Latex satin base coat
Stain and glaze

INSTRUCTIONS

1. Trace and transfer pattern pieces (A) through (D) for canopy bed plus pieces (F), (G), and (H) for privacy bed top to ⅛″ illustration board.
2. Cut all pieces, laminating parts as indicated.

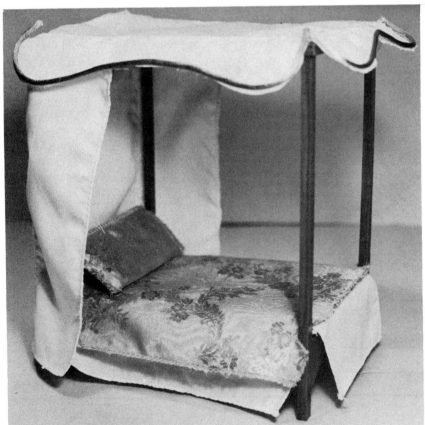

(6³⁄₁₆″ long × 4⅝″ wide × 7⁹⁄₁₆″ high)

3. Laminate headboard (C) and foot (D).
4. Glue base (A) to sides ⅛″ down from top long edges, flush at top and bottom edges.
5. Glue headboard (C) to base (A) ⅞″ up from bottom edge.
6. Glue foot (D) to base (A) ⅛″ down from top edge. Glue in place at all 4 corners, ⅝″ below bottom of headboard and foot. [Top of side posts will be 5¹³⁄₁₆″ above sides (B).]
7. Cut 8 pieces ⅛″ × ¼″ × 7⅜″. Laminate to make 4 corner posts.
8. On underneath side of privacy bed top glue side and end reinforcements as shown by dotted lines on top (F).
9. Glue privacy bed top to corner posts with ⅛″ overhang on all sides.
10. Paint with base coat. Carefully sand where needed.
11. Brush with stain and glaze. Let set 5 to 10 minutes. Wipe lightly with cloth or paper towel until wood grained.

Privacy Bed

All pieces cut from ⅛″ illustration board

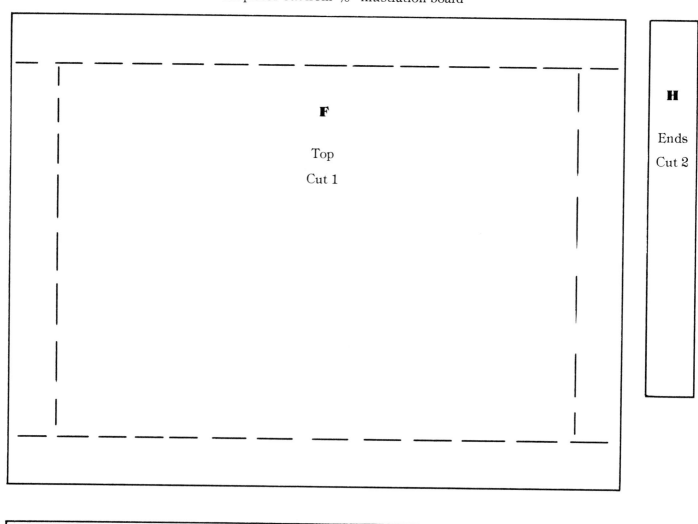

F

Top

Cut 1

H

Ends
Cut 2

Top Sides (Reinforcement)   **G**   Cut 2

Dresser

(3¾″ wide × 2″ deep × 3⅞″ high)

MATERIALS

⅛″ illustration board
1/16″ illustration board
Sobo glue
Straight pins
Latex satin base coat
Stain and glaze
4 drawer pulls
2 doorknobs

INSTRUCTIONS

1. Trace and transfer pattern pieces to ⅛″ and 1/16″ illustration board.

2. Cut all pieces, laminating parts as indicated.

3. Place back (A) on flat surface.

4. Glue sides (B) to back flush with side and top edges (as indicated by dotted line on side pattern, wider base leg toward back of dresser).

5. Glue top (C) to back and sides, flush with back and overhang on sides and front edges.

6. Glue base (D) to back and sides with top edge of base 9/16″ from bottom of side edge leg corner.

7. Glue one drawer spacer to each side of dresser touching underside of top.

8. Glue first drawer partition to sides, back, and spacer bottom edges.

9. Glue in second set of drawer spacers under first partition, to sides and back.

10. Glue second drawer partition to sides, back, and second set of spacer bottom edges.

11. Glue door spacers under bottom partition, sides, back, and top of base.

12. Laminate center door stop. Glue to base, back, and under bottom partition, centering between sides.

13. Glue side trim to bottom of each side (wide base leg at back of dresser).

14. Glue front trim to side trims and base, flush with top of side trims and 1/16″ below top edge of base.

15. Glue drawer sides flush with side edges of drawer bottom.

16. Glue drawer backs to sides and bottom 1/16″ in from back edges.

17. Glue front of drawer flush with bottom and side edges.

18. Paint all pieces with base coat. Sand where needed.

19. Brush with stain and glaze. Let set 5 to 10 minutes. Wipe lightly with cloth or paper towel until wood grained. (This unit may be "doily" trimmed before painted. Check with other pieces in same room to match. Don't combine trimmed and untrimmed pieces in same room. Bedroom furniture must be a matched set.)

20. Pin doors through base and bottom partition ⅛″ from side edges.

21. Attach drawer and door pulls or handles. (See Handles and Pulls, page 196.)

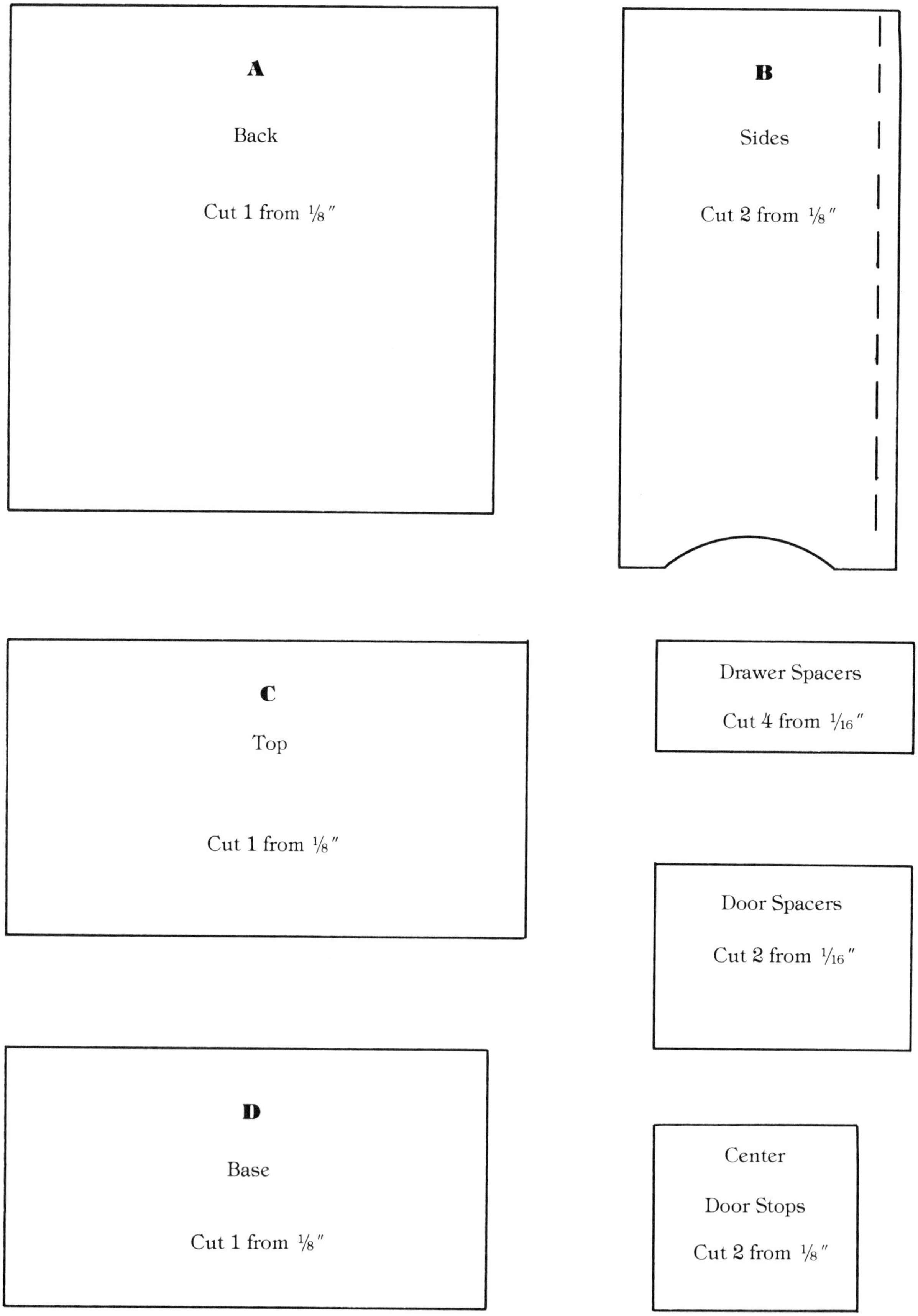

A

Back

Cut 1 from ⅛″

B

Sides

Cut 2 from ⅛″

C

Top

Cut 1 from ⅛″

Drawer Spacers

Cut 4 from ¹⁄₁₆″

Door Spacers

Cut 2 from ¹⁄₁₆″

D

Base

Cut 1 from ⅛″

Center

Door Stops

Cut 2 from ⅛″

E

Drawer Partitions

Cut 2 from ⅛″

F

Doors

Cut 4 from ⅛″

Drawer Bottoms

Cut 2 from ⅛″

Drawer Sides

Cut 4 from ⅛″

Drawer Backs
Cut 2 from ⅛″

Drawer Fronts
Cut 2 from ⅛″

Front Trim   Cut 1 from ⅛″

Side Trim   Cut 2 from ⅛″

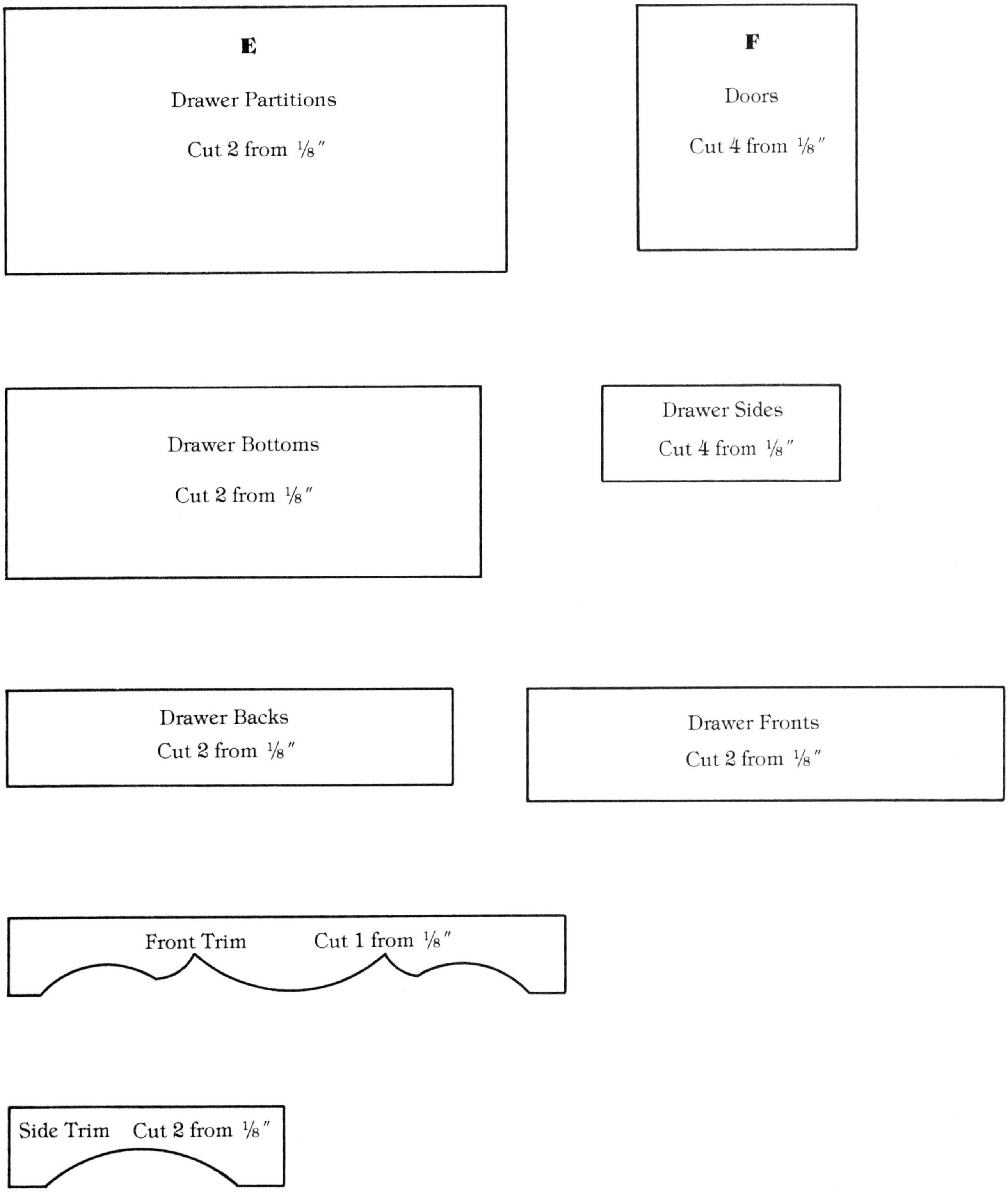

Lowboy Chest

(4¼″ wide × 1⅝″ deep × 2¾″ high)

MATERIALS

Latex satin base coat
Stain and glaze
2 drawer pulls
2 doorknobs

⅛″ illustration board
1/16″ illustration board
Sobo glue
Straight pins

INSTRUCTIONS

1. Trace and transfer pattern pieces to ⅛″ and 1/16″ illustration board.
2. Cut all pieces, laminating parts as indicated.
3. Place back (A) on flat surface.
4. Glue sides (B) to back flush with side edges (back set between sides) and flush at top edges.
5. Glue laminated top (C) to back and sides, flush with back and overhang on sides and front edges.
6. Glue bottom partition (D) to back and sides with top of partition 2 1/16″ below underside of top (C).
7. Glue top spacers to sides and back at underside of top.
8. Glue drawer partitions underneath top spacers, sides, and back.
9. Glue bottom spacers to sides and back between drawer partition and bottom partition.
10. Glue door stop to underside of drawer partition centered between sides.
11. Round side edges of doors and cut an inward slant at center edges. Pin at sides ⅛″ in through drawer and bottom partitions.
12. Glue side trims aligning with sides at bottom edges.
13. Glue choice of front trim (X) or (XX) to side trims and 1/16″ from top of bottom partition.
14. Place drawer bottom on flat surface. Glue laminated front and single back flush with bottom along long edges.
15. Glue drawer sides to bottom, front, and back, all edges flush.
16. Score center of drawer for the appearance of two drawers.
17. Paint with base coat. Carefully sand where needed.
18. Brush with stain and glaze. Let set 5 to 10 minutes. Wipe lightly with cloth or paper towel until wood grained. (Follow instructions on doily trim as for dresser.)
19. Attach drawer and door pulls or handles. (See Handles and Pulls, page 196.)

Lowboy Chest

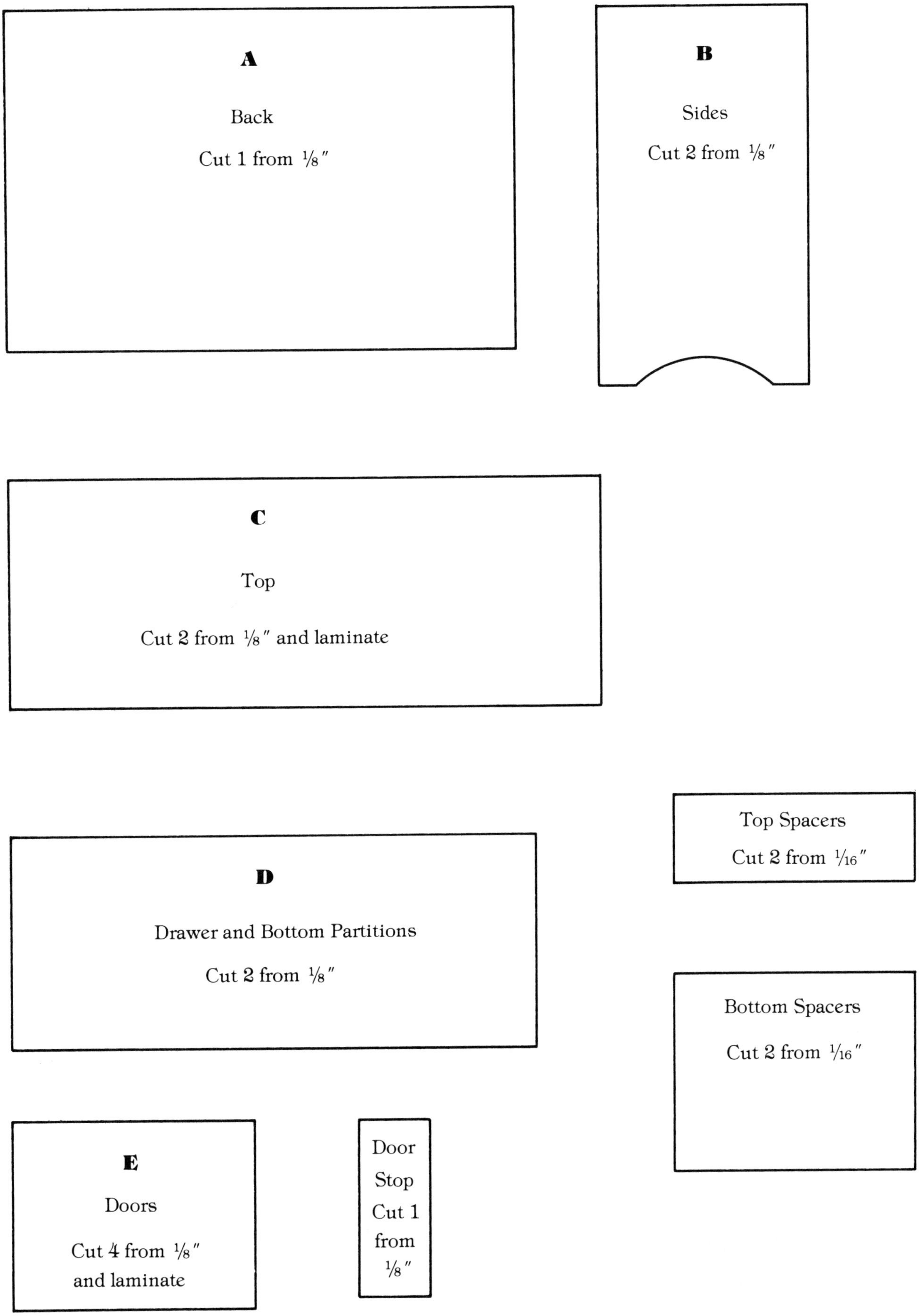

A

Back

Cut 1 from ⅛″

B

Sides

Cut 2 from ⅛″

C

Top

Cut 2 from ⅛″ and laminate

Top Spacers

Cut 2 from 1/16″

D

Drawer and Bottom Partitions

Cut 2 from ⅛″

Bottom Spacers

Cut 2 from 1/16″

E

Doors

Cut 4 from ⅛″
and laminate

Door
Stop
Cut 1
from
⅛″

133

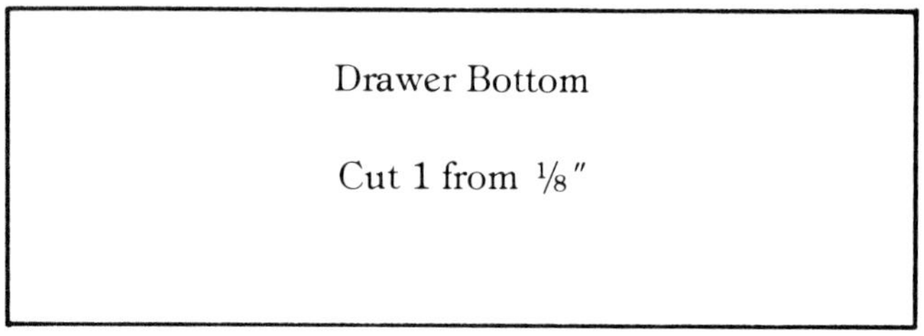

Drawer Bottom

Cut 1 from ⅛″

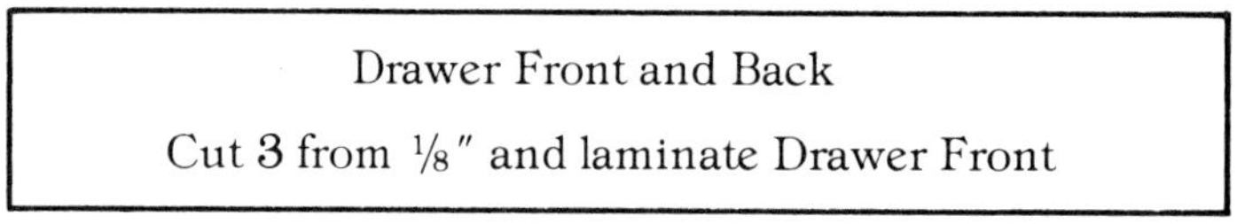

Drawer Front and Back

Cut 3 from ⅛″ and laminate Drawer Front

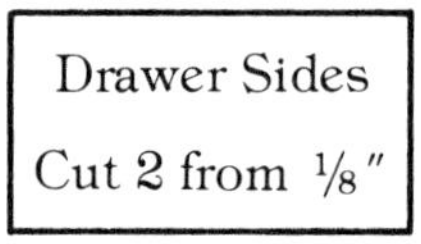

Drawer Sides
Cut 2 from ⅛″

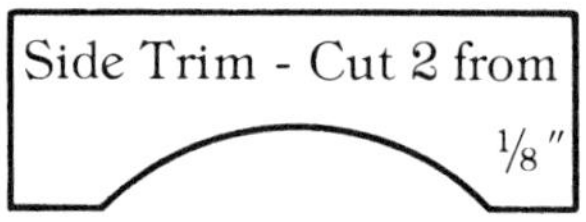

Side Trim - Cut 2 from
⅛″

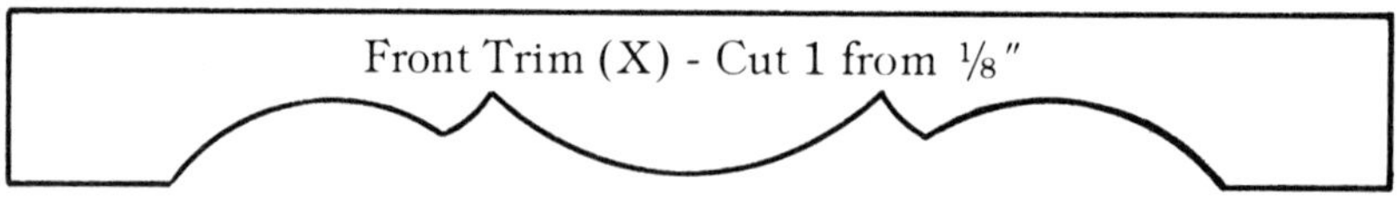

Front Trim (X) - Cut 1 from ⅛″

(Use either Trim (X) or (XX) or pattern of your own creation.)

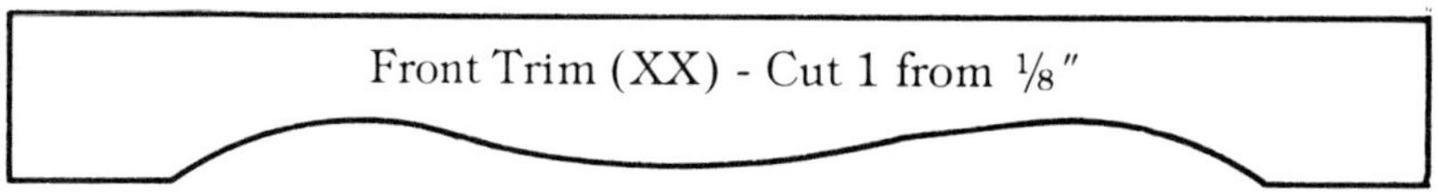

Front Trim (XX) - Cut 1 from ⅛″

Children's Chest
(5-Drawer Chest)

$(3\frac{1}{2}''$ wide $\times$ $1\frac{3}{4}''$ deep $\times$ $4\frac{1}{2}''$ high$)$

MATERIALS

$\frac{1}{8}''$ illustration board
$\frac{1}{16}''$ illustration board
Sobo glue
Latex satin base coat
Stain and glaze
10 drawer pulls

INSTRUCTIONS

1. Trace and transfer pattern pieces to $\frac{1}{8}''$ and $\frac{1}{16}''$ illustration board.
2. Cut all pieces, laminating parts as indicated.
3. Glue back (A) to sides (B) on dotted lines. (Larger base foot on back edge.)
4. Glue laminated top (C) to back and sides flush with back edge and overhang on side and front edges.
5. Glue bottom partition (D) $3\frac{3}{4}''$ down from underside of top.
6. Glue spacers and remaining partitions as follows:

One set of spacers to each side and underside of top;
Partition below spacers, to sides and back;
Second set of spacers to underside of partition, sides and back;
Continue in this manner until all spacers and partitions have been glued in place.

7. Glue $\frac{1}{16}''$ piece of side trim to inside of sides, underside of bottom partition and back.
8. Glue $\frac{1}{8}''$ side trim, matching sides, at bottom, front, and back edges.
9. Glue front trim to sides and side trim and $\frac{1}{16}''$ below top of bottom partition.
10. For each of 5 drawers glue as follows:

Place drawer bottom(s) on flat surface.
Glue back(s) on top of drawer bottoms $\frac{1}{8}''$ from each side.
Glue sides on top of drawer bottom, to backs, flush with back edge and front edge.
Glue front(s) to sides and drawer bottom, flush with bottom of drawer.

11. Paint with base coat. Carefully sand where needed.
12. Brush with stain and glaze. Let set 5 to 10 minutes. Wipe lightly with cloth or paper towel until wood grained.
13. Attach 2 drawer pulls to each drawer, center pull or handle $\frac{5}{8}''$ in from each side of drawer. (See Handles and Pulls, page 196.)

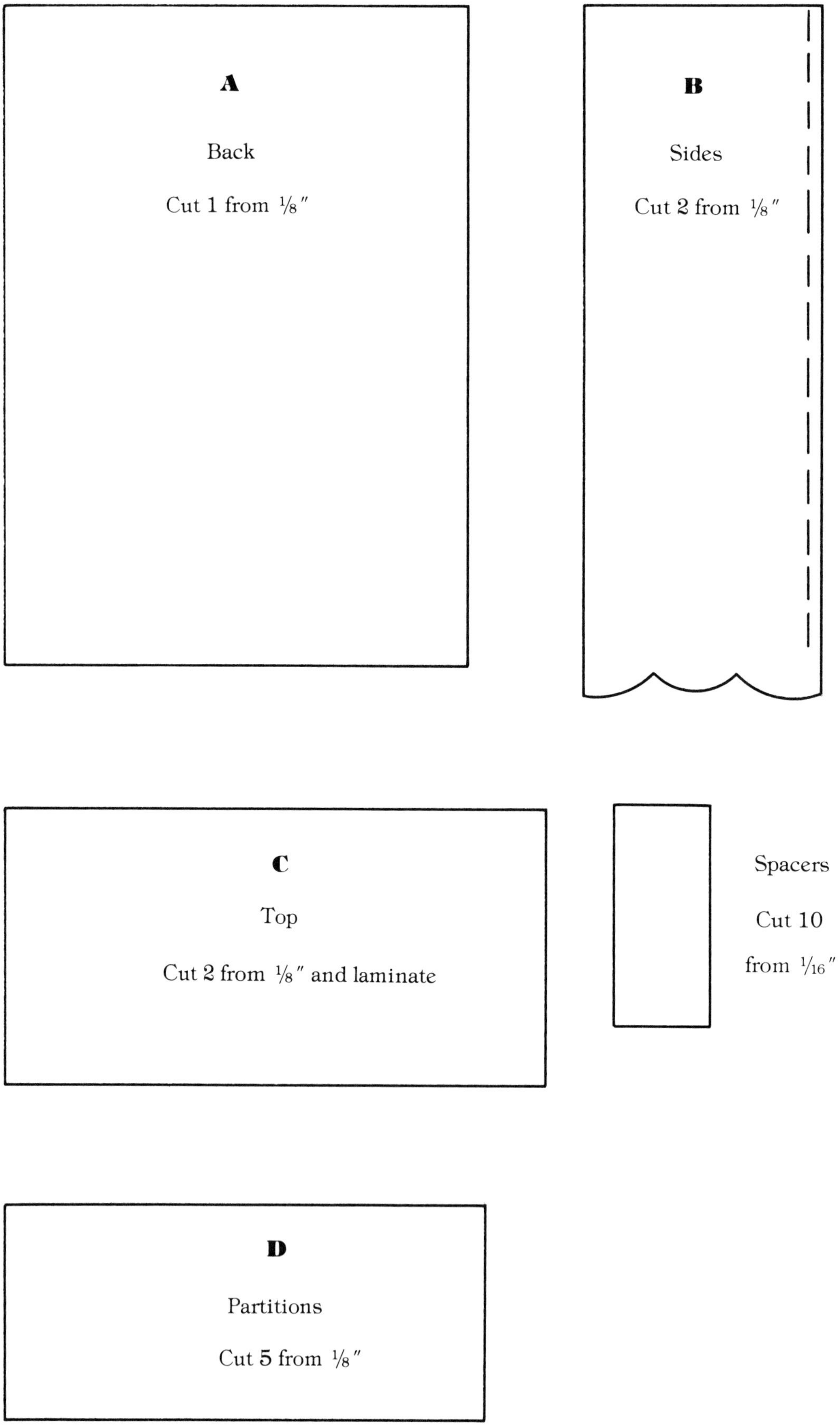

A

Back

Cut 1 from ⅛″

B

Sides

Cut 2 from ⅛″

C

Top

Cut 2 from ⅛″ and laminate

Spacers

Cut 10

from 1/16″

D

Partitions

Cut 5 from ⅛″

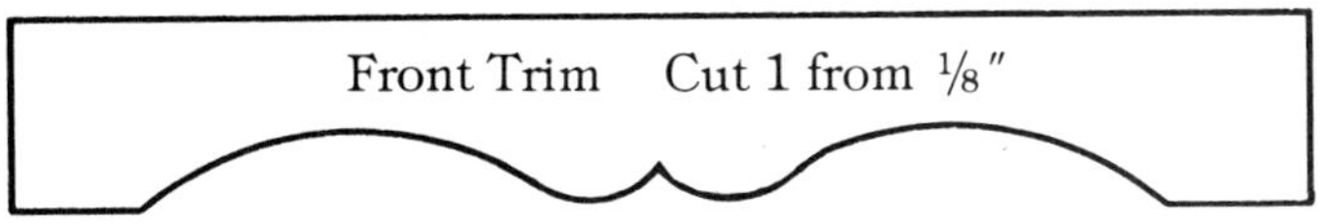

Front Trim   Cut 1 from 1/8"

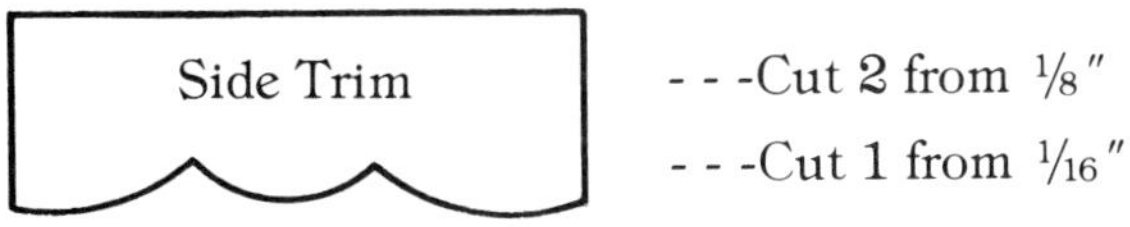

Side Trim

- - -Cut 2 from 1/8"

- - -Cut 1 from 1/16"

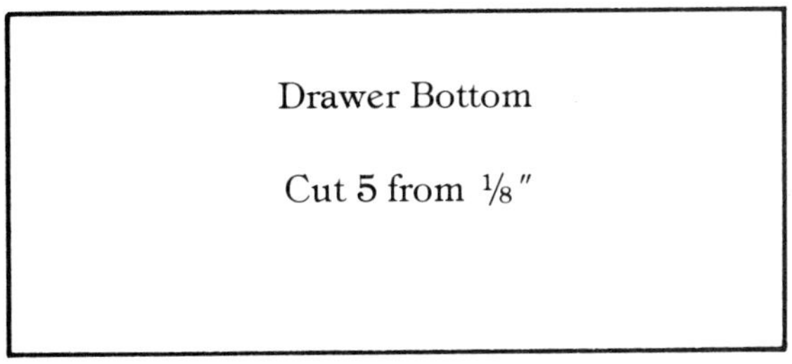

Drawer Bottom

Cut 5 from 1/8"

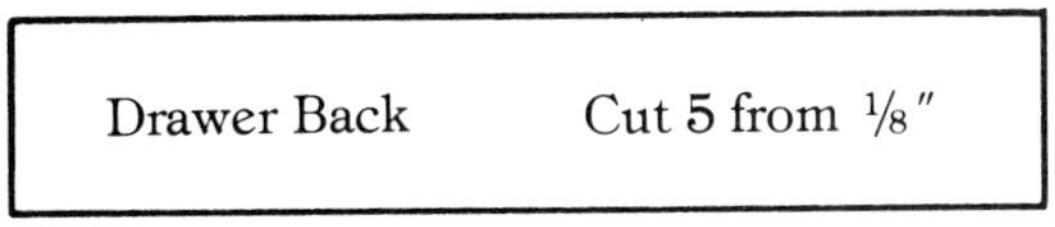

Drawer Back   Cut 5 from 1/8"

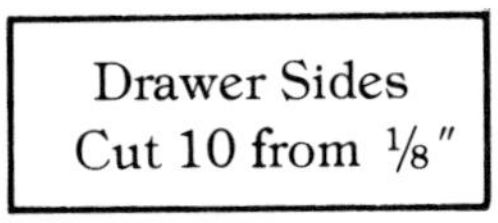

Drawer Sides
Cut 10 from 1/8"

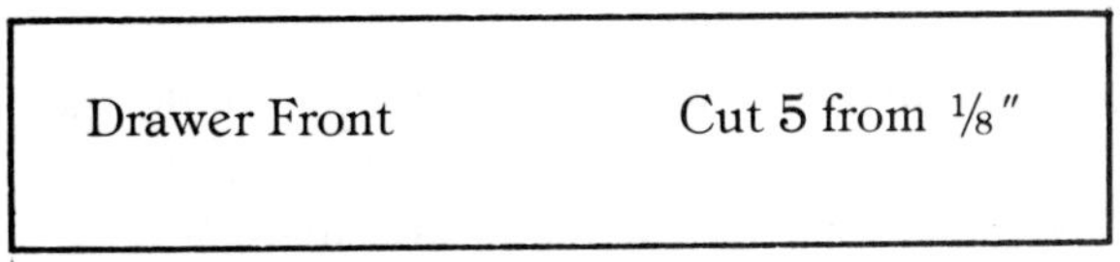

Drawer Front   Cut 5 from 1/8"

Armoire

(4¼″ wide × 2¼″ deep × 6¾″ high. Width and height include top trim.)

MATERIALS

⅛″ illustration board
Sobo glue
Doilies (optional)
⅛″ doweling—1⅞″ long
Latex satin base coat
Stain and glaze
Straight pins

INSTRUCTIONS

1. Trace and transfer pattern pieces to ⅛″ illustration board.
2. Cut all pieces, laminating parts as indicated.
3. Place back (A) on flat surface. Glue sides (B) flush with back ⅛″ from top and ¼″ up from bottom. (Back will be inside of sides.)
4. Glue base (C) to sides and back with bottom of base ⅛″ up from bottom of back and ⅜″ from bottom of sides.
5. Glue top underlayment to sides and back flush with top edges and ⅛″ space in center. (Laminated hanger side to your right with armoire facing you.)
6. Glue top to underlayment, sides, and back, flush with back and overhang on front and sides.
7. Glue center divider (E) to top (between underlayments), back and base, 1⅝″ from laminated side.
8. Glue top shelf spacers to side, center divider, and top underlayment.
9. Glue shelf to back, sides, and center divider under top spacers.
10. Glue center spacers under first shelf to side, back, and center divider.

138

11. Glue second shelf to side, back, center divider under center spacers.
12. Glue bottom spacers under second shelf to side, back, base, and center divider.
13. Laminate doors (F). Round side edges and angle-cut inward at center edges.
14. Glue bottom trim to base and sides, flush with bottom edge of sides.
15. Pin doors in place ⅛″ from side edges through top and bottom trim.
16. Glue top trim from side to side ⅛″ from top front edge.
17. Cut out 3 thicknesses of doily trim (optional) and glue in place on door front. (I used one large center medallion on each door and 4 small corner motifs.)
18. Paint with base coat. (Be careful not to paint doors shut. After painting, leave doors ajar so you won't have this problem.) Sand where needed.
19. Brush with stain and glaze. Let set 5 to 10 minutes. Wipe lightly with cloth or paper towel until wood grained.
20. Attach door pulls where indicated by dot on plans. (See Handles and Pulls, page 196.)

Armoire

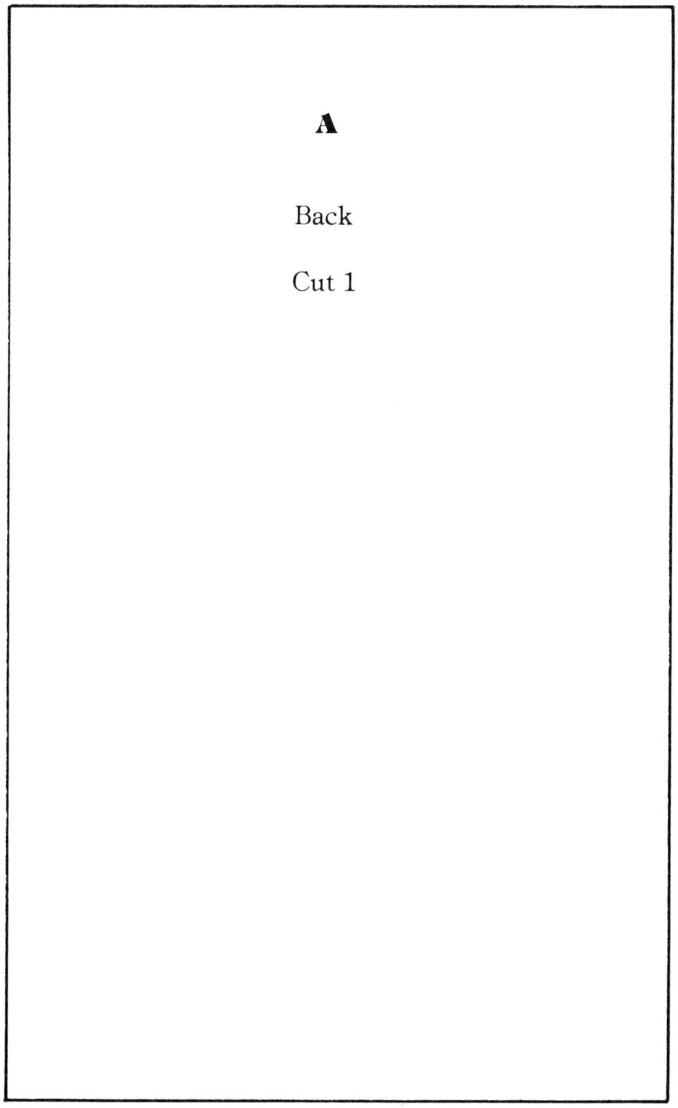

A

Back

Cut 1

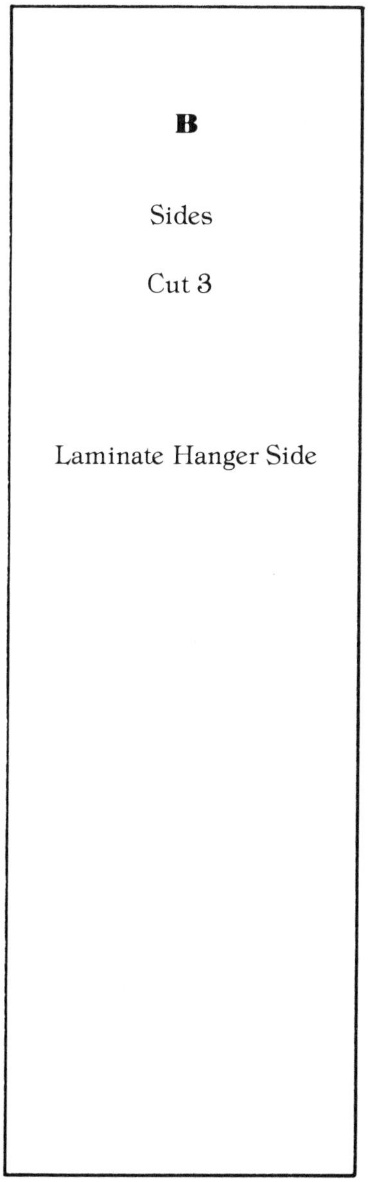

B

Sides

Cut 3

Laminate Hanger Side

All pieces cut from ⅛″ illustration board

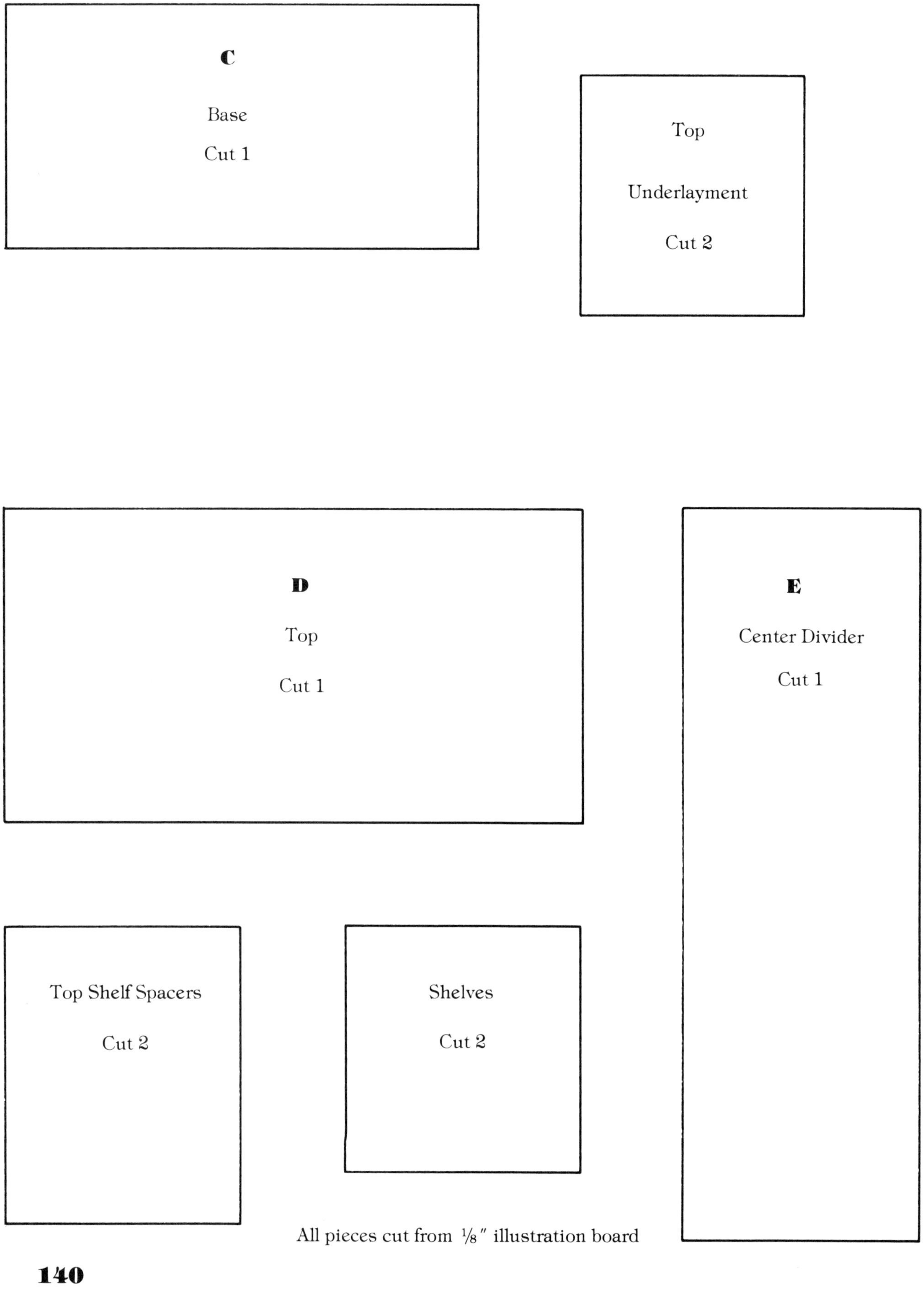

Armoire (continued)

C

Base

Cut 1

Top

Underlayment

Cut 2

D

Top

Cut 1

E

Center Divider

Cut 1

Top Shelf Spacers

Cut 2

Shelves

Cut 2

All pieces cut from ⅛″ illustration board

Center Shelf Spacers

Cut 2

Bottom Shelf Spacers

Cut 2

F

Doors

Cut 4

Laminate

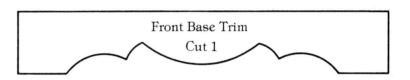

Front Base Trim
Cut 1

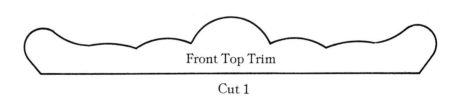

Front Top Trim

Cut 1

All pieces cut from ⅛″ illustration board

Nightstand

(2¼″ wide × 1⁷⁄₁₆″ deep × 2⁷⁄₁₆″ high)

MATERIALS

⅛″ illustration board
¹⁄₁₆″ illustration board
Sobo glue
Doily trim (optional)
Latex satin base coat
Stain and glaze
1 drawer pull

INSTRUCTIONS

1.   Trace and transfer pattern pieces to ⅛″ and ¹⁄₁₆″ illustration board.
2.   Cut all pieces, laminating parts as indicated.
3.   Place back (A) on flat surface. Glue sides (C) outside and flush with back.
4.   Laminate top (B) and glue to sides and back flush with back and overhang on sides and front edges.
5.   Glue small spacers under top to sides and back.
6.   Glue drawer partition underneath spacers to sides and back.
7.   Glue large spacers under drawer partition to sides and back.
8.   Glue base underneath large spacers to sides and back.
9.   Glue side trim to sides matching back larger leg and front smaller leg.
10.   Glue front trim to sides, ¹⁄₁₆″ below top of base.
11.   Glue drawer sides to drawer front and back flush with side edges.
12.   Glue drawer bottom inside the above framework.
13.   Doily-trim front of drawer (optional). Carefully sand before trimming.
14.   Paint with base coat. Carefully sand edges.
15.   Brush with stain and glaze. Let set 5 to 10 minutes. Wipe lightly with cloth or paper towel until wood grained.
16.   Attach drawer pull. (See Handles and Pulls, page 196.)

Nightstand

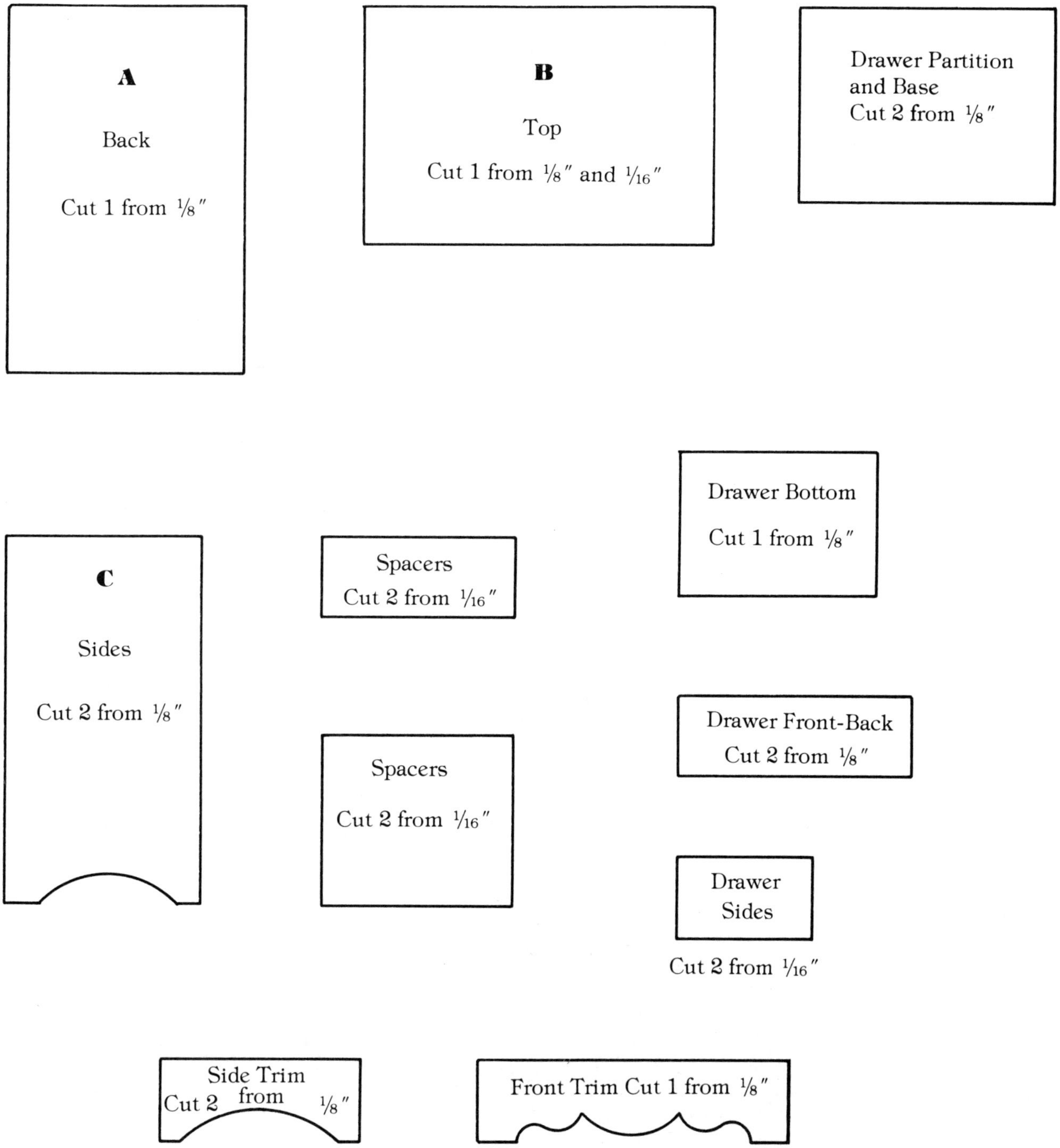
A
Back
Cut 1 from ⅛″
B
Top
Cut 1 from ⅛″ and 1/16″
Drawer Partition and Base
Cut 2 from ⅛″
Drawer Bottom
Cut 1 from ⅛″
C
Sides
Cut 2 from ⅛″
Spacers
Cut 2 from 1/16″
Spacers
Cut 2 from 1/16″
Drawer Front-Back
Cut 2 from ⅛″
Drawer Sides
Cut 2 from 1/16″
Side Trim
Cut 2 from ⅛″
Front Trim Cut 1 from ⅛″

Dressing Table and Bench

(Dressing Table—3 5/8″ wide × 1 7/16″ deep × 2 15/16″ high)
(Bench—1 7/16″ wide × 1 1/4″ deep × 1 1/2″ high—with upholstery.)

MATERIALS (Dressing Table)

1/8″ illustration board
1/16″ illustration board
Sobo glue
Doily trim (optional)
Latex satin base coat
Stain and glaze
2 straight pins
5 drawer pulls
Mirror—1″ × 7/8″ (optional)

INSTRUCTIONS (Dressing Table)

1. Trace and transfer pattern pieces to 1/8″ and 1/16″ illustration board.
2. Cut all pieces, laminating parts as indicated.
3. Place back (A) on flat surface. Glue sides (B) flush with back to outside edges.
4. Glue center partition (C) to back and sides with top edge of partition 3/8″ down from top of back and sides.

144

5. Glue 1 base (D) to left side of table and 1 base (D) to right side of table, ⅛″ up from bottom edge of back and sides.

6. Glue center drawer partitions as follows:

Glue 1 drawer partition to left side of dresser and 1 to right side of dresser flush with edge of base, gluing to base, back, and underside of center partition (C).

Glue remaining 2 drawer partitions to top side of center partitions (C) and back in line with bottom drawer partitions.

7. Dampen center trim and glue flush with front curved edge of center partition and drawer partitions.

8. Cut heads off 2 straight pins. Pin at back side edges of laminated top center (G) ⅛″ from back inserting only halfway.

9. Pin top center (G) to top side (F) for left and right tabletops.

10. Glue top sides (F) to back, sides, and center drawer partitions, flush with back and slight overhang on sides and front. Do *not* glue movable top center.

11. Glue side bottom trims to base and sides with rounded edge toward sides.

12. Make four drawers as follows:

Glue back to drawer bottom ¼″ from back edge.
Glue front to bottom flush with bottom front edge.
Glue sides between backs and fronts ⅛″ in from side edges of bottom.
(Drawers may also be made solid by laminating 3 pieces of ⅛″ × 1¼″ illustration board for each drawer.)

13. Glue legs to underside of base on a 45° angle. Doily-trim top round of legs, if desired. (Sand with emery board before trimming.)

14. Paint with base coat. (Sand where needed, but do *not* sand over doily trim.)

15. Brush with stain and glaze. Let set 5 to 10 minutes. Wipe lightly with cloth or paper towel until wood grained.

16. Glue mirror to inside top center (optional).

17. Attach drawer pulls. (See Handles and Pulls, page 196.)

MATERIALS (Bench)

⅛″ illustration board
¹⁄₁₆″ illustration board
Sobo glue
Latex satin base coat
Stain and glaze
Material for upholstery and padding

INSTRUCTIONS (Bench)

1. Cut 2 bench seats from pattern, do *not* laminate.

2. Cut strip ¹⁄₁₆″ × ⅜″; dampen. Glue around seat ⅛″ up from underside. Cut and glue at seam. You may reinforce seam with a thin piece of paper glued over seam on the inside and outside of trim.

3. Glue legs to base at corners on a 45° angle. Doily trim to round of legs to match dressing table, if desired. (Sand before doily trimming.)

4. Paint with base coat. Do not bother to paint inside seat as this will be covered with upholstery. Carefully sand. Do *not* sand over doily trim.

5. Brush with stain and glaze. Let set 5 to 10 minutes. Wipe lightly with cloth or paper towel until wood grained.

6. Upholster seat. (See Upholstering, page 202.)

Dressing Table and Bench

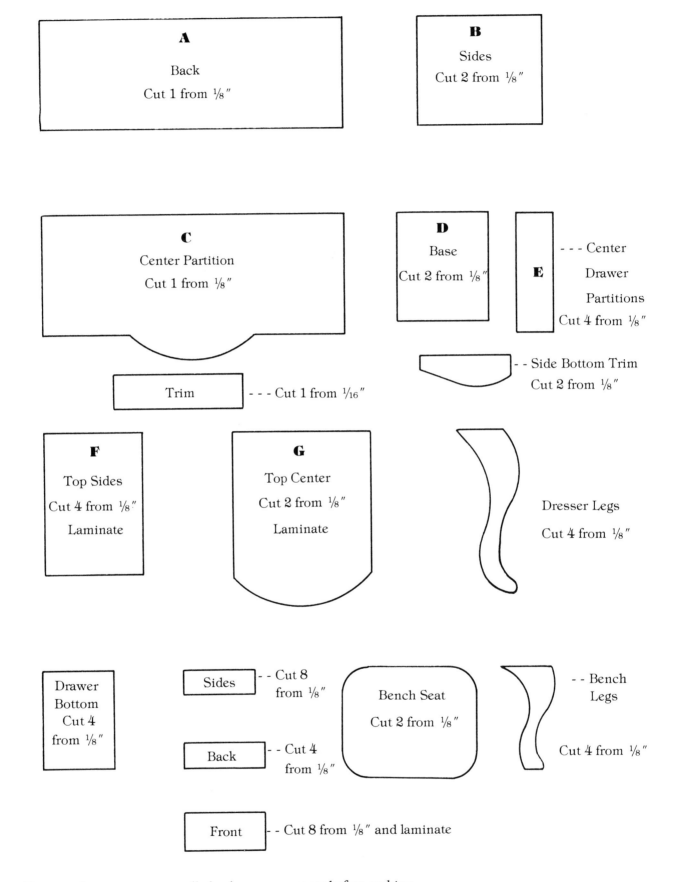

A

Back

Cut 1 from ⅛″

B

Sides

Cut 2 from ⅛″

C

Center Partition

Cut 1 from ⅛″

D

Base

Cut 2 from ⅛″

E

- - - Center

Drawer

Partitions

Cut 4 from ⅛″

Trim   - - - Cut 1 from 1/16″

- - Side Bottom Trim

Cut 2 from ⅛″

F

Top Sides

Cut 4 from ⅛″

Laminate

G

Top Center

Cut 2 from ⅛″

Laminate

Dresser Legs

Cut 4 from ⅛″

Drawer

Bottom

Cut 4

from ⅛″

Sides   - - Cut 8

from ⅛″

Back   - - Cut 4

from ⅛″

Bench Seat

Cut 2 from ⅛″

- - Bench

Legs

Cut 4 from ⅛″

Front   - - Cut 8 from ⅛″ and laminate

Because drawers are so small check measurements before making.

146

Cradle

(4⅛″ long × 2¼″ wide × 2⅞″ high)

MATERIALS

⅛″ illustration board
Sobo glue
Doily or braid trim (optional)
Latex satin base coat
Stain and glaze

INSTRUCTIONS

1. Trace and transfer pattern pieces to ⅛″ illustration board.
2. Cut all pieces, laminating parts as indicated.
3. Glue bottom (D) flush with bottom edges of cradle sides (A).
4. Glue head (B) to high edges of sides (A) flush with outside edges.
5. Glue foot (C) to lower edges of sides (A) flush with outside edges.
6. Glue top (E) to sides and head flush with all outside edges.
7. Glue rocker-bottom brace (F) to center of bottom (D).
8. Glue front and back rockers (G) to bottom (D) and rocker-bottom brace (F).
9. Add doily or braid trim, optional. Sand before trimming.
10. Paint with base coat. Sand carefully, if needed. Do *not* sand doily trim.
11. Brush with stain and glaze. Let set 5 to 10 minutes. Wipe lightly with cloth or paper towel until wood grained.
12. Make mattress for cradle as follows:
    Cut piece of plain or small-print material 3″ × 4″. Use foam or cotton padding approximately ¼″ thick. Cover padding with material and finish edges with overcasting stitch. (See Bed Linens, page 196.)

147

Cradle

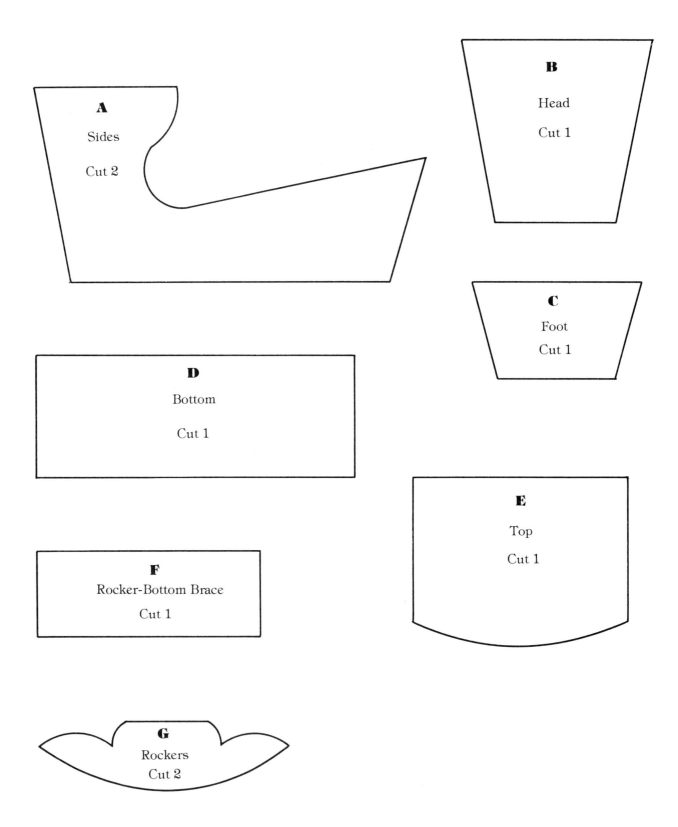

A
Sides
Cut 2

B
Head
Cut 1

C
Foot
Cut 1

D
Bottom
Cut 1

E
Top
Cut 1

F
Rocker-Bottom Brace
Cut 1

G
Rockers
Cut 2

All pieces cut from ⅛″ illustration board

Crib

(4½″ long × 2⅝″ wide × 3½″ high)

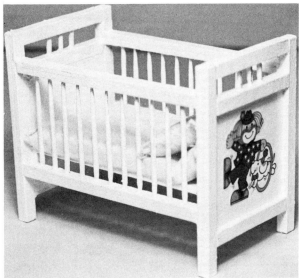

MATERIALS

⅛″ illustration board
Sobo glue
Round toothpicks—24
White paint
Decals or painted designs

INSTRUCTIONS

1. Trace and transfer pieces to ⅛″ illustration board.
2. Cut all pieces.
3. Cut long strips of ⅛″ illustration board ⅛″ wide. (You will need a total of 84″ so cut a little more to allow for errors, etc.)

4. Cut 12 pieces of the ⅛" × ⅛" stripping, 2¹⁄₁₆" long. Laminate for 6 pieces.

5. In center of 4 of the 2¹⁄₁₆" pieces and ¼" each side of center, punch small holes through lamination, not through the white surface area of the illustration board. Cut 6 pieces of round toothpicks ⅝" long; insert and glue into these three holes joining the 4 pieces to make 2 units.

6. Cut 4 pieces of the ⅛" stripping, 3½" long. Laminate for 2 pieces.

7. Place section with toothpicks on flat surface. Glue center panel (A) flush with bottom of this section. Glue 1 laminated 3½" × ⅛" piece flush with top edge of toothpick-trimmed section and side of center panel. Glue 3½" × ⅛" piece to other side of this unit. Glue unpunched 2¹⁄₁₆" piece flush with bottom of center panel and to side pieces. This makes head or foot crib section. Repeat in like manner to other section. This makes both the head and foot crib sections.

8. Glue base supports to inside of head and foot sections with top edge of each 1¼" up from bottom of head and foot sections. (Measured from the foot up, which will be ⅞" up from head and foot 2¹⁄₁₆" framing trim.)

9. Glue mattress base (B) on top of the supports and to inside of both head and foot sections.

10. CRIB SIDES:
Cut 8 pieces of the ⅛" stripping 4" long. Laminate for 4 pieces. Mark 11 equally spaced (¼" apart) lines on white surface of illustration board on all 4 pieces. Punch holes in center of each line, making certain the holes line up on all 4 pieces of 4" laminated stripping. Cut 22 round toothpicks 2" long; insert and glue into holes on top and bottom bed rails, making 2 crib sides.

11. Glue crib sides to head and foot sections with the top railing ½" down from top of end sections and ⅞" up from bottom (measured up from crib "foot").

12. Paint and decorate with small decals or colored pictures cut from glossy catalogs or magazines. (You may, of course, go the stain-and-glaze route, but for variety and the fact that most cribs are painted, it adds a touch of color to your dollhouse. I also deviated and painted the children's chest of drawers.)

13. For mattress, covering, and pillow see page 197.

Crib

A
Center Panel Head and Foot
Cut 2

B
Mattress Base
Cut 1

Base Supports	Cut 2

All pieces cut from ⅛" illustration board

Rocker

(2⅛″ wide × 2¾″ deep × 4″ high. Measured from rockers front to back.)

MATERIALS

⅛″ illustration board
Sobo glue
Round toothpicks—10 to 12
⅛″ doweling—5″ long
Doily or paper cut out trim
Latex satin base coat
Stain and glaze

INSTRUCTIONS

1. Trace and transfer pattern pieces to ⅛″ illustration board.
2. Cut pieces, laminating parts as indicated.
3. With ice pick or sharp nail, punch holes in seat where indicated by o's and x's; punch holes in arms where indicated by o's; punch holes in center of headrest on bottom side where indicated by o's, and punch holes in centers of laminated rocker pieces where indicated by double lines.
4. Cut 7 round toothpicks 2⅜″ long. Glue into holes in headrest and corresponding holes in rocker seat.
5. Cut 2 pieces of round toothpicks 1″ long; glue into front holes on rocker seat. Cut 2 pieces of round toothpicks ⅞″ long; glue into second holes on rocker seat. Cut 2 pieces of round toothpicks ¹³⁄₁₆″ long; glue into third holes on rocker seat. Line up rocker arms with toothpicks in rocker seat with center of notched arm edge ¾″ up from rocker seat. (Do not be concerned if you punch holes through arm pieces (or any other piece. You can sand and paint over these.)

6. Cut 4 pieces of ⅛″ doweling 1¼″ long. With emery board (or carving with your utility knife), sand (or cut) to slight point on each end of doweling pieces. Glue pieces as marked by x's on rocker seat. Glue other ends of the 4 pieces of doweling to rockers as marked with double lines. (Rounded edge of rocker is the front.)

7. Cut sharp point off rounded toothpick and cut 1¾″ long. Glue between front rocker upright doweling ⅝″ down from underside of seat. Cut sharp points off 2 more rounded toothpicks and cut 1¼″ long. Glue between front and back rocker upright doweling ¾″ down from underside of seat. Cut sharp points off rounded toothpick and cut 1³⁄₁₆″ long. Glue between back rocker upright dowelings ⅝″ down from underside of seat.

8. Glue doily or paper cutout trim along front of rocker headrest. Carefully sand headrest before trimming.

9. Paint with base coat. Sand edges, carefully, if needed.

10. Brush with stain and glaze. Let set 5 to 10 minutes. Wipe lightly with cloth or paper towel until wood grained.

Rocker

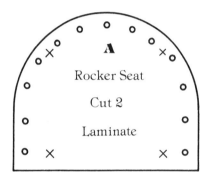

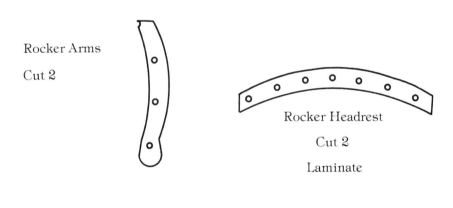

Rocker Arms

Cut 2

Rocker Headrest

Cut 2

Laminate

Rockers

Cut 4

Laminate

All pieces cut from ⅛″ illustration board

7

THE LIVING ROOM

Sofa
Low-Back Chair
High-Back Chair
Foot Stool
Coffee Table
End Table
Round Occasional Table

Sofa

(6¼″ long × 2″ deep × 4¼″ high)

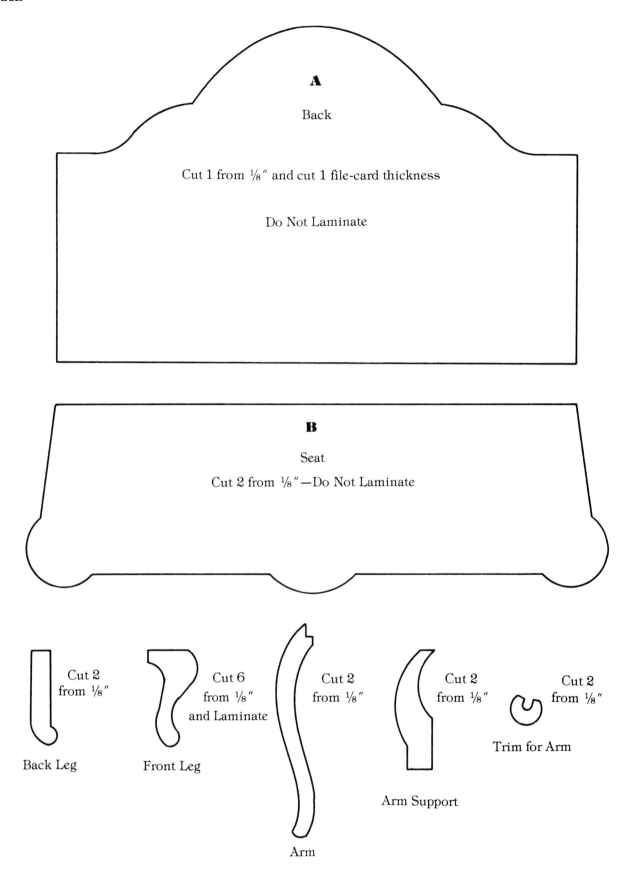

A

Back

Cut 1 from ⅛″ and cut 1 file-card thickness

Do Not Laminate

B

Seat
Cut 2 from ⅛″—Do Not Laminate

Cut 2
from ⅛″

Back Leg

Cut 6
from ⅛″
and Laminate

Front Leg

Cut 2
from ⅛″

Arm

Cut 2
from ⅛″

Arm Support

Cut 2
from ⅛″

Trim for Arm

(Do Not Paint or Upholster Until You Read Section on "Upholstery.")

MATERIALS

⅛" illustration board
1/16" illustration board
Sobo glue
Doily trim
Latex satin base coat
Stain and glaze
Padding
Fabric
File-card cardboard (I used the insert from a frozen pie). Should small pieces be too difficult to cut from ⅛", cut them from 2 pieces of 1/16" and laminate. This would apply for the delicate leg-and-arm supports and arm trim.

INSTRUCTIONS

1. Trace and transfer patterns for back (A) and seat (B) to ⅛" illustration board.

2. Cut pieces.

3. Trace and transfer leg and arm patterns as follows:

Back leg: Cut 2 from ⅛" illustration board.
Front leg: Cut 3 each from ⅛" and 1/16" illustration board and laminate for 3/16" thickness for each leg.
Arm: Cut 2 from ⅛" illustration board.
Arm supports: Cut 2 from ⅛" illustration board.
Trim for arm: Cut 2 from ⅛" illustration board or use small bead.

4. Trace and transfer pattern for back (A) to file-card cardboard.

5. Cut 10½" long piece of 1/16" × 3/8" illustration board.

6. Place back (A) on flat surface. Glue seat (B) to back flush with bottom straight edge. Glue on slant leaning toward back at top.

7. Dampen 1/16" × 3/8" strip and glue flush with bottom edge of seat (B), carefully curving around curves on seat. When glue is dry, cut off excess so trim is flush with back of edge of sofa back.

8. Glue back legs in each corner underneath seat with curved foot toward open end.

9. Glue 1 front leg underneath center curve in sofa seat; glue the corner front legs at corner rounds on a 45° angle.

10. Glue straight end of arm supports flush with bottom of 1/16" trim with long straight side against back of corner round of trim.

11. Glue notched corner of arm ¾" down from top side corner of sofa back with arm support glued flush with inside edge of arm.

12. Glue small round arm trim to the underside of arm directly under front curve flush with end of arm.

13. Doily trim (optional) fronts of legs under the rounds of sofa seat.

14. Paint with base coat. When dry, lightly sand edges.

15. Brush with stain and glaze. Let set 5 to 10 minutes. Wipe lightly with cloth or paper towel until wood grained.

16. Upholster. (See Upholstering, page 202.)

Low-Back Chair

$(2\frac{7}{8}''$ wide $\times$ $2\frac{1}{4}''$ deep $\times$ $3\frac{3}{4}''$ high$)$

High-Back Chair

$(2\frac{7}{8}''$ wide $\times$ $2\frac{1}{4}''$ deep $\times$ $4\frac{1}{4}''$ high$)$

MATERIALS

$\frac{1}{8}''$ illustration board
$\frac{1}{16}''$ illustration board
Sobo glue
Doily trim
Latex satin base coat
Stain and glaze
Padding
Fabric
File-card weight cardboard

INSTRUCTIONS

1. Trace and transfer patterns for backs (A) and (AA) and seat(s) (B) to $\frac{1}{8}''$ illustration board.
2. Trace and transfer leg and arm patterns as shown for sofa with the exception of only 2 front legs for each chair.
3. Trace and transfer backs (A) and (AA) to file-card cardboard.
4. Cut pieces.
5. For each chair cut 7" long piece of $\frac{1}{16}'' \times \frac{3}{8}''$ illustration board.
6. Place back(s) (A) and (AA) on flat surface. Glue seat(s) (B) to back(s) flush with bottom straight edge. Glue on slant, leaning back at top.
7. Dampen $\frac{1}{16}'' \times \frac{3}{8}''$ strip and glue flush with bottom edge of seat(s) (B), carefully curving around corners. When glue is dry, cut off excess so trim is flush with back edges.
8. Glue back legs in each corner underneath seat(s) with curved foot toward open end.

9. Glue front legs underneath seat(s) at corner rounds on a 45° angle.

10. Glue straight end of arm supports flush with bottom of ¹⁄₁₆″ trim with long straight side against back round of corner trim.

11. Glue notched corner of arm ⁷⁄₈″ down from top side corner of low-back chair and 1³⁄₈″ down from top side corner of high-back chair with arm support glued flush with inside edge of arm.

12. Glue small round arm trim to the underside of arm directly under front curve flush with end of arm.

13. Doily trim (optional) fronts of legs under the rounds of seat(s).

14. Paint with base coat. When dry, lightly sand edges.

15. Brush with stain and glaze. Let set 5 to 10 minutes. Wipe lightly with cloth or paper towel until wood grained.

16. Upholster. (See Upholstering, page 202.)

Low-Back Chair

High-Back Chair

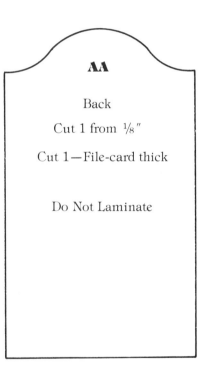

A

Back

Cut 1 from ¹⁄₈″

Cut 1—File-card thick

Do Not Laminate

AA

Back

Cut 1 from ¹⁄₈″

Cut 1—File-card thick

Do Not Laminate

B

Seat

Low-Back and High-Back Chairs

Cut 2 from ¹⁄₈″ for each chair

Do Not Laminate

(Do Not Paint or Upholster Until You Read Section on "Upholstery.")

Foot Stool

(2″ long × 1 ½″ wide × 1 ⅜″ high)

MATERIALS

⅛″ illustration board
1/16″ illustration board
Sobo glue
Latex satin base coat
Stain and glaze
Padding
Fabric

INSTRUCTIONS

1. Trace and transfer pattern pieces to ⅛″ and 1/16″ illustration board. (Pieces designated 3/16″ are easier cut of ⅛″ and 1/16″ and laminated.)
2. Cut pieces.
3. Make frame for base (A) with front and back edges (B) and side edges (C) with mitered corners as shown in top-view detail. Keep frame square.
4. Glue base (A) into frame flush with bottom edges. Base (A) is not laminated. Keep the 1/16″ piece cut for base for applying padding and fabric for upholstering.
5. Glue center brace between legs flush with bottom of legs, rounded edge of brace toward underside of base (A).
6. Glue leg assembly to underside of base 3/16″ from side edges and ⅛″ from front and back edges.
7. For **FIRESIDE BENCH:**
Follow steps 1 through 5 for foot stool. Cut arm rests of ⅛″ and 1/16″ illustration board and laminate. Glue to side edges (C).
8. Paint with base coat. When dry, sand lightly.
9. Brush with stain and glaze. Let set 5 to 10 minutes. Wipe lightly with cloth or paper towel until wood grained.
10. Upholster. (See Upholstering, page 202.)

Foot Stool

A
Base
Cut 1 from ⅛″
Cut 1 from 1/16″

Do Not Laminate
Base A

Top View

Detailing

Mitered Corners

Foot Stool (continued)

Cut 2 from ³⁄₁₆″

B	Front and Back Edges

Cut 2 from ³⁄₁₆″

C	Side Edges

(See instructions for cutting and/or laminating Edges B and C.)

Legs
Cut 2 from ³⁄₁₆″ —see instructions for cutting and/or laminating Legs

Center Brace
Cut 1 from ⅛″

Fireside Bench

Arm Rests— Cut 2 from ³⁄₁₆″

(See instructions for cutting and/or laminating Arm Rests.)

(Do Not Paint or Upholster Until You Read Section on "Upholstery.")

Coffee Table

(3¼″ long × 1⅝″ deep × 1⅝″ high)

MATERIALS

⅛″ illustration board
Sobo glue
Doily trim (optional)
Latex satin base coat
Stain and glaze

INSTRUCTIONS

1. Trace and transfer pattern pieces to ⅛″ illustration board.
2. Cut out pieces.
3. Center and glue table underside (B) to tabletop (A). This is the table bottom.
4. Glue legs at corners of table underside on 45° angle.
5. Trim legs with doily cutouts (optional).
6. Paint with base coat. When dry, sand lightly.
7. Brush with stain and glaze. Let set 5 to 10 minutes. Wipe lightly with cloth or paper towel until wood grained.

Coffee Table

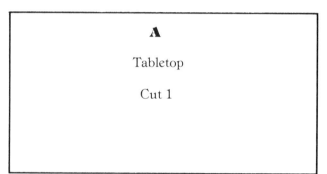

A

Tabletop

Cut 1

B

Table Underside

Cut 1

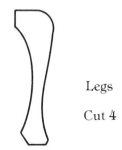

Legs

Cut 4

Cut all pieces from ⅛″ illustration board

End Table

(1 ¾" wide × 1 ⅝" deep × 2 ½" high)

MATERIALS

⅛" illustration board
Sobo glue
Doily trim (optional)
Latex satin base coat
Stain and glaze
Drawer pull

INSTRUCTIONS

1. Trace and transfer pattern pieces to ⅛" illustration board.
2. Cut out pieces.
3. Glue sides (C) to underside of top (A) ⅛" from side edges and back edge.
4. Glue back (E) to underside of table and flush with outside edges of sides.
5. Glue base (B) to sides and back ½" down from underside of top.
6. Dampen front (D) and glue along slight round of base and to front edges of sides and underside of top.
7. Glue legs to underside of base at corners on a 45° angle.
8. Make drawer as follows:
Glue sides to drawer bottom ⅛" from side edges and flush with back edge.
Glue drawer back to sides and back ⅛" in from back edge.
Lightly dampen drawer front. Glue to sides and flush with drawer bottom.
9. Doily trim top curve of legs (optional).
10. Paint with base coat. When dry, sand lightly.
11. Brush with stain and glaze. Let set 5 to 10 minutes. Wipe lightly with cloth or paper towel until wood grained.
12. Attach drawer pull. (See Handles and Pulls, page 196.)

End Table

Cut all pieces from ⅛″ illustration board

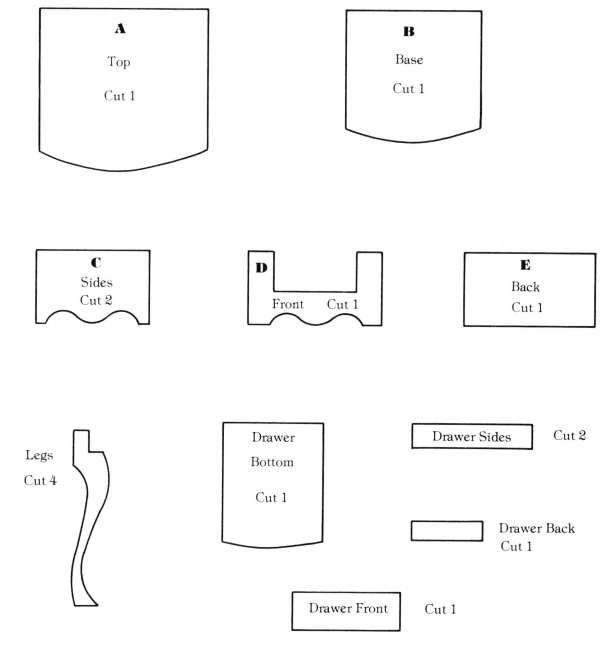

A

Top

Cut 1

B

Base

Cut 1

C

Sides
Cut 2

D

Front   Cut 1

E

Back

Cut 1

Legs

Cut 4

Drawer

Bottom

Cut 1

Drawer Sides   Cut 2

Drawer Back
Cut 1

Drawer Front   Cut 1

162

Round Occasional Table

(3 1/8" diameter × 2 3/4" high)

MATERIALS

    1/8" illustration board
    Sobo glue
    Wood beads—round, flat, and/or elongated
    Long nail or pin—1 1/2" long
    Latex satin base coat
    Stain and glaze

INSTRUCTIONS

1. Trace and transfer pattern pieces to 1/8" illustration board.

2. Cut out pieces.

3. Laminate the 4 pieces of table underside (B) and glue to center of underside of tabletop (A).

4. Make a 1 1/2" high center pedestal from beads in any combination pleasing to you. Nail or pin together and to center of table underside. (I used the following combination of wood beads: Starting at top of pedestal a round wood bead, 1/2 of a wood bead, 3/4" elongated wood bead ending with a small flat wood bead, all beads 3/8" to 1/2" in diameter.)

5. Glue straight edge of legs to pedestal, spaced evenly around pedestal 1/8" from bottom of pedestal.

6. Paint with base coat. When dry, sand lightly.

7. Brush with stain and glaze. Let set 5 to 10 minutes. Wipe lightly with cloth or paper towel until wood grained. (You may decorate this table, but do not overdecorate. A touch of gold paint on the feet and "false" drawers with pulls are all this table needs.)

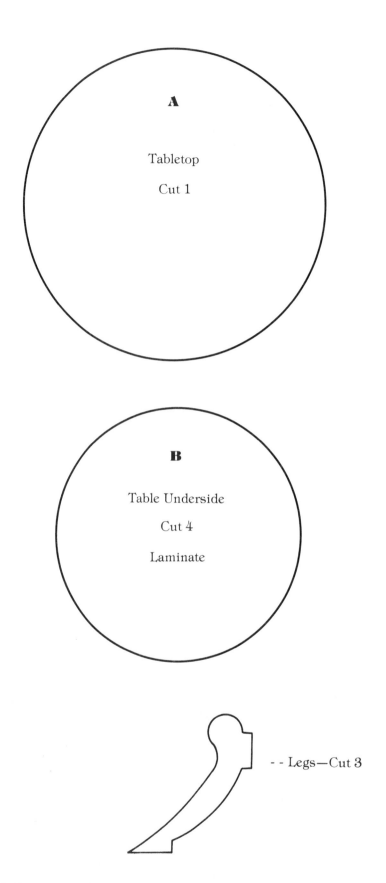

A

Tabletop

Cut 1

B

Table Underside

Cut 4

Laminate

- - Legs—Cut 3

Cut all pieces from ⅛″ illustration board

8

THE DINING ROOM

Dining Table
Dining Chair
Host Chair
Sideboard
Buffet

Dining Table

(7¾" long × 3½" wide × 2½" high)

Dining Table

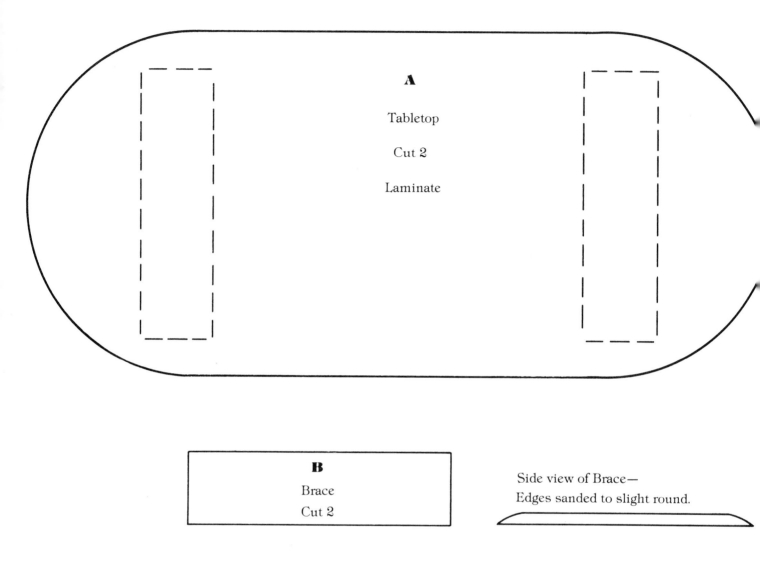

A

Tabletop

Cut 2

Laminate

B

Brace

Cut 2

Side view of Brace—
Edges sanded to slight round.

C

D

C and D form 4-sided leg base. Cut 6 Cs and 12 Ds from ⅛″ and laminate 3 pieces as explained in instructions for each section. A total of 2 complete Cs and 4 complete Ds.

Cut all pieces from ⅛″ illustration board

Post pedestals are made of doweling, beads, buttons in any manner pleasing to you. Instructions explain how I made the pedestals.

MATERIALS

⅛″ illustration board
Sobo glue
Doweling, wooden beads, and/or buttons
Doily or braid trim (optional)
Long nails or pins
Latex satin base coat
Stain and glaze

INSTRUCTIONS

1. Trace and transfer pattern pieces to ⅛″ illustration board.

2. Cut all pieces, laminating parts as indicated.

3. Glue brace (B), after shaping, to underside of laminated tabletop (A) as indicated by dotted lines.

4. Laminate 3 pieces of (C) together for long section of leg base and 3 pieces for second long leg base section.

5. Laminate 3 pieces of small section leg base (D) together; repeat for 4 small sections of leg bases.

6. Glue one section (D) to each side of long section (C) for a 4-cornered leg base. Repeat for second 4-cornered leg base.

7. Pin and glue together any arrangement of doweling, beads, buttons, etc., for 2 pedestals. This arrangement should be 1¾″ high when completed, making table height of 2½″. Pin and glue your pedestal arrangement to centers of braces and 4-cornered legs.

For my pedestals I used the top from a dishwashing detergent with large round Styrofoam ball glued into lafge part of this top.

8. Doily- or braid-trim parts of 4-cornered leg sections, if desired.

9. Paint with base coat. When dry, lightly sand edges; do not sand the doily or braid trim.

10. Brush with stain and glaze. Let set 5 to 10 minutes. Wipe lightly with cloth or paper towel until wood grained.

11. To give your table a high luster, varnished look, paint with light coat of clear polyurethane. (This can be done to any or all of your furniture, but I use it sparingly, as only the most ultra of furniture had a high luster in period settings. You can paint polyurethane on your furniture after selecting pieces for each room.You wouldn't want it in the kitchen or the Nanny's room or your storage and/or playroom.)

Dining Chair

(1¾″ wide × 1⅝″ deep × 3½″ high)

MATERIALS

⅛″ illustration board
1/16″ illustration board
Sobo glue
Doily or braid trim (optional)
Latex satin base coat
Stain and glaze
Padding
Fabric

Dining Chair

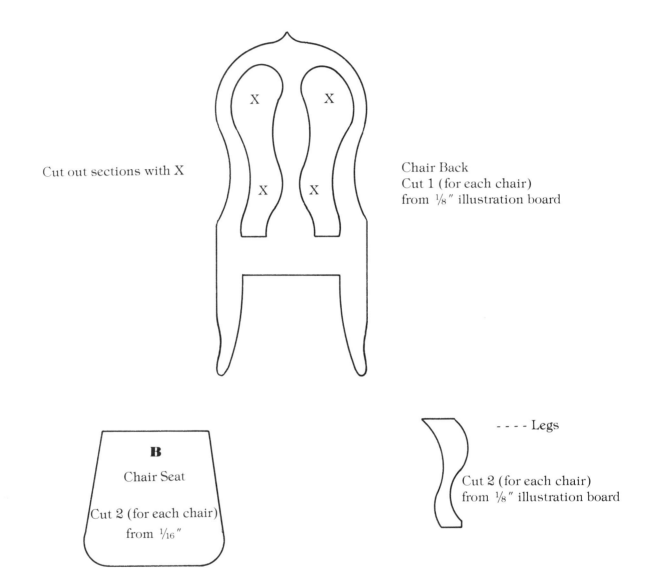

Cut out sections with X

Chair Back
Cut 1 (for each chair)
from ⅛″ illustration board

B
Chair Seat

Cut 2 (for each chair)
from ¹⁄₁₆″

- - - - Legs

Cut 2 (for each chair)
from ⅛″ illustration board

(1 piece of ¹⁄₁₆″ for chair seat is for upholstering.)

Host Chair

Cut **A** Chair Back, **B** Chair Seat and
Legs as for Dining Chair and add Arms.

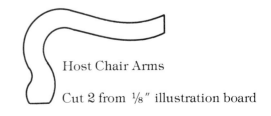

Host Chair Arms

Cut 2 from ⅛″ illustration board

168

(1¾″ wide × 1⅝″ deep × 3½″ high)

INSTRUCTIONS

1. Trace and transfer pattern pieces to ⅛″ and ¹⁄₁₆″ illustration board.
2. Cut out pieces.
3. Cut ⅜″ wide strip of ¹⁄₁₆″ illustration board 4½″ long for each chair. Dampen slightly. Glue to chair seat (B) ¹⁄₁₆″ above bottom edge along sides and curved front. Cut back edges of this strip at a slight slant and glue to chair-back (A) even with top straight edge of cutouts and ¹⁄₁₆″ above bottom straight edge between legs.
4. Glue legs at curved front corners on a 45° angle.
5. Doily- or braid-trim to match table (optional).
6. Paint with base coat. When dry, lightly sand edges; do not sand the doily or braid trim.
7. Brush with stain and glaze. Let set 5 to 10 minutes. Wipe lightly with cloth or paper towel until wood grained.
8. For high luster, to match table, paint with light coat of clear polyurethane.
9. Upholster. (See Upholstering, page 202.)

Host Chair

MATERIALS

See instructions for Dining Chair

($1\frac{3}{4}''$ wide $\times$ $1\frac{5}{8}''$ deep $\times$ $3\frac{1}{2}''$ high)

INSTRUCTIONS

1.—3. Follow instructions for Dining Chair.
4. Glue arms at inward curve of back edges and $\frac{1}{8}''$ from front of chair seat trim.
5.—8. Follow instructions for dining chair, including Step 4.
Doily- or braid-trim to match table (optional).

Sideboard

($3\frac{5}{8}''$ wide $\times$ $2''$ deep $\times$ $3\frac{1}{4}''$ high)

MATERIALS

⅛″ illustration board   Latex satin base coat
1/16″ illustration board   Stain and glaze
Sobo glue   Drawer pulls
Doily trim (optional)

INSTRUCTIONS

1. Trace and transfer pattern pieces to ⅛″ and 1/16″ illustration board.
2. Cut out pieces, laminating parts as indicated.
3. Glue top drawer partitions to sides (B) flush with top, front, and back edges.
4. Glue drawer divider (D) under partitions to sides flush with front.
5. Glue center drawer partitions to sides (B) flush with front and back and to underside of drawer divider.
6. Glue drawer divider (D) under center drawer partitions to sides flush with front.
7. Place back (A) on flat surface. Glue entire unit flush with top, bottom, and side edges of back.
8. Glue laminated top (C) and laminated bottom (C) flush with back edges, overhang on sides and front.
9. Make 3 drawers as follows:
Place bottoms on flat surface.
Glue sides 1/16″ from sides and flush with front edges.
Glue backs between sides ⅛″ from back edge.
Dampen fronts and glue flush with bottom and 1/16″ past sides.
For bottom drawer only: Glue bottom drawer divider in center of drawer from front to back.
10. Laminate 4 pieces of pattern for legs for each leg and glue on 45° angle at corners.
11. Paint with base coat. Sand, if needed.
12. Brush with stain and glaze. Let set 5 to 10 minutes. Wipe lightly with cloth or paper towel until wood grained.
13. For high luster, to match table and chairs, paint with light coat of clear polyurethane.
(For trim I cut small 1/16″ round of illustration board and doily trimmed on each side. Also, small lengths (⅛″) of 1/16″ doweling were used for the drawer pulls. All this was done before painting with base coat. But as to the matter of trim and pulls, this is left to your discretion.)

Sideboard

```
┌─────────────────────┐      ┌─────────────────┐
│          A          │      │        B        │
│                     │      │                 │
│        Back         │      │      Sides      │
│                     │      │                 │
│    Cut 1 from ⅛″    │      │  Cut 2 from ⅛″  │
│                     │      │                 │
└─────────────────────┘      └─────────────────┘
```

C

Top and Bottom

Cut 4 from ⅛" and laminate

D

Drawer Dividers

Cut 2 from ⅛"

Drawer Partitions
(Top and Center)
Cut 4 from 1/16"

Drawer Partition
(Bottom)
Cut 2 from 1/16"

E

Drawer Bottoms

Cut 3 from ⅛"

Drawer Sides
(Top and Center)

Cut 4 from ⅛"

Drawer Side
(Bottom)
Cut 2 from ⅛"

Drawer Backs (Top and Center)
Cut 2 from ⅛"

Drawer Back (Bottom)

Cut 1 from ⅛"

Drawer Fronts (Top and Center)
Cut 2 from 1/16"

Drawer Front (Bottom)

Cut 1 from 1/16"

Bottom Drawer
Divider
Cut 1 from 1/16"

Legs—Cut 4 from ⅛" and laminate for each leg

(Total pieces of ⅛" from this pattern—16)

Buffet

(3⅝″ wide × 2″ deep × 6⅞″ high, not including trim.)

MATERIALS

⅛″ illustration board
1/16″ illustration board
Sobo glue
Doily trim (optional)
Latex satin base coat
Stain and glaze
Drawer pulls

INSTRUCTIONS

1. Trace and transfer pattern pieces to ⅛″ and 1/16″ illustration board.
2. Cut out pieces, laminating parts as indicated.
3. Glue top side partitions to sides (B) flush with top, front, and back edges.
4. Glue bottom side partitions to sides (B) flush with bottom, front, and back edges.
5. Glue drawer divider (D) under top side partitions to sides flush with front.
6. Glue shelf (E) on top of bottom side partitions to sides ⅜″ from front edge.
7. Glue center side partitions to sides between drawer divider and shelf flush with front and back edges.
8. Place back (A) on flat surface. Glue entire unit flush with top, bottom, and side edges of back.
9. Glue laminated top (C) and laminated bottom (C) flush with back edges, overhang on sides and front.
10. Make drawer as follows:
    Place bottom on flat surface.
    Glue sides 1/16″ from sides and flush with front edges.
    Glue backs between sides ⅛″ from back edge.
    Dampen fronts and glue flush with bottom and 1/16″ past sides.
11. Make doors as follows:
    Glue door trim to outside edges of each door and small piece in center of each.
    Pin ⅛″ in from corner edges of each door through bottom and top round partition. There will be an overhang of the top round and doors will sit in from front edge of bottom round.

12. Laminate 4 pieces of pattern for legs for each leg and glue on 45° angle at corners.

13. Place buffet top back (G) on flat surface. Glue top (H) flush with back edge, equal overhang at sides.

14. Glue sides on top of back flush with outside edges and under top.

15. Glue shelves as indicated by dotted lines on sides.

16. Glue top trim to center of top ⅛″ from front round edge.

17. Glue top section to bottom section of buffet, back edges flush and sides of top section lined up with sides of bottom section.

18. Trim to match sideboard. Another nice touch for the buffet is to score a deep line ¼″ from scalloped edge following the lines of the scallops as shown in "carving" detail drawing. Front edges of scalloped edge may be braid- or doily-trimmed. Again, I leave this to your discretion and talents.

19. Paint entire unit with base coat. Sand, if needed.

20. Brush with stain and glaze. Let set 5 to 10 minutes. Wipe lightly with cloth or paper towel until wood grained.

21. For high luster, to match table and chairs, paint with light coat of clear polyurethane.

Buffet

A

Back

Cut 2 from ⅛″

B

Sides

Cut 2 from ⅛″

C

Top and Bottom

Cut 4 from ⅛″ and laminate

D

Drawer Divider

Cut 1 from ⅛″

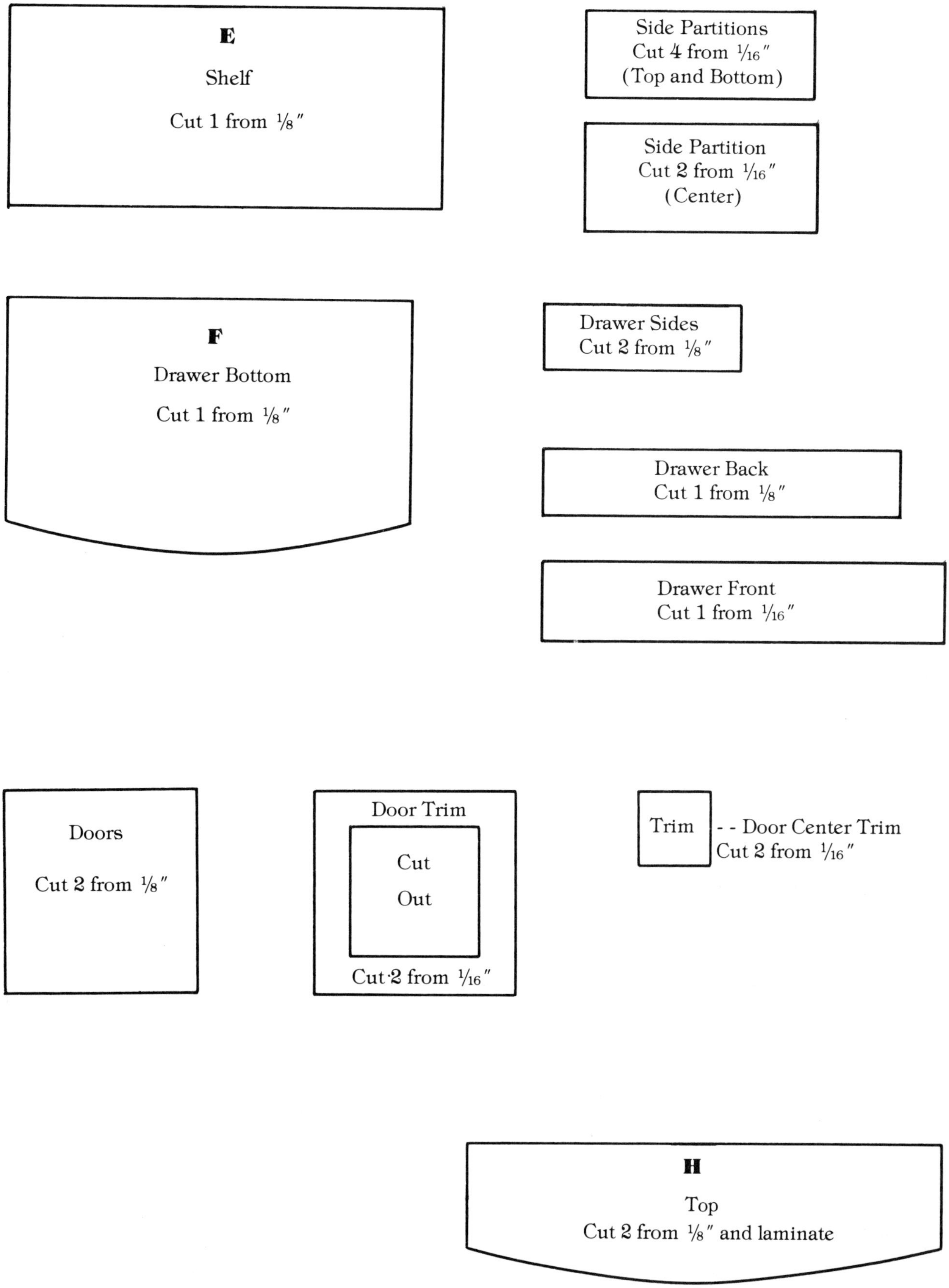

E

Shelf

Cut 1 from ⅛"

Side Partitions
Cut 4 from ¹⁄₁₆"
(Top and Bottom)

Side Partition
Cut 2 from ¹⁄₁₆"
(Center)

F

Drawer Bottom

Cut 1 from ⅛"

Drawer Sides
Cut 2 from ⅛"

Drawer Back
Cut 1 from ⅛"

Drawer Front
Cut 1 from ¹⁄₁₆"

Doors

Cut 2 from ⅛"

Door Trim

Cut

Out

Cut 2 from ¹⁄₁₆"

Trim - - Door Center Trim
Cut 2 from ¹⁄₁₆"

H

Top
Cut 2 from ⅛" and laminate

G

Buffet Top Back

Cut 1 from ⅛″

Shelves
Cut 2 from ⅛″

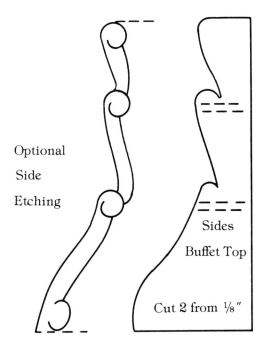

Optional

Side

Etching

Sides

Buffet Top

Cut 2 from ⅛″

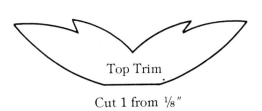

Top Trim

Cut 1 from ⅛″

Legs   Cut 4 from ⅛″
for each leg
and laminate

(Total pieces of ⅛″ from this pattern-16)

9
THE LIBRARY/DEN

Desk
Swivel Chair
Library Breakfront
Settle
Grandfather Clock

Desk

($4\frac{1}{8}$" wide $\times$ $1\frac{7}{8}$" deep $\times$ $4\frac{1}{16}$" high)

MATERIALS

$\frac{1}{8}$" illustration board   Latex satin base coat
$\frac{1}{16}$" illustration board   Stain and glaze
Sobo glue   Drawer pulls

INSTRUCTIONS

1. Trace and transfer pattern pieces to ⅛″ and ¹⁄₁₆″ illustration board.

2. Cut out pieces.

3. Place back (A) on flat surface.

4. Laminate ⅛″ side (B) with the ¹⁄₁₆″ side (B).

5. Notch laminated side (B) as indicated by dotted lines ¹⁄₁₆″ deep, and notch center upright partition in same manner.

6. Glue long drawer partition (C) between notches, flush with front edges of side and front and back edges of center upright partition.

7. Glue above unit to back (A), left side edge outside back and center on top of back with top and bottom edges flush, on right side desk facing you.

8. Glue remaining side (B) to outside of back (A), on left side desk facing you.

9. Glue pieces (E), (F), and (G) as follows:
Glue 2 pieces of (F) to inside of left side and center partition at top.
Glue 1 small drawer partition (E) under first set of side drawer dividers (F) and to side and center upright partition.
Repeat the above two steps for the center and bottom drawers.
Glue (G) under bottom small drawer partition and to side and upright partition.

10. Laminate (H). Glue between right side of desk and center partitions flush with lower edge.

11. Laminate desk top (I), and glue to assembled unit flush with back and slight overhang on sides and front.

12. For long drawer: Make frame with front, sides, and back. Glue bottom inside frame. Make any adjustments to fit in space made for this drawer.

13. For 3 side, small drawers: Glue drawer sides on top of bottom. Glue back inside sides flush with bottom edge of bottom. Glue drawer front flush with bottom and side edges. If needed, laminate piece of ¹⁄₁₆″ illustration board to drawer front to fit spaces for side, small drawers. These are ticklish to make and take a bit of fitting.

14. Top Section: Place back (AA) on flat surface. Glue under shelf uprights (DD) as follows: One flush with either side edge of back and the remaining 2 spaced to make 3 bottom sections as equal as possible. Keep all (DD)s squared and flush with bottom edge of back.

15. Glue shelf (CC) on top of (DD)s and to back.

16. Equally space and glue (EE)s to top of shelf and back to make 7 cubbyholes.

17. Glue sides (BB) to this entire unit flush with bottom and side edges of back.

18. Glue laminated top (FF) flush with back edge, to tops of (EE)s and to tops of sides with slight overhang on front and sides.

19. Glue assembled top unit to bottom of desk, back edges flush and side edges lined up.

20. Paint entire unit with base coat. Sand, if needed.

21. Brush with stain and glaze. Let set 5 to 10 minutes. Wipe lightly with cloth or paper towel until wood grained.

22. Attach drawer pulls. (See Handles and Pulls, page 196.)

Desk

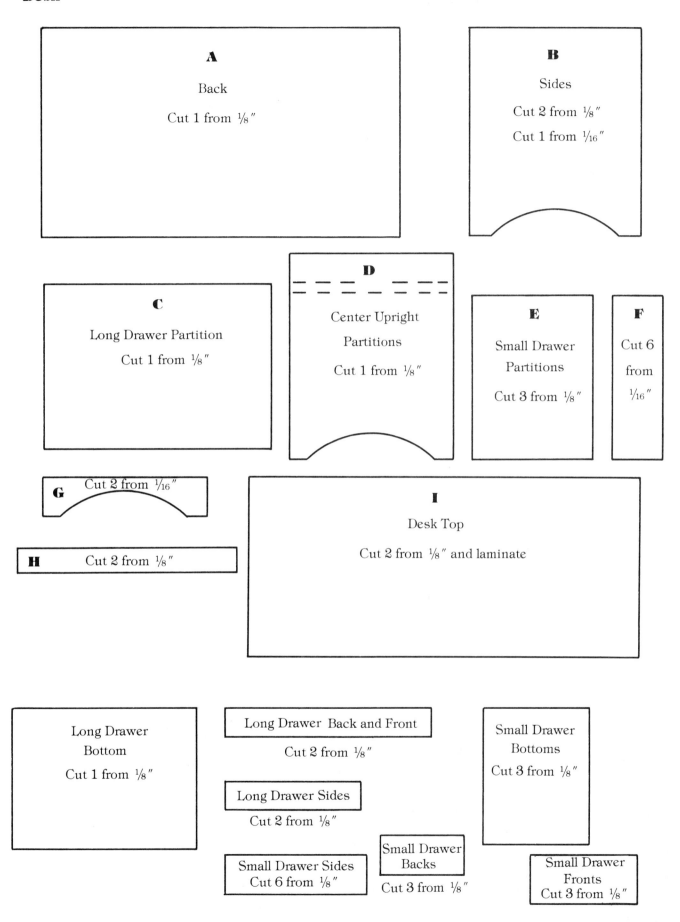

A

Back

Cut 1 from ⅛″

B

Sides

Cut 2 from ⅛″

Cut 1 from ¹⁄₁₆″

C

Long Drawer Partition

Cut 1 from ⅛″

D

Center Upright

Partitions

Cut 1 from ⅛″

E

Small Drawer

Partitions

Cut 3 from ⅛″

F

Cut 6

from

¹⁄₁₆″

G   Cut 2 from ¹⁄₁₆″

H   Cut 2 from ⅛″

I

Desk Top

Cut 2 from ⅛″ and laminate

Long Drawer

Bottom

Cut 1 from ⅛″

Long Drawer Back and Front

Cut 2 from ⅛″

Long Drawer Sides

Cut 2 from ⅛″

Small Drawer Sides

Cut 6 from ⅛″

Small Drawer

Backs

Cut 3 from ⅛″

Small Drawer

Bottoms

Cut 3 from ⅛″

Small Drawer

Fronts

Cut 3 from ⅛″

179

```
┌────────────────────────────────────────────┐
│                    AA                        │
│             Top Section Back                 │
│            Cut 1 from ⅛″                     │
│                                              │
└────────────────────────────────────────────┘
```

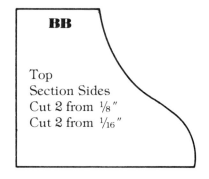

BB

Top
Section Sides
Cut 2 from ⅛″
Cut 2 from ¹⁄₁₆″

```
┌────────────────────────────────────────────┐
│  CC    Shelf          Cut 1 from ⅛″          │
└────────────────────────────────────────────┘
```

DD

*

EE

**

*   Under shelf uprights—Cut 3 from ¹⁄₁₆″

** Above shelf cubbyhole dividers—Cut 6
     from ¹⁄₁₆″

```
┌────────────────────────────────────────────┐
│                    FF                        │
│             Top Section Top                  │
│   Cut 1 from ⅛″ and 1 from ¹⁄₁₆″ and         │
│   laminate                                   │
└────────────────────────────────────────────┘
```

Swivel Chair

(1¾″ wide × 1¾″ deep × 3⁹⁄₁₆″ high)

MATERIALS

⅛″ illustration board
¹⁄₁₆″ illustration board
3 round toothpicks
Sobo glue
Latex satin base coat
Stain and glaze
³⁄₁₆″ bolt cut ½″ long

INSTRUCTIONS

1. Trace and transfer pattern pieces to ⅛″ and ¹⁄₁₆″ illustration board.
2. Cut all pieces, laminating parts as indicated.
3. With pick or small nail mark holes for toothpicks in seat as indicated by dots and bottom edge of back as indicated by dotted lines.
4. Cut toothpicks 1⅛″ long and glue into holes in seat and back.

5. Glue arms to seat flush with side edges and $\frac{3}{8}$″ from front edge. Glue to back along side edges of back slightly more than $\frac{1}{2}$″ higher than top of back.

6. Glue under-seat block in center of bottom of seat.

7. Laminate and shape center post as described on drawing.

8. Glue legs to center post, flush with bottom and centered as indicated by dotted lines.

9. Drill small hole in block and top of center post. Screw in bolt so space between block and center post is $\frac{1}{8}$″.

10. Paint with base coat. Sand, if needed.

11. Brush with stain and glaze. Let set 5 to 10 minutes. Wipe lightly with cloth or paper towel until wood grained.

Swivel Chair

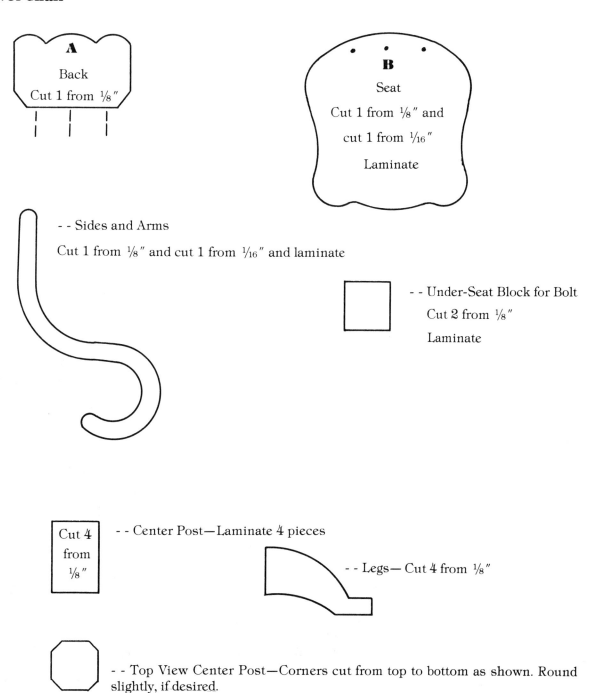

A

Back

Cut 1 from $\frac{1}{8}$″

B

Seat

Cut 1 from $\frac{1}{8}$″ and

cut 1 from $\frac{1}{16}$″

Laminate

- - Sides and Arms

Cut 1 from $\frac{1}{8}$″ and cut 1 from $\frac{1}{16}$″ and laminate

- - Under-Seat Block for Bolt

Cut 2 from $\frac{1}{8}$″

Laminate

Cut 4 from $\frac{1}{8}$″

- - Center Post—Laminate 4 pieces

- - Legs— Cut 4 from $\frac{1}{8}$″

- - Top View Center Post—Corners cut from top to bottom as shown. Round slightly, if desired.

Library Breakfront (Make in three sections)

(2¾″ wide × 1½″ deep × 6⅝″ high. Each section. Depth measured at top.)

(8¼″ wide × 1½″ deep × 6⅝″ high. Measurement of 3-section unit.)

MATERIALS

⅛" illustration board   Latex satin base coat
¹⁄₁₆" illustration board   Stain and glaze
Sobo glue   Door pulls
Pins

INSTRUCTIONS

1.   Trace and transfer pattern pieces to ⅛" and ¹⁄₁₆" illustration board. The 2 side sections are identical, but the middle section has a slight change. Start with the side sections and make each according to the following instructions.
2.   Cut all pieces.
3.   Place back (A) on flat surface. Glue sides (B) to long edge of back flush with back, top and bottom.
4.   Laminate one ⅛" and one ¹⁄₁₆" top (C) together, and glue to top of back and sides, flush with all outside edges.
5.   Glue shelves and base (G) as indicated by dotted lines to back and sides.
6.   Glue top trim (D) under top and flush with outside edges of sides.
7.   Glue trim (E) on top of top trim (D) under top (C), flush with edges of sides.
8.   Glue trim (F) on top of trim (E) under top (C), flush with edges of sides.
9.   Glue 1 brace at bottom of each side under base (G).
10.   Glue door frame to base (G) and shelf (G) flush with bottom and outside edges of sides.
11.   Glue trim (F) flush with top edge of door frame and sides.
12.   Glue trim (E) flush with bottom edges of door frame and sides.
13.   Glue trim (F) on top of trim (E) flush with bottom and side edges.
14.   Glue side frame to each side of unit under top trim (D) to top of door frame flush with side edges.
15.   Make doors as follows:

Glue door frame (X) to top of door.
Glue (XX) in center of door.
Pin doors ⅛" in from outside edges through base and bottom shelf.
Cut small piece of ⅛" illustration board (approximately ⅞" × ½" for door stop.
Glue to top of base centering for flush closing of doors. If necessary, glue another door stop under bottom shelf.

16.   Paint with base coat. Sand if needed.
17.   Brush with stain and glaze. Let set 5 to 10 minutes. Wipe lightly with cloth or paper towel until wood grained.

CENTER UNIT

Follow steps **1** through **4** for side units.

5.   Glue top 3 shelves and base (G) as indicated by dotted lines to back and sides. (The other 2 shelves as indicated by the X's will be glued in later.)

Follow steps **6** through **9** for side units.

10.   Glue bottom panel (Y) flush with sides and bottom.
11.   Glue in remaining 2 shelves. Bottom shelf flush with top edge of bottom panel.
12.   Glue trim (F) flush with top edge of bottom panel and sides.

13. Glue trim (E) flush with bottom edges of bottom panel and sides.

14. Glue trim (F) on top of trim (E) flush with bottom and side edges.

15. Glue center section side frames to each side of unit under top trim (D) to top of bottom panel flush with side edges.

16. Paint with base coat. Sand, if needed.

17. Brush with stain and glaze. Let set 5 to 10 minutes. Wipe lightly with cloth or paper towel until wood grained.

Library Breakfront

Make in 3 sections—2 Side Sections and 1 Center Section. DO NOT join sections.

A

For Each Section:

Cut 1 from $\frac{1}{16}$″

(Total pieces of (A)—3)

X   X

X   X

Cut 2 from $\frac{1}{8}$″ for each section. Total: 6

Brace

B

For Each Section:

Cut 1 from $\frac{1}{16}$″

(Total pieces of (B)—3)

C

Top

For Each Section:

Cut 1 from $\frac{1}{8}$″ and 1 from $\frac{1}{16}$″

Total—3 from $\frac{1}{8}$″ and 3 from $\frac{1}{16}$″

D

Top Trim For Each Section

Cut 1 from $\frac{1}{8}$″   Total: 3

E   Trim

Cut 2 from $\frac{1}{16}$″ for each section—Total: 6

F   Trim

Cut 3 from $\frac{1}{8}$″ for each section—Total: 9

G   Shelves and Base
Cut from $\frac{1}{16}$″ 5 for each side
and 6 for center. Total: 16

Door Frame, Doors, Door Trim, and Side Trims for Side Sections

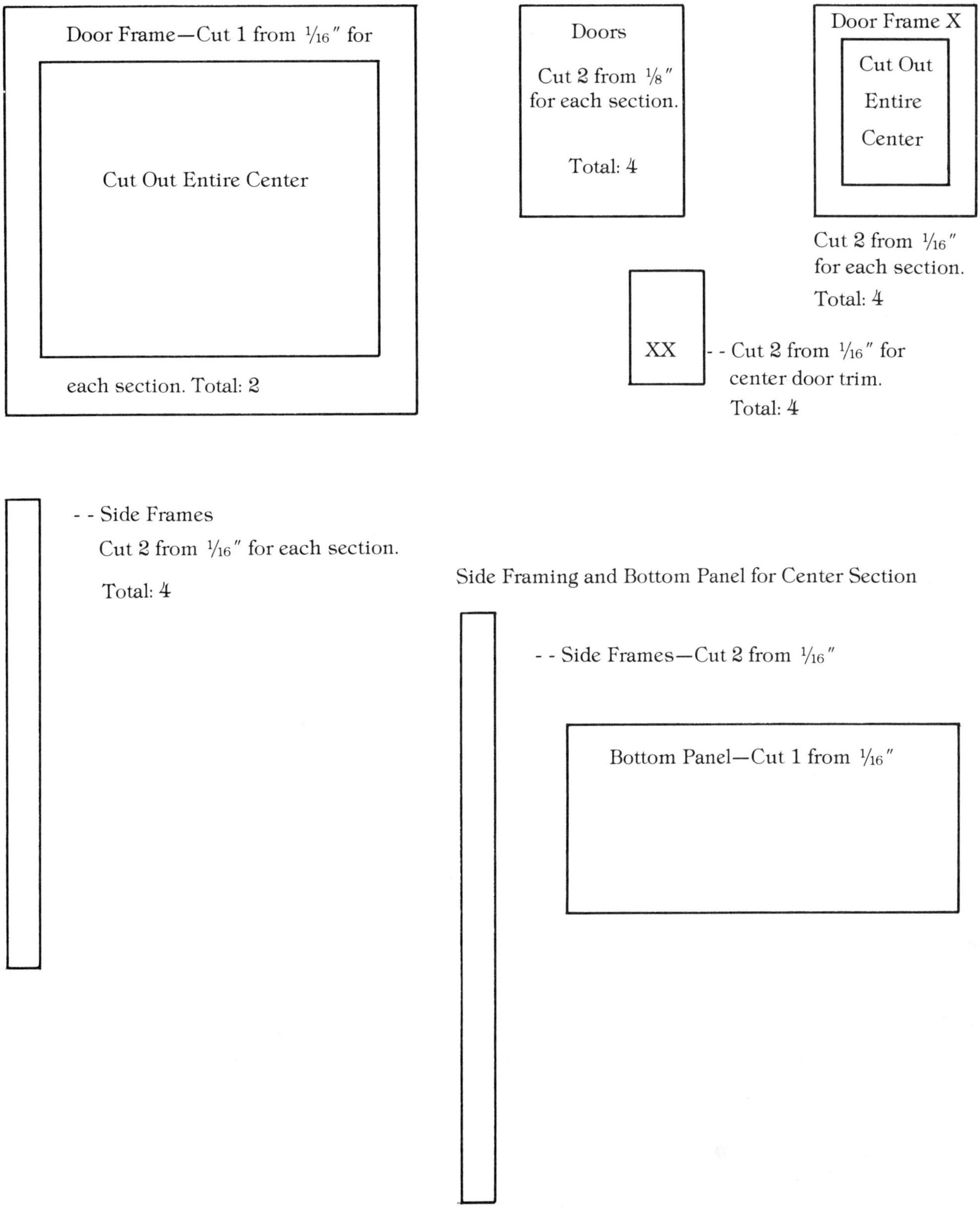

Door Frame—Cut 1 from $\frac{1}{16}$″ for

Cut Out Entire Center

each section. Total: 2

Doors

Cut 2 from $\frac{1}{8}$″
for each section.

Total: 4

Door Frame X

Cut Out

Entire

Center

Cut 2 from $\frac{1}{16}$″
for each section.
Total: 4

XX

- - Cut 2 from $\frac{1}{16}$″ for
center door trim.
Total: 4

- - Side Frames
Cut 2 from $\frac{1}{16}$″ for each section.

Total: 4

Side Framing and Bottom Panel for Center Section

- - Side Frames—Cut 2 from $\frac{1}{16}$″

Bottom Panel—Cut 1 from $\frac{1}{16}$″

Settle

(4 ¾" long × 1 ¹¹⁄₁₆" deep × 3 ½" high)

 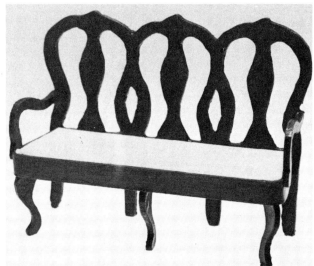

MATERIALS

⅛" illustration board
¹⁄₁₆" illustration board
Sobo glue
Latex satin base coat
Stain and glaze
Padding
Fabric

INSTRUCTIONS

1. Trace and transfer pattern pieces to ⅛" illustration board.
2. Cut all pieces.
3. Cut piece of ¹⁄₁₆" illustration board ⅜" wide × 7¾" long.
4. Glue ⅙" strip around sides and front-curved edge of seat ¹⁄₁₆" up from bottom edge of seat. Cut back edges of ⅜" stripping at slight slant. (Seat back is slanted back slightly.)
5. Glue edged seat to back ¹⁄₁₆" up from top of legs.
6. Glue top edge of arm rest ⅝" up from top of ⅜" stripping on seat to outside edge of seat back. Front of arm rest will be at start of seat front round corner about centered on outside ⅜" stripping (from top to bottom of stripping.)
7. Glue 1 leg under seat at center and the other 2 legs on a 45° angle at both corners under seat.
8. Paint with base coat. Sand, and this will be necessary on this piece.
9. Brush with stain and glaze. Let stand 5 to 10 minutes. Wipe lightly with cloth or paper towel until wood grained.
10. Upholster. (See Upholstering, page 202.)

Settle

Back—Cut 1

Cut out all X
marked sections.

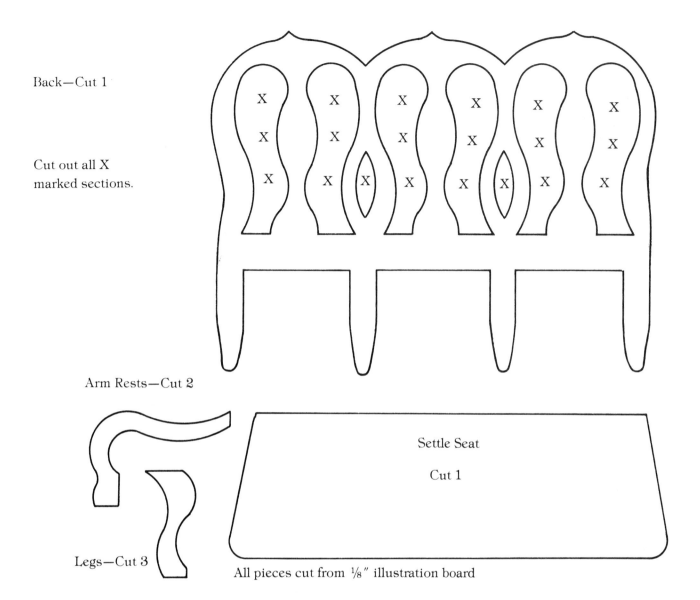

Arm Rests—Cut 2

Settle Seat

Cut 1

Legs—Cut 3

All pieces cut from ⅛″ illustration board

Grandfather Clock

MATERIALS

⅛″ illustration board
Toothpicks
Bead (optional)
Brass wire or ¹⁄₃₂″ doweling painted gold—2″ long
Round brass disc or round piece of file card painted gold—⅜″ diameter
Plastic (optional)—up to ⅛″ thick
Sobo glue
Latex satin base coat
Stain and glaze
Clock face, real or cut from glossy paper
Round gold ring size of clock face or gold doily size of clock face

(1½″ wide × ⅞″ deep × 6¾″ high to top of trim.)

INSTRUCTIONS

1. Trace and transfer pattern pieces to ⅛″ illustration board.

2. Cut all pieces.

3. Base Assembly:

Place 1 piece (A) on flat surface, long edges to front and back.

Laminate all 6 pieces of (B). Glue to (A) flush with back edges, centering on (A) from sides. The measurements of laminated (B) are: 1 3/16″ wide × 11/16″ deep × 1 1/16″ high. Glue second piece of (A) to top of laminated (B) flush with back edges, centered from side to side on (B).

Glue 1 (C) centered from side to side on (A) flush with back edges.

Glue bottom trim centered on front of laminated (B) section.

Body of base is completed. Set aside.

4. Top Assembly:

Starting at top: Place 1 piece (A) on flat surface, long edges to front and back.

Laminate all 4 pieces of (D). Glue to (A) flush with back edges, centered on (A) from side to side. The measurements of laminated (D) are: 1 3/16″ wide × 7/16″ deep × 1 5/16″ high.

Glue second piece of (A) to top of laminated (D) flush with back edges centered on (D) from side to side.

Glue 1 (C) centered on (A) from side to side, back edges flush.

Cut 2 round toothpicks 2⅛″ long; leave one end pointed on each.

Drill or with nail make 4 holes for toothpicks as follows: 2 holes all the way through top piece (A) and partially through (A) which has the (C) piece glued beneath. Insert toothpicks, pointed ends up, down through top holes and glue into bottom holes. Holes should be approximately ⅛″ in from side and front edges.

Glue top trim flush with side edges of top of (A) behind toothpicks.

Top of clock face is completed. Set aside.

5. Center Door Section Assembly:

Place back (E) on flat surface. Glue sides (F) to long edges of back (E) flush with back, top, and bottom edges.

Glue 1 (G) flush with top back and side edges between sides and 1 (G) flush with bottom back and side edges between sides.

Glue center door section (what you have just completed) to top of base flush with back edges, centered from side to side on (C).

Glue center door section to underside of top flush with back edges, centered from side to side on underside of (C). Body of clock is assembled. Set aside.

6. Cut out X'd center section of door (H).

7. Paint with base coat. Sand, if needed.

8. Brush with stain and glaze. Let set 5 to 10 minutes. Wipe lightly with cloth or paper towel until wood grained.

9. Cut (I) of plastic (optional) and glue to inside of door.

10. Pin door at side edges through bottom of top assembly and top of bottom assembly.

11. For Pendulum:

Make small hole in center of center door assembly (G). Insert 2″ brass wire or 1/32″ doweling painted gold. And remember those earring backs we used for faucets? The round disc makes a perfect pendulum glued to small ¼″ × ¼″ × ¼″ laminated illustration board or block of wood. Insert bottom end of brass wire or doweling into this block and you have your completed pendulum.

12.   Use small gold pin for clock door pull centered on door front between cutout and side edges.

13.   Glue paper or real clock face in center of gold doily trim around clock face.

Grandfather Clock

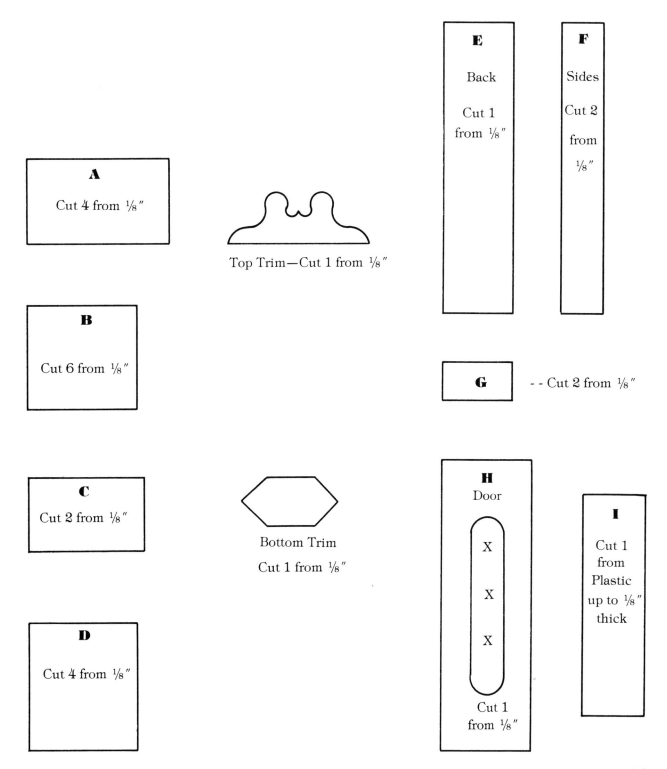

A

Cut 4 from ⅛″

Top Trim—Cut 1 from ⅛″

E

Back

Cut 1

from ⅛″

F

Sides

Cut 2

from

⅛″

B

Cut 6 from ⅛″

G   - - Cut 2 from ⅛″

C

Cut 2 from ⅛″

Bottom Trim

Cut 1 from ⅛″

H

Door

X

X

X

Cut 1

from ⅛″

I

Cut 1

from

Plastic

up to ⅛″

thick

D

Cut 4 from ⅛″

10
STORAGE ITEMS

Toy Chest
Blanket Chest
Trunk

Toy Chest

(3″ long × 1 3/16″ deep × 2″ high, measured to top of back.)

MATERIALS

    1/8″ illustration board
    Sobo glue
    Paint
    Decals, glossy colored magazine pictures, or hand-painted designs with
       children's motif
    Hinges

INSTRUCTIONS

1. Trace and transfer pattern pieces to 1/8″ illustration board.
2. Cut all pieces.
3. Place bottom (A) on flat surface.
4. Glue sides (C) to back (B), bottom and side edges flush.
5. Glue side-back unit to bottom with bottom and front edges flush.
6. Glue front and bottom and sides, all edges flush.
7. Paint with latex satin white or any color you desire. (Don't forget to paint lid and inside of toy chest.)
8. Hinge lid to toy chest by pinning through back 1/4″ from side edges or with outside hinges. (See Hinges, page 195.)
9. Decorate with decals, glossy colored pictures, or hand-painted designs.

```
┌─────────────────────────────────┐     ┌───────────────────────────────────────┐
│                                 │     │                                         │
│               A                 │     │                   B                     │
│                                 │     │                                         │
│            Bottom               │     │                 Back                    │
│                                 │     │                                         │
│            Cut 1                │     │                 Cut 1                   │
│                                 │     │                                         │
└─────────────────────────────────┘     │                                         │
                                         │                                         │
┌─────────────────┐                      │                                         │
│       C         │                      │                                         │
│                 │                      │                                         │
│     Sides       │                      │                                         │
│                 │                      │                                         │
│     Cut 2       │                      └───────────────────────────────────────┘
│                 │
│                 │
│                 │
└─────────────────┘

┌───────────────────────────────┐       ┌───────────────────────────────────────┐
│                               │       │                   D                     │
│              E                │       │                                         │
│            Lid                │       │                 Front                   │
│            Cut 1              │       │                 Cut 1                   │
│                               │       │                                         │
│                               │       │                                         │
│                               │       │                                         │
└───────────────────────────────┘       └───────────────────────────────────────┘
```

All pieces cut from ⅛″ illustration board.

Blanket Chest

(3¾″ long × 1⅝″ deep × 1½″ high)

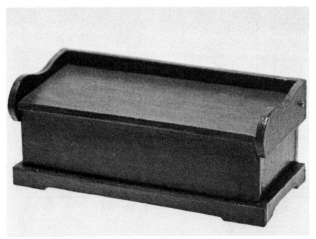

MATERIALS

⅛″ illustration board
Sobo glue
Pins
Latex satin base coat
Stain and glaze

INSTRUCTIONS

1. Trace and transfer pattern pieces to ⅛″ illustration board.
2. Cut all pieces.
3. Glue sides (B), inside back (A), and front (C), bottom and side edges flush. Sides will be flush with top edge of front but ⅜″ below top edge of back.
4. Glue base inside ⅛″ up from bottom edges of sides, back, and front.
5. Glue top side trim outside sides and back edges flush with top of back and ⅞″ up from bottom at front edge.
6. Glue front base trim flush with bottom edge of front (C), extending ⅛″ past side edges.
7. Glue side base trim flush with bottom on sides (B), flush with back edge and behind front base trim.
8. Pin lid (E) through top side trim ⅛″ from back edge of lid.
9. Paint with base coat. Sand, if needed.
10. Brush with stain and glaze. Let set 5 to 10 minutes. Wipe lightly with cloth or paper towel until wood grained.

Blanket Chest

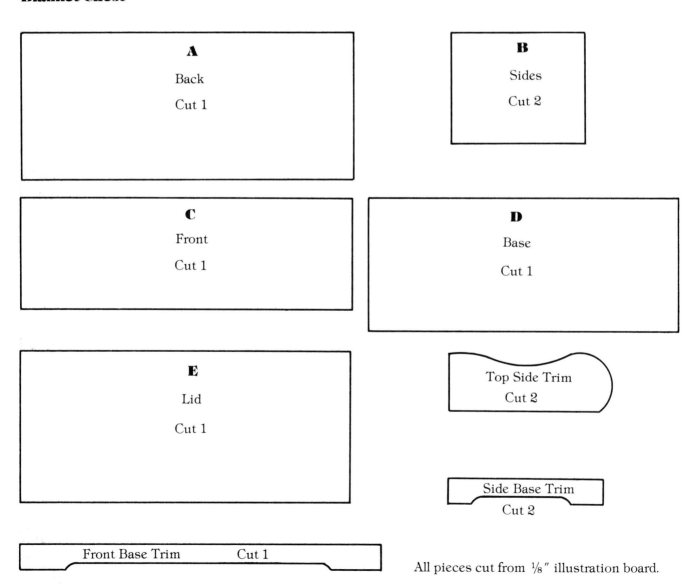

All pieces cut from ⅛″ illustration board.

Trunk

MATERIALS

⅛″ illustration board
1/16″ illustration board
Sobo glue
Latex satin base coat
Stain and glaze
Plastic stripping
Sequin pins

INSTRUCTIONS

1. Trace and transfer pattern pieces to ⅛″ and 1/16″ illustration board.

2. Cut all pieces.

3. Place bottom (A) on flat surface. Glue sides (C) flush with bottom, front, and back edges of bottom (A).

4. Glue front and back (B) to bottom and sides, bottom and side edges flush.

5. Glue trunk liner, front and back (D), inside trunk to front and back. Glue trunk liner sides (E) inside trunk to sides.

6. Glue upright drawer supports at inside corners, edges glued to back, front, and bottom with flat ¼″ surface to sides, ⅝″ high.

7. Glue trunk lid sides (G) inside trunk lid front and back. Angle cut trunk lid front and back corner edges as shown in side view.

8. Dampen trunk lid (H) and glue to edges of trunk lid front, back, and sides.

9. Place drawer bottom (I) on flat surface. Glue drawer sides (K) flush with bottom, front, and back edges of drawer bottom (I).

10. Glue drawer front and back (J) to bottom and sides, bottom and side edges flush. Place drawer in trunk. If drawer is slightly above trunk liner, the upright supports were properly placed.

11. Paint with base coat. Sand, if needed.

12. Brush with stain and glaze. Let set 5 to 10 minutes. Wipe lightly with cloth or paper towel until you have a "distressed wood" effect. Adding a touch of black paint swirled on with a toothpick before wiping will give a truly distressed appearance.

13. To make trunk handles: Drill or punch holes through trunk sides (but not liner) ⅝″ from front and back edges and ¼″ down from top, 2 holes on each side. Cut pieces of black braided shoelace, or similar material, about 1″ long; loop and glue into holes.

14. To make trunk straps: Cut 2 pieces of ¼″ strips of thin black plastic, or similar material, 7½″ long. For each strap, start at lower edge of trunk lid front, ⅝″ from side edges and wrap around entire trunk, ending at top edge of trunk front. Spot glue. Pin ⅛″ above bottom lower edge of front trunk lid, 3 more pins across rounded trunk lid, 1 pin ¼″ above lower edge of back trunk lid, 1 pin ¼″ below top of trunk back (these 2 pins make trunk hinge), 1 pin ¼″ above bottom edge of trunk back, 3 pins across bottom of trunk, 1 pin ¼″ above lower edge of trunk front and 1 pin ⅛″ below top edge of trunk front.

(3″ long × 1⅞″ deep × 2″ high)

Trunk

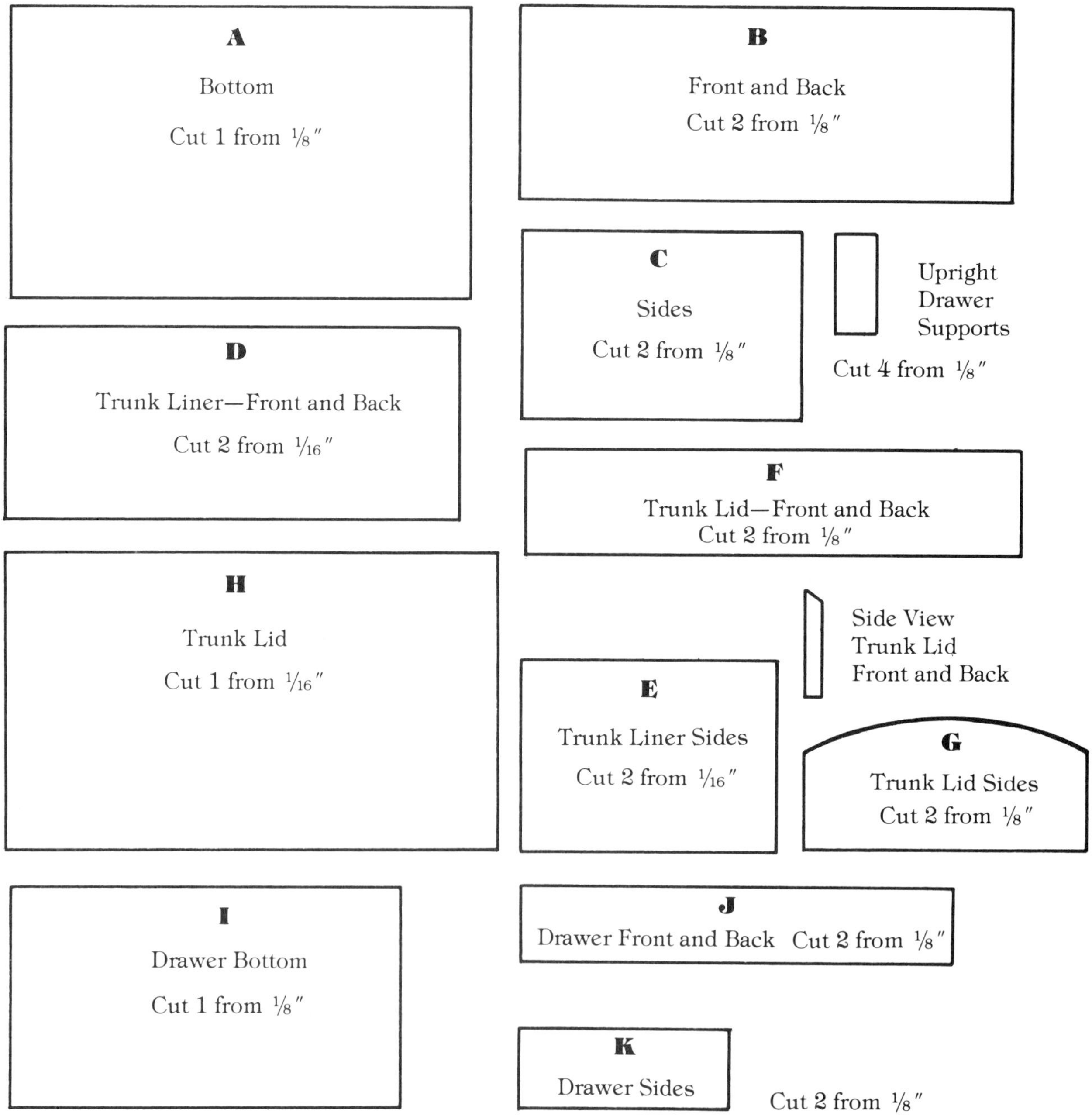

A
Bottom
Cut 1 from ⅛″

B
Front and Back
Cut 2 from ⅛″

C
Sides
Cut 2 from ⅛″

Upright
Drawer
Supports

Cut 4 from ⅛″

D
Trunk Liner—Front and Back
Cut 2 from 1/16″

F
Trunk Lid—Front and Back
Cut 2 from ⅛″

H
Trunk Lid
Cut 1 from 1/16″

Side View
Trunk Lid
Front and Back

E
Trunk Liner Sides
Cut 2 from 1/16″

G
Trunk Lid Sides
Cut 2 from ⅛″

I
Drawer Bottom
Cut 1 from ⅛″

J
Drawer Front and Back   Cut 2 from ⅛″

K
Drawer Sides

Cut 2 from ⅛″

194

11

FINISHING TOUCHES

Hinges
Handles and Pulls
Bed Linens
Curtains
Rugs
Upholstering
Accessories

Hinges

Most of our miniature hinges are "invisible." That is, all flush doors are pinned, no hinge showing. There are a couple of exceptions.

Houseworks #1122 butt hinges are used on the kitchen cupboard and bathroom vanity.

Hinges for the icebox doors and toilet seat are cut from pieces of brass sheet metal or the heavy foil from TV-dinner trays along with straight pins. To make this hinge: Cut head from straight pin. Bend as shown. Wrap brass or heavy foil around pin and tighten with pliers. Insert pin head into frame of icebox and/or toilet seat. Attach metal to doors and seat with a small gold or silver pin. This makes a secure and inexpensive hinge.

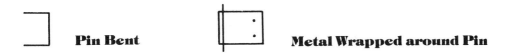

Pin Bent   **Metal Wrapped around Pin**

For all pinned doors, you can cut an outside hinge from doily or foil paper, gold or silver. But never paint a gold or silver outside hinge on doors. Gold and silver paints rub off if care in handling furniture is not always your first priority.

But never "fake" hinge a door that should have a hidden hinge. This can detract from the authen. city of what would otherwise be a beautiful piece of miniature reproduction. If you go the route of fake outside hinges, use sparingly and only where used on real furniture.

Handles and Pulls

Most door pulls are round-topped pins or small gold sequin pins.

On the sideboard and buffet, small rounds were made from $\frac{1}{16}$ illustration board with a paper punch and glued to center of each drawer for the pulls.

The handles on the icebox are Houseworks #1123 handle pulls, which may also be used on other drawers or doors.

Pulls can also be cut in $\frac{1}{8}''$ lengths from $\frac{1}{8}''$ or $\frac{1}{16}''$ wooden pine doweling that you stain before gluing to furniture or glue before stain is applied to furniture piece.

Handles can also be the small metal loops that come on a card of hooks and eyes. These already are in the shape of handles and can be left as is for drawer pulls.

The ideas for handles and pulls are endless. You are restricted only as to proper proportion for each piece of furniture. On small drawers, such as those in the vanity, a gold sequin pin is in proper scale. Larger drawers call for small gold beads with sequin pin to attach them to drawers or doors. Chart or map tacks can be used on larger pieces of furniture, but are usually too large for most pieces.

Once you begin to make miniature furniture and start thinking in Lilliputian dimensions, you'll have no trouble selecting the exact pin, tack, or bead for handles and pulls.

Bed Linens

MATERIALS

Padding. Absorbent cotton or padding of cotton or foam rubber sold for quilting. Use in thickness of no more than $\frac{1}{4}''$ unless stuffing plump pillow or mattress.

Fabrics. Cotton, rayon, satin, silk, synthetic, thin brocade. Your selection is limited only by avoiding heavy materials or prints that are too large to be considered miniature.

Trims. Laces, braids, edge tape (a self-adhesive double-edge tape is perfect for edge trims), rickrack. Again your choice is endless, limited by patterns not in scale.

If you buy any material, never buy more than $\frac{1}{4}$ yard. Measure trims needed and buy the least expensive. In miniature these look just as good as the expensive. Occasionally you can "indulge" and still stay within budget.

If you sew, save all scraps. Have friends and relatives save all their scraps. And never throw away any article of clothing with lace or sheer materials. It is possible to never buy a piece of material or trim for your bed linens, curtain, or upholstery.

Some people, with a fine hand, will sew bedding and/or curtains. Most use glue for hemming and seaming. This takes care of fraying and also eliminates bulky seams that can make a miniature bedspread or curtain look out of scale.

MATTRESSES AND PILLOWS

Cut a piece of $\frac{1}{4}$ foam rubber the same size as bottom pattern of bed and use it without a covering. There is no need to "undress" a miniature bed once you have covered it with a beautiful bedspread, which is usually tacked or in some manner permanently attached to your bed. This foam rubber must be covered only if your bedspread is a sheer fabric. Although the foam padding is an eggshell color, it can be seen through a lacy or sheer fabric.

To make a mattress cover: Cut a piece of white cotton (or similar) material twice the width of your pattern for the bed bottom plus ½″ and the length plus ½″. With a tight, fine overcasting stitch, sew edges of mattress cover to enclose the padding. Or you may overlap edges and glue together with white craft glue.

Pillows are made in the same manner as a covered mattress, cutting pillow to fit the bed. A large bed can have either one bolster or 2 small pillows. Overcast or glue edges of material to cover padding. Trim pillows to match trim of your bedspread if they are used as bolsters. Trim may be glued or sewed to pillow fabric.

CRADLE AND CRIB

Make mattresses for cradle and crib in same manner as described for bed pillows. Make small pillow for crib and/or cradle to fit. If desired, edge-trim mattresses and pillows with dainty lace.

BEDSPREAD FOR BASIC BED

Measure length of bed (6½″) and width plus height from floor to bed bottom plus ½″ (6¾″). Cut material accordingly, 6¾″ wide × 6½″ long. To minimize fraying of lightweight materials, cut material ¼″ longer and wider. Fold back and glue or sew this hem. Never do this on heavy material as it will make edges too thick.

Overcast all four sides of bedspread when hem not used or you have chosen a heavy material.

Fold back sides of bedspread 1¼″ and overcast to form ridge. This makes top edge of bedspread overhang.

For basic bed pillow: Cut a piece of foam 3½″ × 1½″. Or use padding of your choice. Cut material 4″ long × 3¾″ wide; wrap around padding and overcast edges by gluing or sewing.

BEDSPREAD FOR FOUR-POSTER BED

Cut material 6″ long × 4¾″ wide. Overcast edges, or cut ½″ longer and ½″ wider, fold back and glue hem all round.

Cut 2 pieces 1½″ wide × 12″ long. Overcast around all sides of each piece or cut each piece ½″ longer and wider and glue hem. Run a gathering stitch ⅜″ from top edge of long sides; pull thread and fasten, making each piece 6″ long. Stitch or glue gathered trim to bedspread top so top of bedspread measures 4⅛″ wide.

To make plump pillow: Cut 2 pieces of foam (or padding of your choice) 3½″ × 1½″. Cut material to match bedspread 4″ long × 3¾″ wide; wrap around padding and overcast edges with glue or overcasting stitch.

BEDSPREAD FOR CANOPY BED

Cut piece of material 7″ long × 6⅛″ wide. Cut notches 1″ in from side edges and 1⅛″ from bottom edge to accommodate legs at end of bed. Your material will now measure: 6⅛" at headboard, 5¾" along sides, and 4" across foot. Overcast by gluing or stitching material at headboard only.

Using gathered eyelet trim, sew 1 piece of eyelet trim to each side and at foot of bed. Sew or glue eyelet trim ¼" below edge of top trim. Sew 1 more piece of eyelet trim to cut edge of bedspread top on sides and foot. These instructions are for eyelet trim 1¼" wide; adjust for width of eyelet you choose to use.

For pillow: Cut foam (or padding of your choice) 3¼" long × 1¾" wide. Cut piece of bedspread material 4" long × 4½" wide. Wrap around padding. Pin in place. Cut piece of eyelet trim approximately 7¾" long. Pin over material wrapped around padding and stitch or glue in place, allowing ¼" above sewing line. This pillow size is optional. You can make it smaller or you can make 2 small pillows to fit your canopy bed.

For canopy top: Measure top of bed, add ¼" on all sides and sew or glue row of eyelet trim around all sides in same manner as on bedspread.

BEDSPREAD FOR PRIVACY BED

Cut piece for bedspread top 8" wide × 7¾" long. If hemming, add ½" to these measurements. Make cutouts to accommodate legs at bottom of bed. Final piece measures 1" at headboard, 5¾" along sides, and 4" at foot. If hemming, measurements will be ½" more all around. Overcast or hem (glue or stitch) around outside edges, including the cutouts.

For top spread, cut piece of brocade (or satin, velvet, etc.) 6⅜" wide × 6⅛" long. Cut V-shaped notch to accommodate legs at foot of bed, leaving 1" overhang at sides and ⅜" overhang at foot.

Privacy curtain: Cut back curtain the height and width of your privacy bed plus 1" at sides. Cut top of privacy curtain the width and length of the privacy bed plus ½" in width and length. Cut 2 side curtains 2½" wide and height of your privacy bed, rounding bottom corner. Overcast or glue to sides of back curtain and back edge of top. Overcast or hem-glue all outside edges.

Top scalloped valance: Cut 2 pieces the length of top sides, cutting in scallop pattern from 1" to 1½" deep, having deepest scallops at front and back edges. Cut 1 piece of scalloped trim 4¾" long for top of bed at foot end. Overcast scalloped straight edges to sides and foot of top of privacy bed curtains.

Edge-trim scalloped edges and curtain sides with a self-sticking edge tape to match the bedspread brocade top.

For pillow: Cut piece of foam (or padding of your choice) 3½" long × 1⅜" wide Cut a piece of brocade (or material to match top spread) 4" long × 3½" wide. Wrap around padding and overcast edges.

FINAL INSTRUCTIONS

To hold bedspreads and/or pillows securely, tack with small sequin pins or with a product such as Mini-Hold. Never glue bedspreads to bed. Should you ever decide to change your linens, the glue will leave marks on your furniture. With pinning or Mini-Hold this will never happen.

Bedspreads may also be made by knitting or crocheting, but beware! Too often a heavy yarn is used and the bedspread is out of scale. Crochet a granny-square bedspread using size 30 mercerized cotton and a #11 steel crochet hook. Knit with similar yarn and smallest needles available. Experiment with regular afghan and bedspread patterns, using the above-mentioned materials. Or buy patterns for mini-spreads. It is time-consuming to make bedspreads in this fashion, but it also can be most rewarding and gratifying.

Curtains

Ideas for curtains and/or draperies are endless. You are limited only by the miniature size. Never use a lace, print, or material too large or too bulky. Draperies or curtains can overpower a room and detract from the beauty of a miniature setting.

Very little "sewing" is used in making miniature draperies. All hems are either selvage edges or hems are glued. If using a velvet drapery, you can fringe edges desired length. Then on the wrong side of drapery, run a fine line of glue to stop the material from further fraying.

For full sheer curtains, pull a thread both vertically and horizontally on all four sides. This gives you a straight cut. Depending on the sheerness of your material, you will cut material 2½ to 3 times the width of your window. This is about the only style curtain that will take any sewing and that is to gather both top and bottom edges, the bottom gathers will be pulled out when curtains are hung.

To simplify the making of curtains, place pattern of your window, including trim, on a piece of corrugated cardboard or similar material. Over pattern of window, place a piece of wax paper. You are now ready to cut your curtains to proper size. When cut, glue hems, on wrong side of material. When glue is dry, turn curtains over. You will use your corrugated cardboard as a "pin cushion" when making curtains and/or draperies. To show you how several styles of curtains can be made, I'll take you through my dollhouse and show you how the curtains were made.

Starting with the curtains for the third-floor rooms: In the bathroom the curtains were made of 4 pieces of unruffled trim, the length of the window plus about ½". These strips were then glued together, overlapping slightly. When dry, cut a scalloped bottom edge and glue a piece of small ruffled trim to top edge.

The middle room on the third floor uses a 1½" piece of material that was also used for the bedspread on the four-poster bed. Cut this piece 2½ times the width of the window. Overcast edges, gather ¼" down from top edge and pin on window pattern, pulling gathers to fit window.

A sheer material was used in the next room, made in the manner as described for sheer curtains. Pin to window pattern after basting in gathers. Evenly align gathers and pin along gathers vertically to keep a straight line. While curtains are pinned, spray with hair spray to hold gathers in place permanently. When dry, glue a piece of ruffled or braided trim along top edge of gathered window-length curtain. Pull out bottom running stitch.

A short, or even a long, curtain can be made with side panels and valance. Use a 1" wide piece of trim for each side panel. Cut this same trim 2½ times the width of window, and gather. Spray and glue along top of window trim after side panels have been glued in place. Again, here is where a product such as Mini-Hold is used if you plan to change the decor of your room and will want to hang new curtains.

In the two outer rooms on the second floor, floor-length curtains were used, one a sheer, the other a fine cotton. Cut and gather as explained earlier, making 2 panels for each window. Pin over window pattern, spreading gathers evenly, leaving a small space between panels. Pin vertically to keep gathers in straight line from floor to top of window. Spray with hair spray to hold gathers permanently. Pull out bottom running stitch.

In the "canopy" bedroom, an edge of tiny pre-gathered lace was glued to the inside and bottom edges of each panel. A valance of the ruffle used on the canopy bed was used as a valance and glued across the top of the 2-panel curtains.

In the "privacy" bedroom, the 2-panel curtains were used with a plain valance made of ⅛" illustration board covered with the cotton fabric, and the same edging as used on the "privacy" bedspread was used around entire edge of valance. (See instructions below for How to Make a Valance.)

The curtains in the middle room of the second floor are made the same way as those in the parlor.

The curtains in the kitchen were made of strips of small gathered lace trim glued in tiers. To make gluing easier, first place a piece of sheer material over the wax paper over the window patterns. Glue the tiny tiers to this sheer material, pinning edges as you go along. When curtains have dried, cut away the excess, leaving sheer only as backing for the lace trim.

In the parlor and the second-floor study, or den, an elegant lace was used. The wide lace in the study was used horizontally and the wide lace in the parlor was used vertically. Both were glued together, overlapping slightly to make proper width and/or height. Care must be taken when selecting lace of this kind. Check the pattern. It *must* be in scale with the Lilliputian furniture and dollhouse. The elegance of such curtains will be lost if the pattern is out of proportion.

Both lace curtains are topped with a plain valance made of ⅛" illustration board covered with material compatible with decor of each room. These were simple valances but one can make a scalloped or swag valance. This is all a matter of preference.

On the bay window, a fancy valance of ruffled and gold-trim lace was used. The same can be used for the valance of the parlor curtains.

HOW TO MAKE A VALANCE

1. Cut ⅛" illustration board ¼" wider than window and 2" deep.
2. Glue illustration board to back of material, cut 1" wider and longer than illustration board. (As shown by long dashed lines.)
3. Cut corners of material (as shown by smaller dashed lines), coming to within ⅛" of illustration board at corners.
4. Fold over side mitered corners of material and glue to illustration board.
5. Fold over and glue long edges of material and glue to illustration board.
6. Turn over. If corners show raw edge of material, put a drop of glue on each corner and "roll" material until you have a smooth edge.

Word of Caution: If using velvet or similar material, be careful not to overglue as the glue will bleed through and spot. Also, keep your fingers clean, as glue touching the surface of many materials leaves a spot that means making the valance over again. I know. I've been careless and this has happened to me all too frequently.

Rugs

Rugs for dollhouses have been both a problem and an expense. Even the plainest rug costs $2, and the price can go as high as $40 or more. We'll easily have beautiful rugs and at a cost unbelievably low.

For those who like to crochet, you can make round or oval rugs for less than a dollar apiece. Just remember to use yarn or thread in miniature scale.

Miniature rugs can also be needlepointed or hooked. Hooked rugs are the most beautiful and needlepoint ranks a close second. Doreen Sinnett has

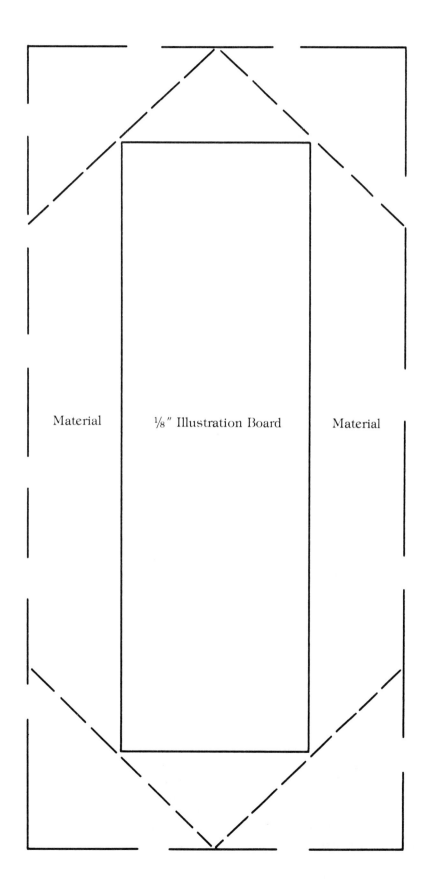

Material   ⅛″ Illustration Board   Material

a beautiful line of hooked rugs. Should your budget allow, a hooked rug from a Doreen Sinnett kit would be a beautiful addition to your dollhouse. But here again, if you are artistic, you can design and hook your own rug using yarn from your own knitting or yarn scraps you can get from friends and relatives.

Some people buy upholstery material for rugs, but few shops will sell the small pieces we need for miniatures. Unless you can get a "sample," never buy upholstery material. You'll have to buy at least ¼ yard, and at today's prices even this small amount is too expensive.

Some people use scraps of carpeting. Rugs made from regular carpeting are hideous in a miniature setting. The pile of the carpeting is so deep, the little legs of chairs and tables get lost in even the tightest pile. And the patterns are so huge the miniature furniture is dwarfed.

Felt rugs for use in the child's and/or Nanny's room can be made in an array of patterns, and the only things needed are pencil to draw patterns, scissors, and glue.

The best place to find rugs for miniature rooms is at an upholstery shop. Outdated sample books can be purchased for as little as 25¢ and no more than 75¢. If you decide to buy a sample book, make certain the patterns are in a miniature scale, and that you'll have enough for all the rooms in your dollhouse, with leftovers so you can change rugs for different decors or give to friends who are miniature enthusiasts.

Besides rugs from sample books, you can use vinyls or suedes to upholster dining room chairs or the settle as was done in the dollhouse pictured.

Upholstering

Upholstering may appear difficult but it really is easier than it looks. Some pieces can be upholstered in the simplest manner, such as the dining room chairs and settle; also the dressing table bench.

Always paint and stain the entire piece of furniture whether you are going to upholster with suede, vinyl, or fabric. Cut a piece of ⅛″ illustration board the size of each seat and glue a piece of upholstery material (as used for rugs) to this top seat. Set in place. If it sinks lower than 1/16″ below rim edges, slip in one or two slats of ⅛″ or 1/16″ illustration board ½″ wide.

The basics for fabric-upholstered furniture are quite similar to the drawings and instructions for How to Make a Valance. Material is cut slightly larger (about an inch) than the seats and backs to be upholstered.

Instructions are given for footstool and the low- and high-back chairs.

When gluing fabric take care to use glue sparingly. It can bleed through velvet or satin. And keep your fingers clean at all times. Glue cannot be washed off velvet or satin. Marring your upholstery with a glue spot means doing it over again, which can be most discouraging.

UPHOLSTERING INSTRUCTIONS FOR FOOT STOOL

1. Cut 1 piece of 1/16″ illustration board the size of (X), foot stool base. If using a thick fabric, cut a fraction smaller to accommodate fabric.
2. Cut piece of padding to fit (X) no more than ¼″ thick and glue to (X).
3. Cut piece of material about size as shown by long broken lines.
4. Glue padded side of base (X) to wrong side of material (gluing optional).
5. Cut corners of material as shown by short broken lines coming to ¼″ of corners.
6. Fold in side edges of material and glue to illustration board. Pull to keep top smooth but not so tight as to force down padding.
7. Fold in front and back edges of material and glue to illustration board, tightening just enough to keep top smooth but not so tight as to force down padding.

Upholstering Instructions for Foot Stool

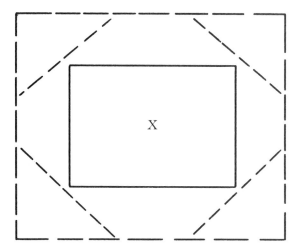

8. If corners are not smooth, place a drop of glue in each and roll material to smooth corners.

9. Drop upholstered seat into foot stool.

UPHOLSTERING INSTRUCTIONS
FOR LOW-BACK AND HIGH-BACK CHAIRS

1. Upholster seats in same manner as for foot stool.

2. Cut piece of padding ¼″ thick and glue to backs of chairs, X and XX.

3. Cut material slightly larger than backs with padding. Notch for arms and bottom edge so material will lie flat on base of chair (this before you slip in upholstered seats). Cut triangular-shaped notches around top of chair backs, checking to see that material will lie flat when glued to backs.

4. Carefully fold material over to backs of chairs and glue, rolling to follow contours of the rounded backs.

Upholstering Instructions for Low-Back and High-Back Chairs

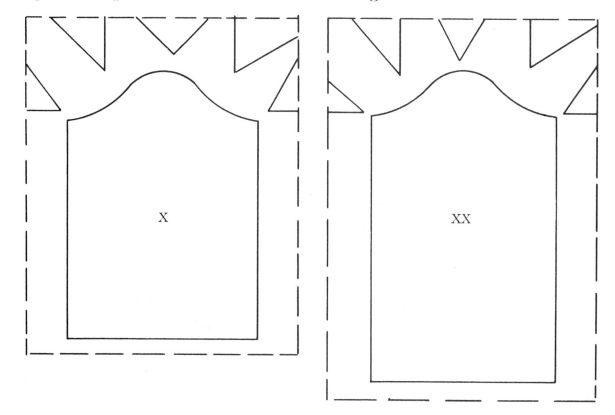

5. Check to make certain corners are carefully squared. If not, put a drop of glue in each corner and roll until smooth.

6. Cut X and XX from index cards or similar-weight paper. Glue to wrong side of material. When dry, cut fabric along edges of X and XX. Glue to chair backs to cover material glued on backs.

7. Drop upholstered seats in place, smoothing corners and back edges.

Caution: If using a velvet or nap material make certain nap goes in the same direction.

Accessories

A house is not a home until you have added those finishing touches. Here is where the accessories come in and where you begin to look at everything from toothpaste caps to buttons to pop bottle caps to small colored pictures in magazines, converting them in your mind's eye to miniatures.

Accessories are a matter of individual preference. You are limited only by your talents, desires, and patience.

Many people like to make items such as pies, cakes, and flowers from bread-dough mixture. But this has a tendency to mold. Others use modeling clay. But this has a tendency to crack. There are two products known as Fimo and Pendo used to make such small items as mentioned.

Fimo seems to work best because it dries slowly giving you more time to shape and mold. Fimo is baked in the oven, after molding and before painting, at 275° for 15 to 45 minutes depending on size of article.

Pendo has a tendency to air-dry. When working with this, keep unused portion in the palm of your hand to keep it warm and pliable.

If you make pies, cakes, flowers, loaves of bread, ham, turkey, etc., using any of these various ways, read instructions and have patience.

Some people stock their pantry with canned goods. Use ¼″ doweling, painted or wrapped with colored paper. Mark with a fine pen or paint product names on your canned goods.

Silverware can be cut from TV-dinner foil trays, using patterns from catalogs or magazines, which often show silverware patterns in a perfect miniature scale.

Buttons that look like china make lovely dishes. Shank buttons are perfect once you file off the shank. Buttons with holes have to be filled with a product such as Gesso, but often when filling the holes it is too easy to cover the beautiful pattern. And one can also find inexpensive buttons that resemble cups. If not, cups can be made from the end of ball-point pens. Or you can cut doweling to resemble cups. Make handles of fine wire or, if you wish, forget the handles and call them demitasse cups.

Towels for kitchen or bath are made from cotton lawn cut 1½″ × 1½″. Fold each towel in thirds lengthwise, selvage edge for finished edge. Steam-press. Fold towels in half and steam press center crease. Draw designs on selvage edge with colored pens. Hang towels on towel bar or wall towel holder made of stiff wire or fine doweling. Soap dish can be made from TV-dinner foil.

Make doilies from cotton lawn and embroider with colored pens, or make doilies from cutouts of paper doilies. Make dresser scarfs in same manner, using the white cotton lawn or whatever material goes with your decor.

To fill desk cubbyholes cut small pieces of index cards ¾″ × ¾″. Use a small piece of green craft paper for blotter. Make books from 1/16″ and ⅛″ illustration board covered with colored paper. Write title in very fine print or fake titles with small lines. These books will sit on desk or help fill empty bookshelves of the library breakfront.

Centerpieces can be made from filigree discs or bell caps, which are opened and ball-shaped filigree caps used as is or to partially cover large beads. Fill with small dried flowers or tiny beads, which you can buy in small vials at any craft store. Candles are round toothpicks and can be set in rounded bell caps.

Lamps are made from assorted bell caps, beads (glass or wooden) and sequins. For examples: In Nanny's room the lamp was made with a silver bell cap for base, a ¾″ long rounded, colored bead topped with a round pearl and a miniature basket with handle cut off for shade.

The lamp in the child's room is made from a small plastic Raggedy Ann using a lampshade made with an index card, pinned with a pearl-headed pin through a piece of thin cardboard cross brace through another pearl under the brace with the point of this pin anchored in Raggedy Ann's head.

In the "canopy" bedroom there is a lamp made with a bell-cap base and white rosebud beads on a long pin with a ¼″ piece of plastic drinking straw glued on top for the "chimney."

The "privacy bedroom" has a lamp made of two wooden beads on a toothpick painted white with red tip for candle flame.

The study has a lamp made of two carved wooden beads, oval pearl bead, and silver bell cap with pearl pinned down from the top.

On the round occasional table in the parlor is a lamp made from a small plastic bottle filled with gold and red beads. A gold fringe trim is glued around base serving both as lamp bottom and "doily" for lamp to sit on. The shade is made from an index card covered with the gold velvet of the furniture, with top and bottom edged with a fine gold braid.

A lipstick top filled with small dried flowers sits in the bay window.

Chandeliers are just large lamps. The study has a wooden-bead chandelier with a small silver filigree disc between the first and second bead with a third bead for the top. Carved beads and disc are held together with a long pearl-headed pin stuck through the ceiling.

The chandelier in the dining room is most elegant. Starting at the top is a large silver bell cap, a heavy silver beaded disc ¼″ deep into which is glued a large pearl bead with another silver disc beneath the pearl bead that is glued to a 2½″ diameter silver filigree disc with a flat glass decorative button glued to the bottom.

The chandelier in the living room/parlor is a small Styrofoam ball covered with silver glitter. Around the center are pinned alternating crystal and red beads with a silver filigree cone pinned with a pearl pin through bottom center into the ceiling.

This should give you a good start on making accessories of your own.

Moving In

Our work is done. Now comes the fun. Moving in!

Hang your curtains. Not with rods or glue but with Mini-Hold. This will secure your curtains in place, but should you wish to change your curtains they can be removed without staining the walls or woodwork. Gluing curtains in place makes them too permanent and should you remove them you will mar or tear the woodwork.

The dining room and living room/parlor chandeliers are also hung with Mini-Hold, even though pinned. If rugs don't lie flat, you can use Mini-Hold for this, also.

Now arrange your furniture. And rearrange it.

Put your lamps in place. Set up your desk. Put the books on the bookshelves in the library. Put your good china in the breakfront. Set your kitchen table. Stock your pantry. Make your beds.

Now stand back and admire your handiwork. You should be very proud of your dollhouse.

Time now for a housewarming. Invite your friends, relatives, and neighbors. Make a real celebration of this day. You'll glow with pride as compliments on your work come from all who view your beautiful dollhouse and furnishings. And you'll deserve all the accolades bestowed you.

Merry miniaturing to you and to you the very best in this Lilliputian World!

ADDING IT ALL UP

As with the dollhouse, there are so many variations in prices and materials used that we will only give both ends of the price range for this dollhouse with all the furnishings and accessories.

Least expensive way to build our dollhouse		$15.33
Furnishings and accessories		29.84
	total	$45.17
Most expensive way to build our dollhouse		$48.97
Furnishings and accessories		29.84
	total	$78.81

And as with the price of the dollhouse, your cost will range between these two figures and, if you bought something you couldn't resist, the price could be a little higher but you should still have built and furnished your dollhouse for $100 or less.